THE PROBLEM OF CRIME

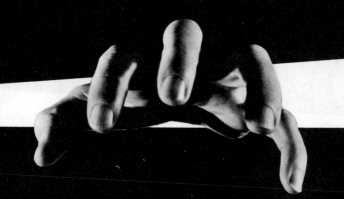

THE PROBLEM OF CRIME:
A CRITICAL INTRODUCTION TO CRIMINOLOGY
SECOND EDITION

RICHARD QUINNEY
JOHN WILDEMAN

HARPER & ROW, PUBLISHERS
NEW YORK   HAGERSTOWN   SAN FRANCISCO   LONDON

Sponsoring Editor: Dale Tharp
Designer: Michel Craig
Production Supervisor: Stefania J. Taflinska
Photo Researcher: Myra Schachne
Compositor: Maryland Linotype Composition Co., Inc.
Printer and Binder: The Murray Printing Company
Art Studio: Danmark & Michaels Inc.
Photo credits: p. 5 Wide World; p. 13, Wide World; p. 25, Culver; p. 32, Wide world; p. 41, Copyright © Nigel Gosling, London, 1973; p. 47, Culver; p. 52, C. Lombroso, *L'homme criminel;* p. 60, Charles Goring, *The English Convict;* p. 73, Copyright © Nigel Gosling, London, 1973; p. 78, UPI; p. 89, Bettmann; p. 100 Muller-May, Woodfin Camp; p. 116, Wide World; p. 119, Atkinson, DPI; p. 123, Beckwith Studios; p. 134 Culver; p. 137, Bettmann; p. 139, Wide World; p. 143, Wide World; p. 152, Mezdy, DPI; p. 156, Daplan, DPI; p. 168, Charles Gatewood; p. 171, Copyright © Alice Neel.

THE PROBLEM OF CRIME: A Critical Introduction to Criminology, Second Edition

Library of Congress Cataloging in Publication Data

Quinney Richard.
  The problem of crime.

  Bibliography: p.
  Includes indexes.
  1. Crime and criminals. I. Wildeman, John,
1937-   joint author. II. Title.
HV6025.Q55 1977   364   76-44271
ISBN 0-06-045311-7

CONTENTS

PREFACE

Our purpose is to provide a critical introduction to criminology. In a revision of the first edition of The Problem of Crime, *we have incorporated and attempted to extend the criminological developments of recent years. The first edition began to examine critically the problem of crime; this second edition extends that critique. The growth of critical-Marxian theory in general is shaping our understanding of crime, and in the process a new criminology is emerging.*

Within this framework we discuss the meaning of crime in reference to the formation of law and the state. In a critical examination of the meaning of crime, it is necessary as well to go beyond the state's definition, a definition limited by the needs of the capitalist order. A critical definition of crime allows us all to expand our understanding of contemporary life. The problem of crime, we argue, is basically and foremost a problem of contemporary society as known particularly in the United States.

The critical approach is then followed by a review of the development of criminology, which similarly presents the current issues in the study of crime and crime control. We then analyze of the principal aspects of crime and punishment in the United States. We attempt, given the existing research, to relate these phenomena to the underlying political economy, the resulting class struggle, and the contradictions of the established order. The book is concluded with a discussion of the contemporary struggle for social justice.

It is our contention that the problem of crime allows us to focus on the important forces of our time. Our understanding is part of the process of transforming our society. The struggle is for the realization of a more humane world, one founded on the principles of socialism.

Richard Quinney
John Wildeman

THE PROBLEM OF CRIME

A CRITICAL UNDERSTANDING OF CRIME

The problem of crime begins as a problem of society. The initial problem is not that of crime, but the failure of a society—consisting of its social, political, and economic organization—to provide an authentic existence. To focus solely on the problem of crime is to avoid the deeper meaning of crime in contemporary society. Likewise, to neglect the larger social order and its internal contradictions is to ignore the possibilities of creating a world liberated from both the oppression that results from these contradictions and the crime that results from that oppression. Our critical understanding of crime is thus related to the larger context that makes crime possible. Our understanding is ultimately for the transformation of society.

THE CONCEPT OF CRIME

Important words have a way of going beyond the assigned boundaries of their dictionary meanings. A critical interpretation of the historical development of words in any language would bear witness to this. "Crime" is one such important word, a word that signifies different meanings to many different people and is always straining at the boundaries of its currently assigned meaning.

To a great extent the meaning of crime depends upon the social location from which one is approaching the problem of crime. Thus, crime begins to have meaning for us in the course of formulating an idea of crime, an idea that is meaningful for our lives. The concept necessarily depends upon the interests and perceptions of those who are constructing the concepts. There are, for instance, the concepts of crime held by the legal authorities of the state, including the police, lawyers, and judges. Criminologists, those who study crime, often construct their own ideas of crime. And there are of course, the various attitudes of the general public toward crime. All of these diverse meanings of the word are ultimately rooted in differential perceptions of reality.

In other words, diverse concepts of crime are employed simultaneously for different purposes and rooted in diverse social histories. Therefore, in order to gain an understanding of crime, we must first consider these various meanings of crime. The objective is to develop a meaning of crime that will be of maximum use in our critical understanding of crime in contemporary society.

The various conceptions of crime differ from one another primarily in the extent to which they refer to the criminal law, that is, to the degree they conform to the state's definition of crime. On the other hand, the non-state definitions of crime go beyond the legal meaning of crime. For example, a completely subjective definition of crime and the criminal was noted by an early sociologist in the suggestion that the criminal is "a person who regards himself as a criminal and is so regarded by society."[1] On other occasions sociologists have argued that because criminal laws change in the course of time, vary from one locality to another, and are sometimes arbitrary, the legal categories of crime do not provide satisfactory units for scientific analysis.[2] Using a different approach, Thorsten Sellin, in broadening the scope of criminology, suggested that criminology includes the study of the violation of all "conduct norms." But it is important to note that Sellin did not extend the concept of crime beyond violation of the criminal law, stating that "it is wiser to retain that term crime for the offenses made punishable by the criminal law and to use the term abnormal conduct for the violations of norms whether legal or not."[3]

Edwin H. Sutherland proposed a definition of crime that has been adopted by most sociologists.

The essential characteristic of crime is that it is behavior which is prohibited by the State as an injury to the State and against which the State may react, at least as a last resort, by punishment. The two abstract criteria generally regarded by legal scholars as necessary elements in a definition of crime are legal descriptions of an act as socially harmful and legal provision of a penalty for the act.[4]

Following this conception, an act is a crime only when it is in violation of a criminal law.

The importance of the criminal law to a definition of crime was forcefully presented in 1933 by Jerome Michael and Mortimer J. Adler in their examination of the field of criminology. According to their argument, there would be no crime without criminal law.

> *If crime is merely an instance of conduct which is proscribed by the criminal code it follows that the criminal law is the formal cause of crime. That does not mean that law produces the behavior which it prohibits, although, as we shall see, the enforcement or administration of the criminal law may be one of the factors which influence human behavior; it means only that the criminal law gives behavior its quality of criminality.[5]*

Michael and Adler concluded that "the most precise and least ambiguous definition of crime is that which defines it as behavior which is prohibited by the criminal code" and that "this is the only possible definition of crime." Later, C. Ray Jeffery was to similarly argue: "Where does crime exist, if not in the legal codes?"[6]

The legalistic definition of crime was taken to its extreme in Paul W. Tappan's suggestion that "only those are criminals who have been adjudicated as such by the courts."[7] But Tappan's conception of crime is not as legalistic as it might appear at first glance. In this conception, Tappan recognized the important and essential point that a person is a criminal by the fact that a definition has been imposed on him or her by others, by the authorities of the state who are charged with the administration of the law. The labeling of persons and behaviors as criminal—the imposition of a legal category—is nothing other than a social enterprise. While not necessarily implying that the person must reach the stage of being adjudicated in the courts before he or she is regarded as criminal, a writer some time ago defined the criminal in terms of the legal action of others:

> *A criminal is one who acts in such a way that organized society, in the form of the community of which he is a part, is compelled to declare that the act and the actual or potential consequences of that act are a menace or injury to it, and is forced to take steps to suppress further activities of his along similar lines.[8]*

In a similar fashion, Richard R. Korn and Lloyd W. McCorkle have offered a definition of crime that indicates that an act is not a crime until

the offender is caught, tried, and punished, crime thus being "an act or omission ascribed to a person when he is punished by the authorities in continuous political control over the territory in which he is."[9] To a number of criminologists, then, crime is a *legal status* that is assigned to behaviors and persons by authorized agents of the state.[10]

More recently the question has been raised as to whether the legalistic concept of crime limits the criminologist to the established order and its official version of reality. The argument has been presented by Herman and Julia Schwendinger, and others following their lead, that a legalistic concept prevents criminology from examining—or even questioning—the existing institutions and arrangements of the society as themselves criminal.[11] There is, indeed, the danger that a sole reliance on the state's definition of crime can lead to an uncritical acceptance of the existing order. As unwitting ancillary agents of power, many criminologists often provide the kind of information that governing elites can find useful in manipulating and controlling those who threaten the established system.[12] This discussion leads us logically into a review of what is to be our principal analytical and theoretical tool in the chapters that follow: critical criminology.

CRITICAL CRIMINOLOGY

Critical criminology, grounded as it is in critical social theory, has a history going back to the Enlightenment. Before discussing the development of a critical criminology, we will review the idea of critical theory.[13]

Critical theory involves a continual and ongoing analysis of modern society in all its multifold aspects. Contemporary critical analysis is rooted in Marxian social theory as opposed to bourgeois social theory. This theoretical analysis is referred to as critical because it begins with the question, Is this particular mode of institutionalized social arrangements the best of all possible ways in which human potential can be fully realized?

Critical theory recognizes that our experience of concrete social reality is in a state of constant flux, while the more basic social institutions and forms persist relatively unchanged. For example, although new laws may be passed and we may enter periods of economic recession or even depression, America persists as a class-divided society based on a capitalist political economy. Critical theory further recognizes that the theoretical constructions of bourgeois sociology are largely dictated by the concrete social reality as opposed to the more basic and persistent social arrangements.

Hence, for social theory to be capable of reaching beyond the immediate, concrete level of social reality and to affect change in the more basic social forms and institutions themselves, it must disabuse itself of those distortions and biases that infect it from this immediate, concrete, and constantly changing level of social experience. Expressed more simply, critical theory seeks to emancipate itself from the ever-changing, concrete social realities and get to an analysis of the basic social forms and institutions, for example, bourgeois, capitalist society.

Consequently, critical theory begins with the Marxian approach to social reality, with social life being understood in terms of the underlying mode of production and class struggle. It deviates from the traditionally received sociological theory of the contemporary Western academic tradition in that it sees such theory as ultimately incapable of examining its own presuppositions. Critical theory strives to rise above the "givens" of the world in which it finds itself at any given moment. At the same time, however, critical theory does build concrete social goals into its analysis, these goals being the human goals of rational production based on real human and social potentials.

A critical criminology, rooted and grounded in critical theory, is thus a new and vigorous development in contemporary crime analysis. It is suspect of "conventional," "liberal," or "applied" criminology as being incapable of critiquing our more basic social forms and institutions. Thus, for example, rejecting a state definition of crime, its advocates argue:

> *In accepting the state and legal definition of crime, the scope of analysis has been constrained to exclude behavior which is not legally defined as "crime" (for example, imperialism, exploitation, racism, and sexism) as well as behavior which is not typically prosecuted (for example, tax-evasion, price-fixing, consumer fraud, government corruption, police homicides, etc.).*[14]

Thus, scholars of the critical school would liberate academic criminology from a comparatively narrow range of subject matter and a comparatively uncritical methodology. This thrust is likewise indicated in a statement by the American Friends Service Committee:

> *Actions that clearly ought to be labeled "criminal," because they bring the greatest harm to the greatest number, are in fact accomplished officially by agencies of government. The overwhelming number of murders in this century has been committed by governments in wartime. Hundreds of unlawful killings by police go unprosecuted each year. The largest forceful acquisitions of property in the United States has been the theft of lands guaranteed by treaty to Indian tribes, thefts sponsored by the government. The largest number of dislocations, tantamount to kidnapping— the evacuation and internment of Japanese-Americans during World War II—was carried out by the government with the approval of the courts. Civil rights demonstrators, struggling to exercise their constitutional rights, have been repeatedly beaten and harassed by police and sheriffs. And in the Vietnam war, America has violated its Constitutional and international law.*[15]

While for some criminologists a legalistic concept of crime has allowed them to at least begin to examine the existence and operation of the legal system, there is now the need for a critical criminology that goes beyond the official, established definitions of crime. The call is for a criminology that serves the needs of all the people rather than the interests of a few narrow segments of our society, segments defined in terms of those elites who enjoy a hegemony of control over access to the state's policy and law-making powers. The call is for a criminology that, having freed itself from service to the few, is capable of laying bare the contradictions in our master institutions, contradictions that have created and continue to create in this country an inhuman and criminogenic social structure. Such a criminology appeals to our most fundamental sense of human dignity and to our basic human needs.

Criminal behavior, according to critical analysis, is best conceptualized not as simply that behavior that the law so defines; for this is far too simplistic an interpretation of our social experience. Criminal behavior is formulated as behavior that results in social injury, social injury arising, for example, from the denial of the right to racial, sexual, and economic equality. (The right to vote, after all, does not constitute the only equality, i.e., political equality.) There are many contradictions in our society that lead to these denials of equality. Regarding the denial of these rights to equality, the Schwendingers write:

> The abrogation of these rights certainly limits the individual's chance to fulfill himself in many spheres of life. These rights therefore are basic because there is so much at stake in their fulfillment. It can be stated, in light of the previous argument, that individuals who deny these rights to others are criminal. Likewise, social relationships and social systems which regularly cause the abrogation of these rights are also criminal. If the terms imperialism, racism, sexism, and poverty are abbreviated signs for theories of social relationships or social systems which cause the systematic abrogation of basic rights, then imperialism, racism, sexism, and poverty can be called crimes according to the logic of our argument.[16]

We must recognize, then, that there are several concepts of crime. Each concept serves the interests of those who treasure it. As shown in the table below, the concepts of crime can be separated into five levels of meaning. The first four levels are incorporated into the legal concept of crime. Crime, according to these four levels of meaning, refers to the legal category that is assigned to conduct by authorized agents in a politically organized society. Each of these first four levels of meaning depends upon the stage of the legal process in which the category of crime is applied —formulation of criminal law, arrest, prosecution, and conviction. The fifth concept of crime is the one of popular usage employed by the public (and sometimes by criminologists) to refer to conduct that does not necessarily involve either the violation of a criminal law or the application of the legal category to the conduct. There are undoubtedly several meanings of crime within this last concept of crime. With a notion of basic human rights, of an authentic human existence, we will use a critical concept of crime in understanding the problem of crime.

THE CONCEPTS OF CRIME

Crime₁	Violation of criminal law formulations	Application of the category of crime at the formulation stage.	
Crime₂	Arrest	Application of the category of crime at the arrest stage.	Crime as a legal category assigned to conduct by authorized agents of the state.
Crime₃	Prosecution	Application of the category of crime at the prosecution stage.	
Crime₄	Conviction	Application of the category of crime at the conviction stage.	
Crime₅	A critical concept of crime	Crime as conduct that does not necessarily involve either the violation of a criminal law or the application of the legal category to the conduct. A violation of *human rights*.	

Critical thinking, the intellectual stance that subsequent generations have inherited from the Enlightenment, points up the contradictory and irrational elements in social structures, which elements lay in the path of human liberation and perfectibility; certainly crime itself is a spin-off of these contradictions in our social structure as well as a drawback to human liberation and freedom. At the same time, the critical mode acts to promote dissatisfactions with "things as they are" and this in itself fosters movement away from inadequately structured social institutions. This notion, then, of crime as social injury, social harm, or a violation of human rights, is most attractive to those who strive to improve the human condition, for it provides the theoretical tools with which we can reconstruct our most basic and at the same time most injurious social institutions: those injurious to the masses of our people.

Thus, for example, the immorality of sexism or the immorality of racism becomes the crime of sexism and the crime of racism. It is precisely this that prompted the following observation:

> . . . I find it difficult to support the position that criminal law can be stripped of its moral judgments. To the contrary, the very stuff of criminal law is moral. The criminal law is moralistic if for no other reason than it takes the position that any *human actions should be limited*. The assumption that either the society or the individual should be regulated is a moral one. And certainly the decision to regulate specific substantive actions is moralistic. A moral decision

is taken when it is decided to protect others by means of the criminal law. Legal reform, or even legal revolution, cannot be achieved by taking morality out of the law.[17]

Critical theory is not positivist in nature, for it does not stop with simply asking for a descriptive analysis of crime formulated as what "is," but it goes on to ask also, How could it be? William Leiss, in an excellent statement on critical theory, observes that "one cannot even fully comprehend what 'is' without also delineating what 'can be' (and what ought to be). The actual incorporates the potential as part of its own structure. The prevailing reality always represents the realization of certain potentialities and the suppression of others. . . ."[18]

Critical criminology, further, challenges conventional criminology's assumption that the law and the state are genuinely impartial agents in maintaining a stable society and balancing the interests of all classes, groups, and individuals according to the dictates of blind justice. In fact, much that critical criminology questions is what conventional theory in criminology naively accepts without question, for conventional criminology is essentially nonreflexive.

A critical theory of crime does not try merely to nail down the "facts" about crime and the social structure. Human conduct cannot be so reified as if it were something capable of being smeared onto a slide for examination under a microscope. Thus, Trent Schroyer comments:

In nailing down the facts about society, the activity of men is reified into a thing-like facticity. A critical theory, on the other hand, transcends its facts, rendering them meaningful, but at the same time placing them in the context of the tension between the given and the possible. Construction of a critical theory follows the principle of an imminent critique. By first expressing what a social totality holds itself to be, and then confronting it with what it is, a critical theory is able to break down the rigidity of the object.[19]

What Schroyer is suggesting here is that what we call academic criminology, or on the wider plane, the social sciences in general, are all inadequate for providing us with an explanation of our multiple experiences in the social world. Technical control of the people through the dual tools of science and technology may not be what we want, after all. According to Schroyer, "Established, official, social science understands itself as having the interest of the strict sciences. In practice, this means that established social science, although it conceives of itself as neutral, is actually an inquiry which has the theoretical interest and societal consequence of maintaining technical control."[20]

The issue of critical criminology versus established criminology resolves itself eventually into an issue of emancipation. Critical criminology seeks in a nonmanipulative way to analyze and expose those contradictory dynamics and contradictory social arrangements that enslave the majority of our people. We again quote Schroyer:

> *The question for social science is how to develop a mode of analysis which is both explanatory and able to interpret symbolic communication. This form of science would have a still different research guiding interest—that of emancipation. Established social science is essentially manipulative because it has allowed itself to be conceived as having the same research-guiding interest as the strict sciences. Insofar as technical control is the guiding interest of social science, it is consistent with the technocratic trend and overtly legitimate class or elite exploitation. On the other hand, a social science guided only by the practical interest would have very little explanatory power. Thus the need for the synthetic critical science.[21]*

A critical criminology focuses on the connections between the perceived need for criminal law and the class-rooted need to protect the interests of those who have much to lose from the potential threat coming from those classes that have little to lose. It looks for the necessary and sufficient conditions of criminality in:

> *material living conditions of a given society, in its economic, class, and other relationships and structures, in the influence of various negative phenomena which act on society, in social conditions which have a decisive influence on the disintegration and alienation of man. . . . The personality of the delinquent is formed under the influence of social factors and the conditions of the concrete living situation.[22]*

A critical criminology, then, attempts to do essentially two things: First, it begins its analysis of crime in American life with a negative-critical inspection of the contradictions in our master institutions, and second, it defines crime as social harm, a violation of basic human rights.

We are now in a position to look at how such a theory would define the role of law in American society and the relation of law to the political economy of our society. Critical criminology, following the Marxian conception of the state and the legal system, sees them as essentially the creation and tool of the dominant class of society. Criminal law in this motif, while undeniably of some utility to all classes and serving some of the interests of all classes in a liberal democracy, nevertheless remains the principal tool serving the interests of the capitalist class. Criminal law is also seen as the coercive instrument of the state, a state under the control of that dominant economic class. Modern capitalist society is thus founded on the control of one class by another with the state securing this arrangement.[23]

The whole idea of the American criminal justice system, then, according to critical criminology is characterized by internal contradictions that give rise to a host of new questions about the nature of and "etiology" of crime. Our criminal justice system is no longer the simple reflection of community custom, but rather the reflection of the breakdown of communal solidarity, the reflection of our underlying class divisions.[24] For critical criminology, the state and its law, rather than serving all the people in an impartial manner, fracture the social solidarity of our society in the interest of the capitalist class.

With this critical understanding of the legal order, we begin to see the contradictory nature of law as the synonym of order. Law in fact becomes the antonym of order. It has its origins in the pathology of social relations brought about by the state itself. Stanley Diamond writes: "Law arises in the breach of a prior customary order and increases in force with the conflicts that divide political societies internally and among themselves. Law *and* order is the historical illusion; law versus order is the historical reality."[25] Modern capitalist society, with its state and legal order, is the one least likely to serve as a guide and model for building a more human society.

According to critical criminology, as capitalist society is further threatened by its own contradictions, as capitalism continues to develop, criminal law is increasingly used in the attempt to maintain domestic order. The working-class, the class that must remain oppressed for the triumph of the dominant capitalist class, will continue to be the object of criminal law as long as the dominant class seeks to perpetuate itself. To remove the oppression, to eliminate the need for further revolt, would necessarily mean a radical change in our present class structure and in our present capitalist economy. The crimes of those who profit from the capitalist system, particularly the crimes of criminal syndicates, crimes of political conspiracy such as the entire Watergate affair, and the crimes

committed by American corporations in the course of business operations, are the product of a capitalist society. In the view of radical criminologists, whether criminal law and law enforcement are directed against the working-class or are actions against those who profit from the existing economy, the purpose of the capitalist criminal justice is to protect and strengthen capitalism.[26]

LEGAL ORDER AND THE STATE

It is the legal order of a society that is officially recognized as the regulator of the various realms of social life. While several different kinds of normative systems operate to control behavior, the law of the state establishes the formal restraints for all members of the society. And associated with law are the formal means of assuring compliance with the official regulations.

The legal system in a society is thus regarded as the prime example of formal social control. Accordingly, the law consists of (1) explicit rules of conduct, (2) planned use of sanctions to support the rules, and (3) designated officials to interpret and enforce the rules.[27] Roscoe Pound, the legal scholar, observed that as societies have increased in complexity, the law as a formal means of control has developed to regulate social life. Regulation of the members of society has tended to shift from the informal controls of the family and religion to the formal control of the state. Pound noted that "in the modern world law has become the paramount agent of social control. Our main reliance is upon force of a politically organized state."[28]

In addition to the concept of law as a type of formal social control, virtually all legal scholars and social scientists have defined it in terms of the body of rules created and enforced by a sovereign state. The state is seen as a political community that governs a territory and all the inhabitants within it through the use of authorized power and through the threat or application of punitive sanctions. Yet, certain scholars have departed from this prevailing view of law. Max Weber, for example, conceived of legality as a legitimized pattern of normative rules, whether the rules are of the state or fall outside the province of the state. According to Weber, all legal orders are "externally guaranteed by the probability that coercion (physical or psychological), to bring about conformity or avenge violation, will be applied by a *staff* of people holding themselves specially ready for that purpose."[29] However, Weber was clear in distinguishing between the law of the state and the law of other bodies:

> We shall speak of "state" law, i.e., of law guaranteed by the state, only when, and to the extent that, the guaranty for it, that is, legal coercion, is exercised through the specific, i.e., normally direct and

physical, *means of coercion of the political community. . . .*
Wherever the means of coercion which constitute the guaranty of
a "right" belong to some authority other than the political, for
instance, a hierocracy, we shall speak of "extra-state law."[30]

More recent writers, taking Weber as a point of departure, have
argued that "the traditional view of law as an integral part of the state has
tended to obscure the fact that law exists in nonstate contexts as well."[31]
They point out that the growth of large-scale organizations is the representative characteristic of modern life and that in industry, government, education, medicine, and so on, the bureaucratic principle—the principle of
rational coordination—prevails. Moreover, there is a modern trend toward
a convergence of governmental and nongovernmental forms of organization
and modes of action, a blurring of the public and private sectors of economy
and society. Government today includes many activities not directly related
to the functions of the state, and many private organizations tend to be
quasi-public in operation. This phenomenon has prompted Philip Selznick
to write the following in regard to the concept of legality:

> *A kind of legality seems to develop within these large enterprises.*
> *In both public and private bureaucracies, authority and rule-making*
> *tend to take on the impersonality, the objectivity, and the ration-*
> *ality of a legal system.*[32]

While in basic agreement with Weber's concept of legality, Selznick takes
exception to the notion that a legal order exists only when there is a coercive
apparatus for purposes of norm enforcement. In modern organizations,
legality may be achieved through *authority* rather than coercion.[33] The legal
order, according to this conception, is primarily an authoritative order, and
to understand the distinctively legal the observer must look to that special
kind of obligation in which persons act in accordance with authoritatively
determined norms.

A major reason for expanding the concept of legality to include
rules outside those of the political state is that such an expansion may
provide for the comparative study of public and private normative orders
in modern society. Likewise, the traditional concept of legality is called into
question when there is a desire for the comparative study of primitive and
early historical normative orders in relation to the legal systems of modern
societies. To the anthropologist, interested in the study of primitive law,
the problem is that of differentiating between custom and law in primitive

society. Bronislav Malinowski, in his study of a primitive society on the Trobriand Archipelago, proposed and utilized the following "anthropological definition of law":

> *The rules of law stand out from the rest in that they are felt and regarded as the obligations of one person and the rightful claims of another. They are sanctioned not by a mere psychological motive, but by a definite social machinery or binding force, based, as we know, upon mutual dependence, and realized in the equivalent arrangement of reciprocal services, as well as in the combination of such claims into strands of multiple relationship. The ceremonial manner in which most transactions are carried out, which entails public control and criticism, adds still more to their binding force.*[34]

The anthropologist Hoebel, using a more restricted definition of law in distinguishing between law and other kinds of norms and sanctions, suggested that "a social norm is legal if its neglect or infraction is regularly met, in threat or in fact, by the application of physical force by an individual or group possessing the socially recognized privilege of so acting."[35] A definition of law that is even more limited in range is the one proposed by A. R. Radcliffe-Brown: "Law will therefore be regarded as coterminous with that of organized legal sanctions. The obligations imposed on individuals in societies where there are no legal sanctions will be regarded as matters of custom and convention but not of law."[36] In this latter conception of law, some societies have no law, only customs that are supported by other kinds of sanctions. After reviewing the various anthropological definitions of law, Ronald L. Akers has proposed a formulation for comparative purposes that, while not as restrictive as the definition by Radcliffe-Brown nor as broad as some other definitions, limits law to a normative system that is sanctioned by a third party (person or agency) other than the offender, the offended, or their relatives: "A social norm is law if its breach is met by physical force or the threat of physical force in a socially approved and regular way by a socially authorized third person."[37]

Each definition of law is formulated for a particular purpose. For comparative purposes, either the comparison of highly complex normative orders in modern societies or the comparison of primitive and modern orders, a broad definition of law or legality may be useful. Moreover, what is essential to any definition, in addition to purpose, are the *theoretical assumptions* that underlie the formulation of the definition. For example, an assumption about the importance of rationality in social order will lead to one definition of law; a belief in the importance of sanctions will lead to another definition. And related both to the purpose of the observer and the theoretical assumptions is a more general theory about the role of law in society and the relation of law to the political and economic organization of the state.

THE NATURE OF CRIMINAL LAW

Criminal law is the ultimate form of legal control in the state. With its provisions for punishment and sanction, the criminal law stands ready to repress, among other things, any conduct that threatens the state. The concept of criminal law developed when the custom of private or community redress of wrong was replaced by the principle that the state is injured when it or one of its subjects is harmed. Thus, the right of the community to deal with wrongdoing was taken over by the state as the "representative" of the people. The state could now act by means of the criminal law to protect its own interests and those of the dominant economic class that it served.

In formalized language, what is criminal law and how does it differ from other forms of law? In answering this question, Henry M. Hart, Jr., has suggested that such inquiry should be approached from the view that criminal law is a "method," a way of doing something. The criminal law "is concerned with the pursuit of human purposes through the forms and modes of social organization, and it needs always to be thought about in the context as a method or process of doing something."[38] What then are the characteristics of this method?

1. The method operates by means of a series of directions, or commands, formulated in general terms, telling people what they must or must not do. Mostly, the commands of the criminal law are "must-nots," or prohibitions, which can be satisfied by inaction. "Do not murder, rape, or rob." But some of them are "musts," or affirmative requirements, which can be satisfied only by taking a specifically, or relatively specifically described kind of action. "Support your wife and children," and "File your income tax return."
2. The commands are taken as valid and binding upon all those who fall within their terms when the time comes for complying with them, whether or not they have been formulated in advance in a single authoritative set of words. They speak to

members of the community; in other words, in the community's behalf, with all the power and prestige of the community behind them.

3. The commands are subject to one or more sanctions for disobedience which the community is prepared to enforce.

4. What distinguishes a criminal from a civil sanction, and all that distinguishes it, is the judgment of community condemnation which accompanies and justifies its imposition. . . . If this is what a "criminal" penalty is, then we can say readily enough what a "crime" is. It is not simply anything which a legislature chooses to call a "crime." It is not simply anti-social conduct which public officers are given a responsibility to suppress. It is not simply any conduct to which a legislature chooses to attach a "criminal" penalty. It is conduct which, if duly shown to have taken place, will incur a formal and solemn pronouncement of the moral condemnation of the community.

5. The method of the criminal law, of course, involves something more than threat (and, on due occasion, the expression) of community condemnation of anti-social conduct. It involves, in addition, the threat (and, on due occasion, the imposition) of unpleasant physical consequences, commonly called punishment. . . . The condemnation plus the added consequences may be considered compendiously, as constituting the punishment.[39]

The above attempt to distinguish criminal law from other types of law is basically consistent with the long legal tradition that places emphasis on (1) the relation of the act or omission to society and (2) the nature of the reaction to the violation. Thus, Ronald M. Perkins has defined a crime as "any social harm defined and punishable by law."[40] From this definition it is obvious that not all conduct that may be regarded as "social harm" in a society is regulated by law. For example, the tremendous social harm wrought by an unemployment figure on the national level of 8 or 9 percent in our capitalist economy is not regarded as criminal according to Perkins's definition. Likewise, not all conduct subject to punishment by the law is recognized in the society as "social harm." These latter forms of conduct, while technically part of the written law, are not usually subjected to formal detection and prosecution by the state. In other words, law consists of more than the written law. There is, in addition, a "law in operation" that relies upon considerable discretion in the interpretation and application of the laws on the statute books. When the living law is considered along-side the written law, it is possible to regard criminal law as a regulation of behavior that is deemed harmful to the society and that is subject to punishment by the state. Thus, rules are criminal laws if, and only if, they (1) have been created by the state, (2) contain provisions for punishment to be administered upon substantiation of their violation, and (3) provide for the punishment to be administered by the state in the name of society.

The basic conceptual difference, then, between criminal and civil law defines conduct that is *believed* to be against the interest of the *society* while civil law refers to conduct that is against the interest of the *individual*. In other words, a *crime* in the legal sense is a social wrong and a *tort* is a civil or private wrong. The distinction, however, is not always easy to maintain in practice. The practical difficulty is that any given act or omission may at the same time involve both a criminal and a civil wrong.

> *The conventional view is that crime is an offense against the state, while, in contrast a tort in violation of civil law is an offense against an individual. A particular act may be considered as an offense against an individual and also against the state, and is either a tort or a crime or both according to the way it is handled. A person who has committed an act of assault, for example, may be ordered by the civil court to pay the victim a sum of $500 for the damages to his interests, and he may also be ordered by the criminal court to pay a fine of $500 to the state. The payment of the first $500 is not punishment, but payment of the second $500 is punishment.*
> *This distinction between individual damage and social harm is extremely difficult to make in the legal systems of nonliterate societies, where court procedures are relatively informal. Even in in modern society, the distinction is dubious, for it rests upon the assumption that "individual" and "group" or "state" are mutually exclusive. For practical purposes, the individual is treated as if he were autonomous, but in fact an act that harms an individual also harms the group in which he has membership. Also, in modern society the indefiniteness of the distinction between torts and crimes is apparent when the victim of an act which is both a tort and a crime uses the criminal law as a method of forcing restitution which could not be secured with equal facility in the civil courts.*[41]

Regardless of the practical problem of administering criminal and civil law, there is the question of the origin of the legal concept of crime.

Some legal scholars maintain, as did Weber, that the distinction between tort and crime was unknown in primitive law and in the otherwise complex legal systems of ancient societies.[42] One difficulty in establishing the beginnings of criminal law has been the failure to distinguish between crime as a concept and crime as a term. The *Oxford English Dictionary* gives the fourteenth century as the date of the earliest reference to the word "crime." If one is looking for "crime" in the English vocabulary, this may be true. On the Continent, the term *causae criminales* was recorded as early as A.D. 614 in the edict of the Merovingian King Chlotar. Thus, since the word "crime" is French, and French was not a part of the English legal vocabulary until after the Norman Conquest of 1066, one would hardly expect to find "crime" in early English legal terminology. An early English legal concept of crime was most likely incorporated in the Anglo-Saxon terms *synn, gylt,* and *undoed.*

It is apparent, nevertheless, that the modern concept of crime did not become firmly established in English law until the reign of Henry II (1154–1189). Before Henry's time, crime was basically a wrong against an individual and the kinship group, to be remedied by either blood or money. Cases were decided almost solely by battle and compurgation. As a vigorous king, Henry was instrumental in strengthening his government and in reorganizing the judicial system.[43] He created the *Curia Regis*, a legislative, executive, administrative body, which was a court of law as well. In doing this, Henry centralized the government in the king, removing authority from the local courts of the barons and the Church. With a centralized government and the machinery for its effective administration, Henry could insist that crime was a wrong against the state. Crime consequently violated the "King's Peace."

On the basis of recent scholarship, Gerhard O. W. Mueller has shown that crime exists as a concept in early formalized codes of law.[44] The concept of crime appears in the Babylonian code of Hammurabi of about 2270 B.C., in the law codes of ancient Palestine, in the Twelve Tables of Roman law, and in Germanic law. In the Germanic legal code, *Legas Barbarorum*, tort law is indicated in section *Lex Thuringorum*: "Who not wilfully by some accident kills a human being or wounds him, shall pay lawful compensation." And the concept of crime is indicated in section *Lex Saxonum*: "Who conspires either against the kingdom or the life of the king of the Francs or his sons, shall be punished with capital punishment." We may thus conclude that, while not always expressed in the most explicit terms, the concept of crime as a *wrong against society* has been a part of most modern systems of law. Crime in the modern sense of the concept, then, means a wrong against a politically organized society represented by the state.

SOURCES OF CRIMINAL LAW

Contemporary criminal law is actually composed of two separate and distinct bodies of rules, the *substantive* criminal law and the *procedural* criminal law. The substantive criminal law consists of a description of the acts that are forbidden and the punishments that may be imposed when the laws are violated.

The procedural law describes how the state will deal with violators. At the same time, procedural law provides the alleged violator with protection from unjust treatment by the state. Procedural law specifies the course of action that is to be followed at several stages of the legal process, that is, the appropriate procedure for (1) the complaint, (2) the warrant, (3) the arrest, (4) the preliminary hearing, (5) the accusation, (6) the arraignment, (7) the trial, (8) the sentence, (9) appellate review, and (10) executive clemency.

Modern criminal law, both substantive and procedural, is derived from four basic sources. The majority of rules that define conduct as criminal are found in (1) constitutions, (2) statutes, (3) court decisions, and (4) administrative regulations. *Constitutional law* consists primarily of procedural rules and basic principles that serve as guides for future enactments and decisions. *Statutory law* is composed of the enactments of legislative bodies. These laws are for the most part compiled in state and federal volumes, variously termed *The Criminal Code, The Penal Code, Penal Law*, and the like. In addition to such compilations, many "noncode" criminal statutes have been enacted by legislatures. These statutes, pertaining primarily to commerce, agriculture, health, and welfare, are not found in the respective criminal codes but are scattered throughout the statute books.[45]

Common law, the third basic source of criminal law consists of precedents derived from earlier judicial decisions. Court decisions, sometime collectively called case law, coming from particular cases before the courts, become a part of the body of rules that are used for future determinations in similar or analogous cases. This application by courts of rules announced in previous decisions is referred to as *stare decisis*, which means "let the decision stand." This principle is fundamental to English and American law, although it is the practice on occasion for a higher court to overrule judicial precedents.[46]

Administrative law, the fourth source of criminal law, is composed of the regulations and rulings that are made by the numerous federal, state, and local administrative agencies. These agencies are granted authority by the legislative and executive branches of government to establish and enforce policies for the sphere of activity for which they are responsible. Within the last hundred years in the United States, and in many other countries as well, there has developed an elaborate system of administrative agencies concerned with business and public welfare.[47] The result has been that a vast bulk of criminal law has been created by these agencies. The laws are enforced and the cases are adjudicated by these agencies in the name of the government.

In recent years, utilizing all of these sources of criminal law, statutory law in particular, the state has entered a *new stage* of crime control. Orchestrated largely by the *executive* branch of government, there has been a rapid increase in criminal legislation, law enforcement programs, and judicial activity. These recent efforts in crime control mark the attempt by the state to respond to the crisis in contemporary society. Instead of changing the social and economic system to relieve or eliminate the contradictions inherent in them, the state has reacted by *protecting the existing order*. In waging "war on crime," the state has sought to preserve domestic order by means of the criminal law.[48]

Beginning in the early 1960s, the nation's problems began to be focused simply and conveniently on a domestic enemy: crime. Crime and the fear of crime played a crucial role in the political campaigns of the decade. The Johnson administration finally assumed the task of launching the war on crime. In a presidential message to the 89th Congress in 1965, Lyndon Johnson declared that "we must arrest and reverse the trend toward lawlessness."[49] Suggesting that "crime has become a malignant enemy in America's midst," Johnson charted a course of action based on legal control and law enforcement: "This active combat against crime calls for a fair and efficient system of law enforcement to deal with those who break the law. It means giving new priority to the methods and institutions of law enforcement." The problem was conceived to be a national one, with crime prevention and crime fighting to be intensified at all levels of government. The federal effort, Johnson continued, would consist of "(1) increased federal law enforcement efforts, (2) assistance to local enforcement efforts, and (3) a comprehensive, penetrating analysis of the origins and nature of crime in modern America."

Johnson appointed a commission, the President's Commission on Law Enforcement and Administration of Justice, to study the crime problem and to make recommendations for action. Hearings were held by the Senate Judiciary Committee (Subcommittee on Criminal Laws and Procedures) and by the House Judiciary Committee. The hearings provided the framework for defining the crime problem in modern terms, suggesting new criminal laws, stricter law enforcement, denial of basic rights for defendants, and the use of modern technology in the war on crime. The Senate committee's chairman, John McClellan, opened the hearings on March 7, 1967, by stating, "It is quite probable that these hearings and the bills we will be considering will mark the turning point in the struggle against lawlessness in this nation.[50] The survival of the state and the current social and economic order (the "society") was presented to the American people as being at stake: "The rate of increase in crime cannot continue if our society is to remain safe and secure and our people protected against the ravages of crime."

The result of these efforts was the enactment of the Omnibus Crime Control and Safe Streets Act of 1968. The new crime legislation initially assisted state and local governments in increasing the effectiveness of law enforcement and criminal administration—in trying more effectively to secure domestic order. By the time the bill was passed, several amendments were added that deliberately attempted to overturn previous Supreme Court decisions that supposedly "coddled criminals" and "handcuffed the police." For example, one amendment provided that all voluntary confessions and eyewitness identifications—regardless of whether a defendant had been informed of his rights to counsel—could be admitted in federal trials. In another provision, federal, state, and local law-enforcement agencies were given broad license to tap telephones and engage in other forms of eavesdropping without obtaining a court order. It subsequently was revealed that even these broad licenses were not sufficient for the Justice Department. Under the infamous leadership of John Mitchell, the department illegally eavesdropped on some six hundred citizens, whose resulting convictions were eventually overturned as unconstitutional. Another amendment provided that any persons convicted of "inciting a riot or civil disorder," "organizing, promoting, encouraging, or participating in a riot or disorder," or "aiding and abetting any person in committing" such offenses, would be disqualified from employment by the federal government for five years.

The government has continued to rely on these sources of criminal law in its course of controlling crime. The administration and several congressional committees have worked to construct a comprehensive program of crime control, including a crime bill for the District of Columbia, drug control legislation, an organized crime bill, and a series of proposals for future legislation.

As in the Omnibus Crime Bill, the recent crime control laws contain many repressive measures. Fundamental procedure policies are instituted covering such matters as preventive detention, "no-knock" searches, extension of grand jury powers, long-term sentencing, and reversals in the due process of law. Upon passage of this legislation, the Senate majority leader could state: "After the passage of these bills, we may then direct ourselves to the more difficult tasks of identifying and addressing ourselves to the task of eradicating the causes of criminal behavior."[51] If the state were to seriously turn its attention to the social structural contradictions that underlie criminally defined behavior, it would find itself faced with the task of launching a critical examination of contemporary society.

ADMINISTRATION OF CRIMINAL JUSTICE

In juridical terminology, the actual operation of criminal law is usually called the administration of justice. Every actual or perceived violation of the law is supposed to be judged according to a number of criteria, in determining whether or not the conduct constitutes a crime. Delegated officials of the state, through defined procedures, determine the criminality of any conduct that is brought to their attention. Before any act or omission can be officially labeled as crime, four principles have to be established: (1) that the conduct actually occurred, (2) that the conduct was in violation of the criminal law, (3) that the conduct was committed with intent, and (4) that the alleged violator was capable of the conduct.

A number of legal terms and concepts have been used at various times to refer to the above principles. In the administration of the criminal law there probably is no general doctrine more important than that of *mens rea*. This ancient legal doctrine has been used for centuries in a variety of legal systems to refer in a general way to the idea that no person shall be punished for conduct in which their mind is innocent. *Mens rea* has been intertwined with a host of interrelated legal issues and concepts in the administration of criminal law, including those of intention, liability, negligence, moral wrong, malice aforethought, culpability, insanity, responsibility, and the recent concept of recklessness.

Basic to the traditional meaning of *mens rea* is a moral connotation expressed in terms of "evil mind" or "evil will" by early writers and in terms of "guilty mind" or "moral culpability" by modern writers.[52] Today, as in the past, determination of the criminality of an accused person depends upon a consideration of his or her ability to commit an offense and his or her responsibility for that offense. Over a period of many centuries, there gradually developed in English law the recognition that certain persons were not wholly responsible for their actions. This recognition was to later form the basis for Weber's distinction between substantive and formal rationality in his work on the sociology of law. Included among these were the insane, mental defectives, and minors. The belief that minors were not

responsible for their law-violating acts was incorporated into the English principle of *parens patriae*, in which the king was regarded as the ultimate protector of all minors, as well as father of the country. In early chancery, jurisdiction, children received protection in a host of matters. Chancery jurisdiction was eventually applied to the criminal-court procedure in handling child offenders. The juvenile court was an outgrowth of these early developments.[53] The earliest American juvenile court was established in Cook County (Chicago), Illinois, in 1899. The movement spread rapidly throughout the United States. Thus, today violations by minors, which would be judged as crimes if committed by adults, are usually handled in juvenile courts. Minors are not likely to be charged with crimes, but their cases are "heard" and a "disposition" is administered under supervision of the court. Such differential handling of minors has, however, been modified through the Supreme Court's decision in the *Gault* case. On the basis of the 1967 ruling, juvenile courts must now grant children many of the constitutional rights observed in adult courts.

The first major test in Anglo-American law of the mental condition of an offender was formulated in the *M'Naghten* case of 1843. At that time, Daniel M'Naghten was acquitted for an attempt on the life of the British prime minister, an attempt that nevertheless resulted in the death of the prime minister's secretary. M'Naghten was acquitted on the ground of insanity. Believing that a stiffer test for insanity was required, the law lords responded by issuing what came to be called the M'Naghten Rule. According to the rule, a person is sane if "the accused at the time of doing the act knew the difference between right and wrong." This rule remained in the procedural law of England and most of the United States for the next century, although increasingly coming under critical fire.

A major change in the insanity test came in 1954 when the Court of Appeals of the District of Columbia, in a trial, finally rejected the M'Naghten Rule in favor of a new test called the Durham Rule (which had effect only in the District of Columbia). It held that a person is not responsible for a criminal act if the crime "was the product of a mental disease or defect." Later the court defined "mental disease or defect" as including "any abnormal condition of the mind which substantially affects mental or emotional processes and substantially *impairs behavior control*." This gave the psychiatrist the power to tell the jury the details of a defendant's background and the personality factors that caused his mental condition. Juries began to find with increasing frequency that certain offenses were the result of abnormal mental states. The number of insanity acquittals rose from one in 1953, to 100 in 1959, and to 104 in 1960. The courts responded by tightening the interpretation of the Durham Rule, and the number of insanity acquittals dropped to 74 in 1962 and to only 12 in 1965.

Some authorities on the historical development of legal doctrine are currently arguing that since the landmark case of *Durham* v *United States*, judicial decisions have increasingly reflected lack of judicial respect for the civil and constitutional rights of persons suffering from mental illness. There is also evidence that in the twenty-two years since the Durham decision its liberalized position has been more or less completely rejected by the psychiatric profession; and it is the cooperation of the psychiatrst as expert witness that is essential for its success. Furthermore, during these past two decades, "The poor were forced to rely on mediocre and prosecution-oriented government psychiatrists and the success of the insanity defense was dictated by a psychiatric *fiat* founded on considerations of a hospital housing shortage rather than pure diagnostic judgment. Only the wealthy could afford to challenge the judgment of the government psychiatrists."[54]

More recently, in 1966, the United States Congress proposed a District of Columbia crime bill that would have substituted the Durham Rule for a test of responsibility recommended by the American Law Institute, a body composed of members from the bench and bar of the entire country, in the Model Penal Code of 1962. The test, which was earlier adopted by the United States Court of Appeals for the Second Circuit and by the Third Circuit Court of Appeals (in the Currens Rule), holds that "a person is not responsible for his conduct if he lacks substantial capacity either to know or appreciate the wrongfulness of his conduct or to conform his conduct to the requirements of law." The new rule represents a move back to the M'Naghten Rule and gives the jury more freedom to use its judgment as to whether the defendant was mentally capable of committing a crime.[55] Legislation is also being proposed that would prevent a defendant from pleading not guilty by reason of insanity as long as the prosecution can establish the presence of all the elements of the crime. The mental state of the defendant would arise only if the condition was so serious that the prosecution could not prove criminal intent at the time of the crime. It is debatable whether the new definitions clarify the issue of *mens rea.* The issue of *mens rea* seems likely to remain at the heart of the administration of criminal justice for some time.

The mental state of the offender is not the only criterion used in determining the criminality of conduct. The criteria of liability and responsibility, however defined, have been used in a consideration of the intent of the person and of his capacity to commit a crime. The recently proposed Model Penal Code by the American Law Institute deals explicitly with the issues of liability and responsibility. The Model Penal Code submits that only four concepts are needed to describe the kinds of culpability sufficient to establish liability: purpose, knowledge, recklessness, and negligence.[56] The code recognizes that the kinds of culpability required by the law may vary from one crime to another and from one circumstance to another. Also considered in the code is the issue of strict liability. Strict liability, meaning the liability to punitive sanction despite the lack of intent, has become an issue in criminal law with the increasing use of regulative law, such as the regulations pertaining to the public's welfare in housing and in food and drug purchases. The practical solution proposed in the Model Penal Code involves the creation of a grade of offense that is not denominated as crime and that entails upon conviction no severer sentence than a fine, civil penalty, or forfeiture.

No matter what criteria may be used to establish criminal liability, and various criteria have been used in historically different legal systems, it is clear that they are based on certain underlying assumptions about the nature of human life and society. In the administration of criminal law, the two philosophies of *rationalism* and *determinism* have served as alternative assumptions about the criminal and his environment. These two philosophies have provided diverse concepts of liability and responsibility.[57] Rationalism, with its modern development in the latter half of the eighteenth century and the first part of the nineteenth century, was a response to the administration of arbitrary and barbarous criminal procedures. Liberal writers of the period, taking little account of social conditions, viewed the violator as an independent, reasoning individual who weighs the consequences of his or her crime. The proposed system of justice was on the basis of a reasoned retribution for clearly defined legal categories of crime.

The deterministic position, on the other hand, developing shortly after rationalism, was founded on an awareness of the relation between the criminal and the social order. Writers in the positivistic tradition contend that criminal responsibility should be based not on free will but upon the needs of society. The potential danger of the offender to the community rather than his or her guilt served as the basis for establishing criminal responsibility. In other words, the classicists assumed the existence of criminal responsibility as an essential part of the liberal doctrine of individual choice. The determinists denied this form of responsibility as incompatible with social and psychological determinism, suggesting instead a concept of responsibility that considered the social danger of the offense. Subsequent national codes of criminal law adopted one or the other philosophy of criminal responsibility, although the rationalistic philosophy of responsibility was most commonly adopted in criminal codes.[58]

In the United States a contradiction has generally existed between the philosophy underlying the administration of criminal law and the explanation of criminal behavior, that is, between legalistic and scientific thought. The explanation of criminal behavior by the social scientists has tended to rest on a deterministic approach, while the problem of establishing the criminality of an accused person, the problem of the legalist, has depended upon a rationalistic approach. In the administration of justice, the primary concern is with whether the person is guilty. The principles of crime (criminal law, conduct, intent, and capacity) must be considered for every given case. In the administration of criminal law, the problem is not one of why people violate the law but one of whether the accused person violated a law and should be convicted of the offense. In the explanation of criminal behavior, on the other hand, the criminologist attempts to generalize beyond the particular case. Criminologists have traditionally attempted to find regularities in behavior. They have sought explain criminal behavior in terms of factors and conditions outside the offender and beyond the immediate act. Such an endeavor tends to lead to a deterministic model, a search for conditions that produce other conditions or behaviors.[59]

The breach between the administration of criminal law and criminology is not necessarily inevitable and unalterable. As we have witnessed in recent years, efforts to control crime have involved the suspension of many of the traditional concepts of justice, even including frequently due process of law. As this happens, the interests of the agents of legal order and those of criminologists and other social scientists begin to converge. The scientists' explanations of crime are based on an interest in establishing social order; and the administration of justice is for the preservation of the existing social order.

THE RULE OF LAW

An understanding of crime in America must recognize the relation between law and the moral order. Any legal system claims to rest on a moral order that legitimizes the prevailing law, including the laws of crime control. The moral basis of the law, that we are all to be bound by the law, is also known as the rule of law. To accept the principle of the rule of law, however, is to run the risk of also uncritically accepting the legal system and the political economy upon which that entire legal system rests. Therefore, if we are to understand law and crime in the state, we have to be aware of the ideological foundations of the legal order.[60] This is to say that if we are concerned about the problem of crime in our society, we must by that fact be married to an equal concern with how the ideology of law defines criminal behavior in the first place and how it defines the duties and responsibilities of "good citizens."

What is the nature of the legal ideology in the United States, and how does that ideology come to prevail in the society at large? The superstructure of the legal system and its ideology is a reflection of the substructure of capitalism. As such, the ideology of law, the rule of law, prevails by the very fact that the dominant reality in America is capitalist. Thus, alternatives to our present legal order and all its contradictions, the results of which are recognized and bemoaned by all, are not easily perceivable within the existing framework. Except in dialectical thinking, which is not the methodology of conventional criminology, existing reality always rejects alternative possibilities. For example, an American society without centralized, capitalist law, is rarely suggested. The capitalist ideology of law successfully keeps alternatives from arising; and that in fact is one of its purposes.

The second basic way the legal ideology is ensured, protected, and strengthened is through the repressive efforts of privileged groups in our liberal democratic society. Alan Wolfe, in *The Seamy Side of Democracy: Repression in America*, constructs a convincing argument, based upon historical analysis, to the effect that Amercian society is at heart a repressive society; he bases his demonstration on the history of organizational and ideological heretics to the official legal ideology, groups such as the anarchists, the Communist party, the I.W.W., the Black Panther party, and others.[61] The eventual destruction of these renegade organizations reflects conscious, institutionalized, and systematic process, not temporary and chance aberrations in our system. Wolfe defines repression as "a process by which those in power try to keep themselves in power by consciously attempting to destroy or render harmless organizations and ideologies that threaten their power."[62] He then demonstrates the contradictions of inherent ambiguity in our liberal democratic state: While the Constitution gives individual freedom, it also gives the state the power to suppress that freedom—generally in the name of crime-fighting. The argument against the official legal ideology is based on the proposition that "other things being equal, in any conflict between privileged groups and those challenging those privileges, the state will support the former."[63] Thus, the state supports the powerful and suppresses the powerless, especially when these latter attempt to organize themselves under the banner of an alternate ideology. The state aids and assists those outside the dominant, privileged class only when it is to the enlightened interest of the dominant capitalist class to do so.

Furthermore, Bertell Ollman conceives of the state as an "illusory community" that expresses the relationship of each atomized individual to society as a whole in just the same manner that the concept of class expresses individuals' relations to all those others who share his or her socio-economic conditions of existence.[64] The state expresses the division between caring for oneself and caring for others, a condition of alienation in the genuine Marxian sense, because in the state we have been separated from our truly "human, that is, social mode of existence." In this manner the radical Marxian distinction is drawn between state existence and social existence. Ollman writes:

> In capitalism, the state is an abstraction in political life on the same plane that value is in economic life; the one is the abstract product of alienated political activity, just as the other is the abstract product of alienated productive activity. And just as value becomes a power over man when realized in the concrete forms of commodity, capital, money and so on, the state exercises power over him when expressed in the real institutions of government— in legislatures, executive agencies, courts, political parties, constitutions and laws.[65]

Thus, from this "spurious equality" our liberal democratic society derives its legal ideology of the rule of law: We are to treat the law as holy writ.

The bond between the worker and the owner in a capitalist economy is reproduced in the state between the citizens and the people who occupy the pinnacles of state power and control the machinery of government. In the symbolic realm the citizen is manipulated by the false ideal of patriotism to submit to these arrangements and their supporting legal ideology; but according to the above analysis, patriotism becomes "the detached impersonal kind of belonging that is associated with the state. To be patriotic is to recognize one's duties not to real living people, but to the abstract community, to the very links of alienation which bind the social whole after the human ties have been cut."[66]

Thus it is that the state destroys genuine communal interest, leaving the way open for the swarms of competing class, group, and individual "particular interests" to reduce society to a battleground. This is called pluralism, and it is all held together under the false aegis of a legal ideology called the rule of law.[67] The legal ideology perpetuates the existing system, a system that depends upon the fundamental contradiction of class divisions in the political economy.

Finally, perhaps the most powerful of the pervasive forces that support the rule of law are the moral values of the society. Underlying most societies is a belief in a *natural* moral order. This natural order assumes some kind of relation between human-made law ("positive law") and a higher law. The relation of the natural law to the human-made law is recognized in most legal systems. The result is a moral basis for the legal order.

The prevailing moral view of law in Western societies is basically the Greek conception; that is, the citizen has a moral duty to obey the law, even when that law seems to be immoral. According to the Greek conception, "human law may conflict with moral law but the citizen must still obey the law of his state though he may and indeed should labour to persuade the state to change its law to conform with morality."[68] This view has tended to dominate most Western ideologies of law since Greek times.

The same moral basis of the rule of law continues to this day. It is this legal ideology that underpins the recent efforts to control crime in this country. The American way of life is at stake, we are told, in this war on crime. This moral challenge is providing the state and the capitalist ruling class with the rationale to institute new forms of control. Crime today, as always, is a moral problem. This is what gives the ideology of law its force and consequence.

NOTES

1. Ernest W. Burgess, "Comment on Frank E. Hartung's White Collar Offenses in the Wholesale Meat Industry in Detroit," *American Journal of Sociology,* 56 (July 1950), p. 35.
2. Alfred R. Lindesmith and H. Warren Dunham, "Some Principles of Criminal Typology," *Social Forces* (March 1941), pp. 307–314.
3. Thorsten Sellin, *Culture Conflict and Crime* (New York: Social Science Research Council, 1938), p. 32.
4. Edwin H. Sutherland, *White Collar Crime* (New York: Holt, Rinehart and Winston, 1949), p. 31.
5. Jerome Michael and Mortimer J. Adler, *Crime, Law and Social Science* (New York: Harcourt Brace Jovanovich, 1933), p. 5.
6. C. Ray Jeffery, "The Structure of American Criminological Thinking," *Journal of Criminal Law, Criminology and Police Science,* 46 (January–February 1956), p. 671.
7. Paul W. Tappan, "Who is the Criminal?," *American Sociological Review,* 12 (February 1947), p. 100.
8. Albert Levitt, "Some Societal Aspects of the Criminal Law," *Journal of Criminal Law, Criminology and Police Science,* 13 (May–June 1922), p. 90.
9. Richard R. Korn and Lloyd W. McCorkle, *Criminology and Penology* (New York: Holt, Rinehart and Winston, 1959), p. 46.
10. See Austin T. Turk, "Prospects for Theories of Criminal Behavior," *Journal of Criminal Law, Criminology and Police Science,* 55 (December 1964), pp. 454–461.
11. Herman and Julia Schwendinger, "Defenders of Order or Guardians of Human Rights?," *Issues in Criminology,* 5 (Summer 1970), pp. 123–157.
12. Clayton A. Hartjen, "Legalism and Humanism: A Reply to the Schwendingers," *Issues in Criminology,* 7 (Winter 1972), pp. 59–69. See also Hartjen's discussion of this whole issue in his *Crime and Criminalization,* (New York: Praeger, 1974), pp. 2–5.
13. This discussion of critical theory is based on William Leiss, "The Critical Theory of Society," in Paul Breines ed., *Critical Interruptions* (N.Y.: Herder & Herder, 1972), pp. 74–100.
14. Tony Platt, "Prospects for a Radical Criminology in the United States," *Crime and Social Justice: A Journal of Radical Criminology,* 1 (Spring–Summer 1974), p. 2.
15. American Friends Service Committee, *Struggle for Justice,* (New York: Hill and Wang, 1971), pp. 10 and 11; quoted in Platt, op. cit., pp. 2 and 3.
16. Schwendingers, "Defenders of Order or Guardians of Human Rights?," p. 148.
17. Richard Quinney, "The Ideology of Law: Notes for a Radical Alternative to Legal Oppression," *Issues in Criminology,* 7:1 (Winter 1972), p. 24.
18. William Leiss, "The Critical Theory of Society," p. 80.
19. Trent Schroyer, "A Reconceptualization of Critical Theory," in David Colfax and Jack Roach, eds., *Radical Sociology,* (New York: Basic Books, 1971), p. 132.
20. Ibid., p. 137.
21. Ibid., p. 141.
22. M. Milutinovic, "Contemporary Criminological Thought: Main Trends in Contemporary Criminology," *International Journal of Criminology and Penology,* 2 (August 1974), p. 221.
23. For a fuller, historical exposition of this thesis, see Frederick Engels, *The Origin of the Family, Private Property, and the State* (New York: International Publishers, 1942).
24. On this theme see Stanley Diamond, "The Rule of Law Versus the Order of Custom," *Social Research,* 38 (Spring 1971), pp. 42–72.
25. Ibid., p. 71.
26. For an extended development of these themes, see Richard Quinney, *Critique of Legal Order: Crime Control in Capitalist Society* (Boston: Little, Brown, 1974).
27. F. James Davis, "Law as a Type of Social Control," in F. James Davis, Henry H. Foster, Jr., C. Ray Jeffery, and E. Eugene Davis, *Society and the Law* (New York: Free Press, 1962), p. 43.

28. Roscoe Pound, *Social Control Through Law* (New Haven: Yale University Press, 1943), p. 20.

29. Max Weber, *Law in Economy and Society,* ed. Max Rheinstein (Cambridge: Harvard University Press, 1954), p. 5.

30. Ibid., pp. 14 and 16.

31. William M. Evan, "Public and Private Legal Systems," in William M. Evan, ed., *Law and Sociology* (New York: Free Press, 1962), p. 183.

32. Philip Selznick, "Legal Institutions and Social Controls," *Vanderbilt Law Review,* 17 (December 1963), p. 88. Also see Philip Selznick, "Sociology and Natural Law," *Natural Law Forum,* 6 (1961), pp. 84–108.

33. Philip Selznick, "Sociology of Law," *International Encyclopedia of the Social Sciences,* vol. 9 (New York: Macmillan and Free Press, 1968), pp. 50–59.

34. Bronislav Malinowski, *Crime and Custom in Savage Society* (Boston: Routledge & Kegan Paul, 1926), p. 55.

35. E. Adamson Hoebel, *The Law of Primitive Man* (Cambridge: Harvard University Press, 1954), p. 28.

36. A. R. Radcliffe-Brown, *Structure and Function in Primitive Society* (New York: Free Press, 1956), p. 212.

37. Ronald L. Akers, "Toward a Comparative Definition of Law," *Journal of Criminal Law, Criminology and Police Science,* 56 (September 1965), p. 306.

38. Henry M. Hart, Jr., "The Aims of the Criminal Law," *Law and Contemporary Problems,* 23 (Summer 1958), p. 403.

39. Ibid., p. 403.

40. Rollin M. Perkins, *Criminal Law* (Brooklyn: Foundation Press, 1957), p. 5.

41. Edwin H. Sutherland and Donald R. Cressey, *Criminology,* 9th ed. (Philadelphia: Lippincott, 1974), p. 8.

42. Weber, *Law in Economy and Society,* p. 50.

43. See G. O. Sayles, *The Medieval Foundations of England* (London: Methuen, 1966), chap. 21.

44. Gerhard O. W. Mueller, "Tort, Crime and the Primitive," *Journal of Criminal Law, Criminology and Police Science,* 46 (September–October 1955), pp. 303–332.

45. Stanford J. Fox, "Statutory Criminal Law: the Neglected Part," *Journal of Criminal Law, Criminology and Police Science,* 52 (November–December 1961), pp. 392–404.

46. See C. Gordon Post, *An Introduction to the Law* (Englewood Cliffs, N.J.: Prentice-Hall, 1965), chap. 6.

47. See, for example, Frank E. Cooper, *State Administrative Law* (Indianapolis: Bobbs-Merrill, 1965); Kenneth C. Davis, *Administrative Law and Government* (St. Paul: West Publishing Co., 1960); Urban A. Lavery, *Federal Administrative Law* (St. Paul: West Publishing Co., 1952); Bernard Schwartz, *An Introduction to American Administrative Law,* 2d ed. (New York: Oceana, 1962); and Peter Woll, *Administrative Law: The Informal Process* (University of California Press, 1963).

48. For a detailed discussion of crime control in the last decade, see Quinney, *Critique of Legal Order,* especially pp. 51–135.

49. "Crime, Its Prevalence, and Measures of Prevention," Message from the President of the United States, House of Representatives, 89th Congress, March 8, 1965, Document No. 103.

50. "Controlling Crime Through More Effective Law Enforcement," *Hearings* Before the Subcommittee on Criminal Laws and Procedures of the Committee on the Judiciary, United States Senate, 90th Congress (Washington, D.C.: U.S. Government Printing Office, 1967), p. 1.

51. *Congressional Record,* Vol. 16, Part 2, 91st Congress, January 28, 1970 (Washington, D.C.: U.S. Government Printing Office, 1960), p. 1690.

52. See Jerome Hall, *General Principles of Criminal Law,* 2d ed., (Indianapolis: Bobbs-Merrill, 1960), chap. 3.

53. Anthony M. Platt, *The Child Savers* (University of Chicago Press, 1969). For a discussion of the legal definitions of juvenile delinquency and the operation of the juvenile court, see Donald J. Newman, "Legal Aspects of Juvenile Delinquency," in Joseph Roucek, ed., *Juvenile Delinquency* (New York: Philosophical Library, 1958), chap. 2.

54. Richard Arens, *Insanity Defense* (New York: Philosophical Library, 1974).

55. The various insanity defenses are presented in Abraham S. Goldstein, *The Insanity Defense* (New Haven: Yale University Press, 1967).

56. Herbert Wechsler, "On Culpability and Crime: The Treatment of *Men Rea* in the Model Penal Code," *Annals of the American Academy of Political and Social Science,* 339 (January 1962), pp. 24–41.

57. See Leon Radzinowicz, *Ideology and Crime* (New York: Columbia University Press, 1966), chaps. 1 and 2.

58. For an excellent analysis of this contradiction from a historical and developmental perspective, see Ian Taylor, Paul Walton, and Jack Young, *The New Criminology: For a Social Theory of Deviance* (New York: Harper & Row, 1974), pp. 1–30.

59. For the differences between legalistic and scientific approaches to "truth," see Michael Barkum, ed., *Law and the Social System* (New York: Lieber-Atherton, 1973), Introduction, pp. 1–15.

60. For a more detailed discussion, see Quinney, "The Ideology of Law," pp. 1–35.

61. Alan Wolfe, *The Seamy Side of Democracy: Repression in America,* (New York: McKay, 1973). For a compatible and comparable analysis, see also Roberta Ash, *Social Movements in America* (Chicago: Markham Publishing Co., 1972).

62. Ibid., p. 6.

63. Ibid., p. 25.

64. Bertell Ollman, *Alienation: Marx's Conception of Man in Capitalist Society* (Cambridge University Press, 1971).

65. Ibid., p. 216.

66. Ibid., p. 56.

67. See Ralph Miliband, *The State Capitalist Society* (New York: Basic Books, 1969), p. 182.

68. Dennis Lloyd, *The Idea of Law* (Baltimore: Penguin Books, 1964), p. 55.

THE DEVELOPMENT OF CRIMINOLOGY

The history of criminology has been a search for a stable social order.[1] In fact, criminology developed as a reaction to the various revolutions that were occurring in eighteenth- and nineteenth-century Europe. At that time the developing social sciences, responding to the turmoil and disorder of those eras, were attempting to discover the natural laws of society in hopes of establishing a stable social order.[2]

In the effort to discover these elusive "laws of society," early, and contemporary criminologists have tended to favor existing social arrangements. That which threatens the given social order is regarded as a violation of the natural laws of society. Crime has thus appeared to be something that disturbs society. Criminologists, rather than conceiving of crime as a form of rebellion or as a force of social change, have historically regarded it as a pathology that must be controlled or prevented. The development of criminology can thus be viewed as an ongoing attempt to explain crime in terms of established social order.

The history of criminology, nevertheless, lacks any clear accumulative theoretical growth. No line of theoretical development can be found that leads to a well-developed body of knowledge.[3] The study of crime is characterized by a number of divergent theoretical perspectives that exist in relative isolation from one another.

In order to review the development of criminology, the major theoretical perspectives can be presented according to the periods of time in which they served as the dominant themes or paradigms for the study of crime. Five theoretical perspectives, or paradigms, may thus be delimited in the development of criminology, perspectives embraced roughly by five time periods: (1) early and classical criminological thought, (2) nineteenth-century sociological criminology, (3) nineteenth-century biological criminology, (4) twentieth-century eclectic criminology, and (5) twentieth-century sociological criminology.

EARLY AND CLASSICAL CRIMINOLOGICAL THOUGHT

While it may be correct to date the beginnings of modern criminology in the first half of the last century, crime has been a topic of speculative thought for centuries. Most social philosophers have found it necessary to make observations about crime.[4] Plato, in *Republic*, suggested in regard to crime causation that "man's gold has always been the cause of many crimes." Aristotle noted in *Politics* that "poverty engenders rebellion and crime." The permissibility of theft "in the greatest need" was expressed by St. Thomas Aquinas in his *Summa Theologica.* Sir Thomas More in his *Utopia* argued that criminality is a reflection of society. These early writers found a discussion of crime necessary for observations on man, society, and the ideal condition of mankind.

While much of the writing of early social philosophers focused on the relation of crime to factors in the temporal world, it was common to attribute crime to the influence of powers outside this world. George B. Vold refers to this kind of explanation of crime as the "demonological."[5] Demonological explanations can be found in various forms. In primitive and preliterate animism it is held that evil spirits cause crime. During the Middle Ages, demons and devils were thought to be responsible for crime and other deviant acts. A great deal of attention has been given to this theme by Thomas Szaz, chiefly as it relates to the social attribution of crime and mental aberrations to diabolic possession.[6] The ideas of "sin" and "moral defect" occupied popular thought and much of the writing between the sixteenth and early nineteenth centuries. The criminal was viewed as having in some way an improper relation to other world powers.

The writers of the Enlightenment of the eighteenth century mark the beginning of a naturalistic approach to criminal behavior. In their philosophy the explanations of human behavior were to be found in man himself, not in supernatural forces. When they devoted their attention to crime, it was primarily in respect to the relation of the offender to the criminal law. Among the French were Montesquieu, who in 1748 in *L'Esprit des Lois* considered criminal justice at length; Voltaire, who expressed opposition to the arbitrariness of justice; and Marat, who criticized legislation in 1780 in his *Plan de legislation criminelle*. French socialists also gave considerable attention to crime, especially Fourier and Enfantin. A number of English utopian writers, anarchists, and socialists observed and criticized the administration of the criminal law and penal policies in relation to social conditions. Among their works were William Godwin's *Inquiry Concerning Political Justice* in 1793, Charles Hall's *The Effects of Civilization on the People of European States* in 1805, W. Thompson's *Inquiry into the Principles of the Distribution of Wealth, Most Conducive to Human Happiness* in 1824, Thomas Hodgskin's *Labour Defended* in 1825, and Robert Owen's *A New View of Society* in 1816 and *The Book of the New Moral World* in 1844. A Russian anarchist prince, Peter Kropotkin, wrote in 1883 an influential pamphlet, *Prisons and Their Moral Influence on Prisoners*, that proved to be an early forerunner of numerous modern critiques of penal systems.

Perhaps the most important ideas in criminological thought prior to the nineteenth century are to be found in what is commonly referred to as the classical school. The classical school in criminology represents the culmination of the eighteenth-century humanitarian rationalism that preceded the application of scientific methods to the study of human behavior. Guided by the assumption of a human ability to reason and control human destiny, the classical writers directed their attention to the relation of people to the legal structure of the state. In reaction to contemporary legal practices, these writers protested against the inconsistencies and injustices of the criminal law and its administration, proposing reforms that were more in keeping with their conception of human nature. The publication of *Tratto dei Delitti e delle Pene* by Cesare Beccaria (1738–1794) in 1764 (translated in 1767 as *Essay on Crimes and Punishment*) established the classical school of criminological thought for the period. Other classical writers of the period included Jeremy Bentham, William Blackstone, Samuel Romilly, Ludwig Feuerbach, and Robert Peel.[7]

By far, the most influential of these classical writers was Beccaria. Among the most enlightened and progressive humanists of his day, this Jesuit-trained scholar was strongly influenced by the negative-critical thought of the philosophers of the Enlightenment. He saw the criminal justice system of his time as a massive obstacle to human liberation, and he was outraged by the arbitrary administration of justice that characterized this criminal justice system. To correct these contradictions, he urged that criminal law be restructured in accordance with what he saw as "the natural rights of man," rights that people possess independent of the state. Human justice had to be brought more into line with divine and natural justice. Accordingly, he argued that justices should not interpret the criminal law in their judgments; and to make this arbitrary interpretation less neces-

sary, he pressed for more clear and more concise wordings of penal statutes. Obscure law filled with cryptic references and phrases must be discarded. It can be said today that Beccaria launched a moral crusade for the rule of law over the rule of people, for formal rationality of the law over substantive rationality. Beccaria was also an enlightened humanist in his ideas for penal reform, urging only that amount of punishment of the criminal that was deemed necessary for society's protection. His place in the history of criminology is secured by the fact that he laid a solid foundation for the far-reaching legislative changes in substantive and procedural criminal law that were to come later.[8]

A concern for justice and reform of the criminal law characterized the main body of thought of the classical writers. Also important for the development of criminology was the emphasis that classical thought placed on rational discourse. According to Bentham's slogan of "the greatest happiness of the greatest numbers," utility was the measure of all goodness. In practice, however, this tended to mean that the good of the society was placed before the rights of the people. The whole of classical theory has been summed up as follows:

1. All men being by nature self-seeking are liable to commit crime.
2. There is a consensus in society as to the desirability of protecting private property and personal welfare.
3. In order to prevent a "war of all against all," men freely enter into a contract with the state to preserve the peace within the terms of this consensus.
4. Punishment must be utilized to deter the individual from violating the interests of others. It is the prerogative of the state, granted to it by the individuals making up the social contract, to act against these violations.
5. Punishments must be proportional to the interests violated by the crime. It must not be in excess of this, neither must it be used for reformation; for this would encroach on the rights of the individual and transgress the social contract.
6. There should be as little law as possible, and its implementation should be closely delineated by due process.
7. The individual is responsible for his actions and is equal, no matter what his rank, in the eyes of the law. Mitigating circumstances or excuses are therefore inadmissable.[9]

Thus, classical theory essentially was a theory of social control. As such it represented the interests of the rising bourgeoisie.

NINETEENTH-CENTURY SOCIOLOGICAL CRIMINOLOGY

Modern criminology has been dated by Willem A. Bonger as beginning in the 1830s with the study of crime as a social phenomenon.[10] Before individualistic theories came into vogue, explanations of crime were largely in terms of factors in the social environment. The origins of the sociological study of crime were in part the result of the rise of the social sciences in general. The collection of criminal statistics in a number of European countries provided early criminologists with a great source of material on crime and also gave direction to the kind of research that could be conducted.

EUROPEAN CRIMINOLOGY

During the early and middle nineteenth century a number of scholars in the continental European countries gathered and analyzed crime statistics. Alexander von Oettingen of Germany, one of the pioneers in the analysis of crime statistics, devoted considerable attention to problems on the measurement of crime in his *Moralstatistik*. In Belgium, statisticians such as Adolphe Quételet studied the social nature of crime as reflected in crime statistics. A. M. Guerry, in charge of judicial statistics for Paris, analyzed (through the use of ecological maps) rates of crime against the person and against property for the regions of France. Numerous other European writers of the period interpreted crime as a function of the social environment.[11] A number of Italian socialists were also active in making observations about crime as a social phenomenon.[12] During this period two journals were instrumental in providing a source of publication for European studies of the social aspects of crime. In 1836, Antoine Marcellin Lacassagne established the *Archives de l'Anthropologie Criminelle,* and in 1896 Emilè Durkheim founded *L'Année Sociologique.* Other members of the early sociological school of criminology created the International Criminological Association.

In England, roughly between 1830 and 1860, there was a great deal of interest in the geographical distribution of crime.[13] Influenced by the impact of social change brought about by industrialization and the growth of cities, several English writers turned their attention to social problems, especially crime, brought about by these changes. In 1839, Rawson W. Rawson published a paper on "An Inquiry into the Statistics of Crime in England and Wales" in the *Journal of the Statistical Society of London.* In the same journal, Joseph Fletcher, Rawson's successor as honorary secretary of the Statistical Society of London, reported on rates of crime in relation to social characteristics of geographical areas. In an attempt to associate crime rates with characteristics of the countries of England and Wales, Fletcher refuted theories based on poverty, ignorance, and density of population, and proposed a theory that crime was a profession in which persons receive training in certain kinds of neighborhoods and in prisons and jails. Henry Mayhew, one of the founders of *Punch*, made detailed ecological analyses of crime in London. In a book titled *Those Who Will Not*, Mayhew noted for various types of crimes the locations of the offenses and residences of the offenders. Other works by Mayhew included *London Labour and London Poor*, published in 1854, and *The Criminal Prisons of London*, published in 1862. John Glyde, in an examination of the relation between population density and crime, published an article in 1856 on "The Localities of Crime in Suffolk" based on an analysis of the records of persons awaiting trial. In his *Irish*

Facts and Wakefield Figures, John T. Burt in 1863 suggested that habitual crime is the result of "criminal classes already existing" and that "crime is reproductive."

As one reviewer of these early works concludes, such studies cannot be classed with the ecological studies of the twentieth century because of their lack of a specific body of theory.[14] Yet, these works have been unduly ignored by contemporary criminologists. These early English ecological studies were, unfortunately, to be eclipsed by the individualistic theories of the biological positivists.

In addition to the studies noted above, several monumental works that related in one way or another to social conditions and crime were published during the nineteenth century in England. At the beginning of the century, Patrick Colquhoun, a magistrate for the counties of Middlesex, Surrey, Kent, and Essex, published the seventh edition ("Corrected and considerably enlarged") of *Treatise on the Police of the Metropolis.*[15] As indicated by the subtitle of the book ("Containing a Detail of the Various Crimes and Misdemeanors by which Public and Private Property and Security are, at present, Injured and Endangered: and Suggested Remedies for their Prevention"), Colquhoun devoted his attention to a discussion of forms of criminal behavior. Chapters of the book consist of such titles as "On Burglaries and Highway Robberies," "On Cheats and Swindlers," "On Gaining and Lottery," "On the Coinage of Counterfeit Money," and "On River Plunder." In regard to an explanation of crime, Colquhoun in his chapter on "The Origin of Criminal Offenses" made observations on such topics as deficient laws, ill-regulated police, habits of "the lower orders," bad education, idle servants, depraved morals of "aquatic labourers," and ill-regulated public houses. The primary purpose of the book was to criticize existing criminal law, punishment, and police procedures.

At the end of the century, Luke O. Pike published in two volumes *A History of Crime in England* subtitled "Illustrating the Changes in the Laws in the Progress of Civilisation; Written From the Public Records and Other Contemporary Evidence."[16] The book is an impressive work of scholarship, extensively documented, and for the criminologist, a source of descriptive material on crime over a great period of time, including material on the reactions to crime. Crime is discussed by Pike as being relative to changing criminal laws.

Another notable contribution to the study of social conditions and social life, including crime, is the monumental, multivolumed work of Charles Booth, *Life and Labour of the People of London.*[17] While first published as a two-volume work in 1889 and 1891, Booth's book was expanded in subsequent editions to include nine volumes in one edition and seventeen volumes in another. Booth was a merchant, shipowner, and manufacturer who, while benefiting from industrialization, was concerned about the changes in social conditions brought about by industrialization. Booth, apparently like others in his station, felt a moral obligation to improve society. As his biographers, T. S. and M. B. Simey, observe: "Booth appears to be a true Victorian insofar as he acclaimed the positive values of industrial and commercial enterprise, but sought at the same time to devise methods of combating the evils that had resulted from it."[18] Booth was a practical man who believed that social policy should be guided by facts, and he set out to gather the facts. What resulted was essentially an application of scientific inquiry to the understanding of social problems. As the Simeys have noted, "Objectivity and obligation were fused together by him into a new system of thought and inquiry."[19] Apparently, however, Booth's potential influence on British sociology was diminished by the continuing confidence in deductive reasoning in academic circles.

AMERICAN REFORMISM AND THE STUDY OF CRIME

There was the tendency in nineteenth-century American thought to equate crime with sin, pauperism, and immorality. Even when crime was recognized as a distinct phenomenon, it was usually regarded as an ill that had no place in social life. Crime was one of those conditions that fell within the domain of the reformism that characterized roughly the last fifty years of the nineteenth century in the United States.

This reformism, rooted in and shaped by principles of romanticism, humanitarianism, democracy, and the religious idea of community, created an awareness of social problems. Various behaviors and conditions became defined as problems inappropriate to the American ideal. Crusades, movements, and organizations flourished in the attempt to attack such evils as intemperance, slavery, poverty, mental illness, idleness, defective education, war, and discrimination against women. Criminal and penal codes were rewritten in an attempt to achieve a more humane and rational justice. There was specific agitation for prison reform, resulting in new concepts of imprisonment.

Reform efforts by no means went unchallenged. The teachings of classical, laissez faire, individualistic economics, and the eventual popularity of conservative Social Darwinism were counter themes for any attempt at reform and social planning. Yet, many persons in positions of responsibility and authority were impressed with the need for more adequate knowledge that would guide their endeavors, especially in charity and philanthropic work, and supply them with rational grounds for implementation. The social science movement in the second half of the century was to a great extent stimulated by such a need. The conception of social science as a systematic body of knowledge for the purpose of reform became an important part of the American academic community.[20] In colleges and universities such as the University of Chicago in the Midwest, Stanford in the West, and Columbia in the East, newly established social science departments designed courses on the basis of specific social problems, with criminology among the first sociology courses offered in the curriculum. Thus, the study of crime, as well as the study of other social problems, became at an early time an integral part of the academic sociology.

In addition to the academic beginnings of the sociological study of crime, crime received study as a social phenomenon by a number of persons engaged in prison and welfare work. In a study of these writers, Guillot documents that a sociological criminology flourished in the United States around the period of the Civil War. In evaluation of the work of these writers, Ellen Elizabeth Guillot comments: "Their efforts may seem naive to the criminologist of today, but there was a groping toward objectivity. Students obtained their data at first hand, they recorded and analyzed what they saw with their own eyes, and they put their common sense to work in a quantitative framework."[21]

Among these early criminologists were Z. B. Brockway, superintendent of Elmira Reformatory; Michael Cassidy, prison administrator; E. C. Wines, secretary of the Prison Association of New York; Franklin B. Sanborn, chairman of the Massachusetts Board of State Charities; and Richard Vaux, president of the Board of Inspectors of Eastern State Penitentiary as well as lawyer and one-time mayor of Philadelphia. Other writings on the social causes of crime came from persons associated with such organizations as the National Prison Reform Congress, the National Conference of Charities and Corrections, National Prison Congress, and the Society for Alleviating the Miseries of Public Prisons.

The writers of this period, 1860 to 1885, viewed crime as a product of "disharmony" in the operation of social forces, "constituents," or institutions of society. As Guillot comments on this viewpoint: "When these institutions were not soundly constructed, or when their functions were not realized competently and responsibly, and when the patterns of behavior characteristic of groups of people differed from predominating standards, crime was a natural consequence."[22] In their explanation of crime in terms of social conditions, most of the writers assumed that the operation of any one factor could only partially explain the phenomenon of crime. While they pointed to associations, they believed that a multiplicity of social causes operated to produce crime. Of the many factors considered, most popular in the explanation of crime were drinking, lack of trade education,

desire for luxuries, poverty, oblivion of religious and moral principles, idleness, abnormal family relations, bad company, and, in general, civilization.

Crime in the growing city became a problem and focus of attention for several writers in the last half of the nineteenth century. Charles Loring Brace, in a life devoted to the organization of charities, found the causes of crime to be rooted in the way of life of a significant segment of the urban population. In his fascinating book, *The Dangerous Classes of New York* (subtitled "And Twenty Years Among Them"), Brace described in considerable detail the life conditions of numerous groups in New York with which he worked as secretary of the Children's Aid Society.[23] The groups included were what he defined as German ragpickers, the street rovers, the poor, the little Italian organ-grinders, homeless girls, the ignorant, the outcast street children, and the Nineteenth Street gang of ruffians.

Another commentator on urban crime was the journalist Edward Crapsey. In *The Nether Side of New York* (subtitled "Or the Vice, Crime and Poverty of the Great Metropolis") Crapsey, in a fine example of an early empirical study of crime, utilized the records of the police department, coroners' records, interviews with officials, and the records of courts, public meetings, and various agencies. He then described and analyzed types of crime, modes of operation, and the locations of crime in New York. His underlying theory was that crime had developed in the city because of the lack of community integration and because of the corruption that permeated the political structure. As Crapsey stated his position:

> *With its middle classes in large part self-exiled, its laboring*
> *population being brutalized in tenements, and its citizens of*
> *the highest class indifferent to the common weal, New York drifted*
> *from bad to worse, and became the prey of professional*
> *thieves, ruffians, and political jugglers. The municipal government*
> *shared in the vices of the people, and New York became a*
> *city paralyzed in the hands of its rulers.*[24]

The religious temper of the latter part of the nineteenth century, especially as found in the social gospel, was attuned to the crime problem. The social-gospel movement was an outgrowth of a reaction within Protestantism to the perils attributed to the new industrial capitalism and to the failure of the church to grapple with social conditions. A number of religious leaders, such as Washington Gladden in *Applied Christianity* and Walter Rauschenbusch in *Christianity and the Social Order*, argued at the turn of the century for a religion that would adjust Christianity to the problems of this world, wishing to create a kingdom of God on earth. The social-gospel movement helped to revolutionize attitudes toward social problems, including crime. One of the results was the development of urban neighborhood programs and settlement houses.

Religious and humanitarian indignation of social problems was also expressed to the public in such popular books as *In His Steps* by Charles M. Sheldon and *If Christ Came to Chicago* by W. T. Stead. Thus, a combination of social, religious, and political movements, including the social gospel, humanitarianism, premuckraking thought, and emerging progressivism, joined to focus critical public and intellectual attention on crime as a social problem. Crime was a condition that was not appropriate to the American character.

The social sources of the administration of justice also came under scrutiny during the last quarter of the nineteenth century and the beginnig of the twentieth. A judge in Denver, Ben Lindsey, began to question the severe handling of juvenile offenders.[25] Viewing juvenile delinquency as a product of the social and economic environment, Lindsey found a clause in a Colorado school law that could be interpreted to mean that juvenile delinquents were wards of the state and were to be treated by the state. Lindsey transformed his court into a juvenile court. He avoided the concept of punishment and instituted a plan to bring juvenile delinquents into an environment of new opportunities. Similar efforts toward reform of juvenile justice were also taking place in other parts of the country, particularly the creation of special juvenile institutions in New York and legislation on delinquency in Illinois. These experiments, with their emphasis on environmental conditions, spread rapidly throughout the United States.

The use of the environmental theory of crime and delinquency provided a rationale for judicial and correctional reform. In 1884 the theory was forcefully brought to public attention by the publication of Peter Altgeld's *Our Penal Machinery and Its Victims.* Altgeld's passionate argument that poverty lay at the bottom of most crime and delinquency received wide attention. Altgeld, a wealthy reformer, sent copies of the book to every legislator, judge, warden, minister, teacher, lecturer, and social worker he could find on a mailing list. In Ashtabula, Ohio, the book came to the attention of a young county lawyer, Clarence Darrow (1857–1938). Throughout his illustrious career, Darrow defended cases and pursued justice on the basis of the environmental argument. Speaking to an audience of offenders at the Cook County jail in Chicago in 1902, Darrow pushed environmentalism to its limit: "There is no such thing as crime as the word is generally understood. If every man, woman and child in the world had a chance to make a decent, fair, honest living, there would be no jails and no lawyers and no courts."[26]

Academic criminology in the United States, however, was to be influenced only minimally and at most only indirectly by the ideas on crime that emanated from several sources in nineteenth-century America. Sociological criminology in the twentieth century and was more influenced by the new social science, European positivism, and the criminological writings of European thinkers than by the leads provided by the reformers, prison administrators, humanitarians, and socially conscious writers of the nineteenth century.

NINETEENTH-CENTURY BIOLOGICAL CRIMINOLOGY

The beginning of modern criminology is usually marked by work of the Italian physician, Cesare Lombroso, and his immediate followers. For example, Barnes, in his review of criminology in *Encyclopedia of the Social Sciences*, writes: "The originators of modern criminology are Cesare

Lombroso (1836–1909), Enrico Ferri (1856–1928), and Raffaelle Garofalo, who together are designated as the Italian school. Lombroso's work became the point of departure for the science."[27] Recently, in a survey of criminology, Radzinowicz has given a similar evaluation, noting that "virtually every element of value in contemporary criminological knowledge owes its formulation to that remarkable school of Italian criminologists who took pride in describing themselves as 'positivists' "[28] Such judgments on the founding of modern criminology are based on the assumption that there were no efforts before the Italian criminologists to take the discussion of crime out of the realm of theology and metaphysics and into the objective description and analysis of crime as a natural phenomenon.

A reading of the history of criminology, however, shows that there was a scientific study of crime before the appearance of the Italian school, and, furthermore, that the prior writings were more pertinent to the sociological study of crime than the work of the Italian writers. An extensive literature on the social aspects of crime, as scientifically valid as the writings of the Italians, was in existence before Lombroso began his work. There is, thus, a myth in criminology that Lombroso is the founder of scientific criminology. What Lombroso and his followers actually did, as Alfred R. Lindesmith and Yale Levin have noted, was to change the conception of crime and the focus of attention, not necessarily to make the study of crime more scientific or objective: "For centuries the criminal had been regarded as a human being living in society; Lombroso's contribution seems to have been to have inaugurated the study of the criminal as an animal or as a physical organism."[29] In studying the individual criminal, the criminal apart from the social setting, the Lombrosians turned attention away from the perspective that crime is a social phenomenon.

The Italian criminologists are usually regarded as the founders of the "positive school" of criminology. If the term "positive" is used to identify these criminologists, it must not be confused with the substantive theories of the writers. Nor may the term be used to characterize this school's depiction of people convicted of crimes by the state. The theoretical orientation of the Italian criminologists was for the most part substantively biological. Their approach to the study of crime was positivistic in that they utilized or attempted to utilize the point of view and methodology of the natural sciences. Methodologically, then, the positive school of criminology is in contrast to the speculative approach of the classical school. The two schools also differ in their general theoretical orientations. While the classical school emphasized the idea of the choice of right and wrong, the positive school placed the emphasis on the determinism of conduct. In a sense, all of contemporary criminology is positivistic in method and basic formulation, and the sociological criminology of the nineteenth century is as positivistic as the biological criminology of the Lombrosians. Most students of crime are in some sense positivistic.

Other writers before Lombroso presented theories alluding to the criminal as a definite physical type. The physiognomy of Johann Kaspar Lavater in the latter part of the eighteenth century and the phrenology of Franz Joseph Gall at the beginning of the nineteenth are part of the general background of thought on the relation between physique, character, and behavior. From the beginning of the nineteenth century, mental degeneration explanations flourished, as in the writings of Philippe Pinel, Jean Esquirol, and B. A. Morel. In the mid-nineteenth century English prison physicians, including James Bruce Thompson, Forbes Benignus Winslow, George Wilson, and David Nicholson were making references to the physical and psychological anomalies of the criminal.[30] With the aid of statistics, they attempted to demonstrate that the criminal is a distinct physical type, publishing their results under such titles as "Statistics of Prisoners: Their Mental Conditions and Diseases," "Criminal Lunatics of Scotland," "The Hereditary Nature of Crime," "On Moral Imbecility of Habitual Criminals as Exemplified by Cranial Measurement," and "The Morbid Psychology of the Criminal." *The Anatomy of Suicide* by Winslow, published in 1840, presented the results of postmortem examinations of 1333 cases of suicide. Pursuing the thesis that suicide is a result of physical anomalies, for the practical purpose of gaining the abolition of the punishment of the suicide's family, Winslow found it necessary to conclude that "the morbid appearances are so varied and capricious that they cannot lead to sound conclusions." His contradictory conclusions illustrate that empirical evidence need not destroy faith in a theoretical assumption when that assumption is highly valued or when no alternatives are readily available. Study of the criminal as a physical type was also given special attention by anthropologists in the mid-nineteenth century. The peculiarities of skulls and brains of criminals were noted by Broca, who in 1859 initiated criminal anthropology as a part of the Anthropological Society of Paris.

The publication of Lombroso's *L'uomo delinquente* in 1876 marked the synthesis of a line of thought that had been developing in Europe for some time. Lombroso, who spent a considerable part of his career as professor of legal medicine at the University of Turin, presented in dramatic form the thesis of the atavistic criminal. According to Lombroso, the criminal was a *born* criminal, a throwback to a more primitive and savage man. Although Lombroso acknowledged precedents to his thesis, including prehistoric folklore, he expressed excitement in his own revelation. In a speech at the Congress of Criminal Anthropology at Turin in 1906, Lombroso recalled his discovery:

> *In 1870 I was carrying on for several months researches in the prisons and asylums of Pavia upon cadavers and living persons, in order to determine upon substantial differences between the insane and criminals without succeeding very well. Suddenly the morning of a gloomy day in December, I found in the skull of a brigand a very long series of atavistic anomalies, above all an enormous middle occipital fossa and a hypertrophy of the vermis, analogous to those that are found in inferior invertebrates. At the sight of these strange anomalies, as a large plain appears under an inflamed horizon, the problem of the nature and of the origin of the criminal seemed to me resolved; the characters to primitive men and of inferior animals must be reproduced in our time.*[31]

It is true that Lombroso later modified his thoughts on the born criminal. In the book he perpared for American readers, *Crime, Its Causes and Remedies*, published two years after his death, Lombroso included a discussion of many diverse environmental factors assumed to be causally related to criminal behavior.[32] Furthermore, in the division of criminals into three classes (born criminals, insane criminals, and criminaloids), Lombroso conceded that biological atavism did not apply to all criminals. However, in his modifications most criminals were still regarded as being inferior, degenerate, or defective in some way. When environmental factors (climate, rainfall, government, marriage customs, religious belief, etc.) were considered, they were generally viewed as agents in limiting, or conversely, in stimulating, the individual in the expression of physical criminal tendencies.

The most distinguished pupil of Lombroso was a young Socialist, Enrico Ferri. Although he never rejected biological causation of crime, Ferri emphasized the role of various kinds of interrelated factors. Early in his career, in his study of criminality in France for the years 1826–1878, Ferri presented his theory of multiple causation: "Crime is the result of manifold causes, which, although found always linked into an intricate network, can be detected, however, by means of careful study. The factors of crime can be divided into *individual* or *anthropological, physical* or *natural,* and *social.*"[33] Most important, perhaps, Ferri was to carry on the methodology of positivism, rejecting in his dissertation (at the age of twenty-one) and in his

Fig. 1. — P. R., voleur napolitain.

Fig. 2. — B. S., faussaire piémontais.

Fig. 3. — BOGGIA, assassin.

Fig. 4. — CARTOUCHE.

Fig. 5. — G. MARINI, femme de brigand.

Fig. 6. — DESRUES, empoisonneur.

subsequent work, the classical idea of free will. The most complete statement of his thought was published in 1884 in his *La sociologica criminale*. In the introduction to this classic, he alerts his readers:

> *The experimental philosophy of the latter half of our century, combined with human biology and psychology, and with the natural study of human society, had already produced an intellectual atmosphere decidedly favorable to a practical inquiry into the criminal manifestations of individual and social life . . .*
>
> *From this point onwards, nothing could be more natural than the rise of a new school, whose object was to make an experimental study of social pathology in respect to its criminal symptoms, in order to bring theories of crime and punishment into harmony with everyday facts. This is the positive school of criminal law, whereof the fundamental purpose is to study the natural genesis of criminality in the criminal, and in the physical and social conditions of his life, so as to apply the most effectual remedies to the various causes of crime.*[34]

Raffaele Garofalo, the third recognized member of the Italian positivistic criminologists, although placing greater emphasis than the others on psychological factors, similarly rejected the doctrine of free will in support of the positivism of the nineteenth century. Radzinowicz has commented on the decline of the Italian positivists:

> *Once these men completed the initial exploration of their particular fields nothing was done to re-examine them in light of new knowledge and in the context of a changing social and political milieu. In the absence of such a movement, those early explorations became frozen into a rigid system of premises and conclusions.*[35]

The failure of positivistic criminology in Italy is probably directly related to its stance on the issue of criminal responsibility. The classical school's ideas of criminal responsibility, as grounded in the concept of free will, continued to be the basis for the penal codes of Italy. Francesco Carrara, the leader of the Italian classical school, was instrumental in securing the adoption of a classically oriented code in the Italian Penal Code of 1889. Later, in 1921, Ferri attempted to gain the adoption of a revised penal code based on positivistic ideas of criminal responsibility but was rejected by the Chamber of Deputies in favor of the classical concept of responsibility.

In contrast to the classical position, the positivists proposed a kind of responsibility based on the needs of society rather than on free will and the moral guilt of the offender. The positivistic position on the responsibility of the individual to society was stated clearly by Ferri: "Man is always responsible for every one of his acts, for the sole reason that he lives in society, and for as long as he does so."[36] Criminal justice, according to the positivists, was to be found in the determination of whether the person is the perpetrator of an offense and then to apply a measure that will prevent the person from committing further offenses. The implications of positivistic ideas of criminal justice can be seen in Garofalo's theory of punishment, which is based on the ability of persons to adapt to society. The positivists' stand on criminal responsibility, being in opposition to classical ideas among Italian intellectuals and the teachings of the Roman Catholic Church, became an extremely unpopular position. Positivistic criminology in general was made suspect and was regarded as dangerous.

In their later careers, both Ferri and Garofalo easily adapted themselves to Mussolini's Fascist regime. Their political alignment may not be accidental or a matter of practical compromise. As Vold has indicated, the general orientation of positivism is consistent with totalitarianism:

> *The end of Ferri's career, assent to Fascism, highlights one of the*
> *implications of positivistic theory, namely, the ease with which*
> *it fits into totalitarian patterns of government. It is centered on the*
> *core idea of the superior knowledge and wisdom of the*
> *scientific expert, who, on the basis of his studies, decides what kind*
> *of human beings his fellow men are who commit crime, and*
> *who, on the basis of this knowledge and scientific insight, prescribes*
> *appropriate treatment without consent from the person so*
> *diagnosed (i.e. the criminal). There is an obvious similarity in*
> *conception of the control of power in society between positivism*
> *and the political reality of centralized control of the life of*
> *the citizen by a government bureaucracy indifferent to democratic*
> *public opinion.*[37]

In the rest of Europe, at the end of the nineteenth century, criminology was marked in large measure by the controversy between the substantive biological theory of the Italian positivists and the sociological orientation of other European scholars. The Lombrosians received sharp criticism from European social scientists, such as Gabriel Tarde, Henri Joly, Georg von Mayr, and W. A. Bonger, who were following the sociological perspective of A. M. Guerry and Adolphe Quételet. According to Herbert

Bloch and Gilbert Geis, "The best criticism of Lombroso remains that of the French anthropologist Paul Topinard (1830–1911), who gave criminology its name and who, when shown a collection of Lombroso's pictures of asymmetric and stigmatic criminals, remarked wryly that the pictures looked no different than those of his own friends."[38] Such was the hostility directed against Lombroso and his followers by other European criminologists at the Second International Congress of Criminal Anthropology in Paris in 1889 that he and his followers, out of protest, did not even attend the Third Congress at Brussels in 1892.[39]

Nevertheless, Lombrosian ideas exerted a significant influence on European criminology, an influence that is found in much of European criminology today.[40] Among the probable reasons for the eventual acceptance of the ideas of Lombroso were:

1. The prestige of the natural sciences, especially biology, which was central to Lombroso's theory.
2. The use of the terms "new" and "positive" gave prestige and excitement to the approach, capturing the spirit of the late nineteenth century.
3. The idea of physical features as indicators of character had a long, acceptable tradition in Europe.
4. The ideas and methods of positivistic, biological criminology were accepted and perpetuated by personnel with high prestige in Europe: physicians, psychiatrists, lawyers, and magistrates.
5. Emphasis on individual inferiority supported nationalistic political structures.
6. The positivist and biological orientation lent itself favorably to increases in social control by the state.

In other words, Lombrosian or biological criminology was accepted to a great extent for reasons usually regarded as contrary to the image of scientific development.

TWENTIETH-CENTURY ECLECTIC CRIMINOLOGY

The first decades of the twentieth century, especially in the United States, were marked by explanations of crime based on a variety of factors. The explanations usually focused on characteristics of the individual. The choice of factors such as emotional development, heredity, mental health, race, family background, and so on was influenced to a great extent by professional controversies and attitudes toward the criminal. Dogmatic adherence to one point of view over others, and the cultish pursuit of a viewpoint characterized the period. The controversy, however, was misplaced because of the failure to recognize that emphasis on a particular factor or collection of factors was a matter of methodological strategy. The selection of one theoretical orientation to the exclusion of other possibilities and the relation of this process to the social context of thought have been succinctly summarized by Bloch and Geis:

> *The fact is that such views need not be antagonistic; they may be complementary. The difficulty seems to be that these disparate points of view are not rooted in self-contained and consistent theoretical frameworks. If they were, it would be recognized that a given theoretical explanation proceeds from its own frame of reference and is solely concerned with certain types of facts which fall exclusively within its purview. Theoretical points of view beginning with different assumptions need not contend for dominance—although the prevailing cultural climate may tend to favor one more than the other. Such cultural preference, however, is not a scientific problem; it is a matter of historical fact.*[41]

Those criminologists who preferred the strategy of trying to explain criminal behavior in terms of a variety of factors, because of dissatisfaction with any one particular explanation, were faced with a unique problem. For them no theory was possible. Those who followed the multiple-factor approach failed in the formulation of criminological theory because they made no attempt to abstract to a common principle, integrate factors into a theoretical scheme, or theoretically relate multiple factors.

As in Europe, nineteenth-century American writers had been relating crime to the individualistic factors. Proposed in the American writings of the nineteenth century were theories of criminal behavior based on phrenology, insanity, anatomy, physiology, heredity, feeblemindedness, personality, and mental degeneration.[42] An especially noteworthy work of the period was Richard Dugdale's *The Jukes*, a study of a family with a history of a large number of criminals.[43] Dugdale, an inspector for the New York Prison Association, while supposedly presenting evidence on hereditary degeneracy, stressed the tentative nature of his work and indicated the likely importance of environmental factors. Actually, Dugdale was suggesting an eclectic approach when he wrote, "The tendency of heredity is to produce an environment which perpetuates that heredity: thus, the licentious parent makes an example which greatly aids in fixing habits of debauchery on the child. The correction is change of environment."

The writings of the Italian positivists were translated for the American audience in the second decade of the twentieth century: Lombroso's *Crime, Its Causes and Remedies* in 1911, Garofalo's *Criminology* in 1914, and Ferri's *Criminal Sociology* in 1917.[44] Their work, however, was known to a number of American writers before the translations. Some had read the summary and interpretation of Lombroso and criminal anthropology that Havelock Ellis had prepared in 1892 for English readers.[45] In the same year, Arthur MacDonald in his *Criminology* acknowledged the influence of Lombroso.[46] The book was dedicated to Cesare Lombroso and contained an introduction by Lombroso. MacDonald was trained in theology in the United States and in medicine and psychiatry in European universities and was employed by the U.S. Bureau of Education as Specialist in Education as Related to the Abnormal and Weakling Classes. Included in MacDonald's book was a discussion of the physical-type criminal. But, like most other early American writers on crime, MacDonald found it necessary to broaden the scope to include psychological and social factors. Such writers, while acknowledging in some way biological factors, were most impressed with the positivistic methodology of the Italian criminologists.

Lombroso, also giving his approval to another American writer, wrote the introduction to August Drähms's *The Criminal, His Personnel and Environment: A Scientific Study.*[47] Drähms, a resident chaplain of San Quentin State Prison, utilized criminal statistics to support a classification of three categories of criminals: (1) the Instinctive Criminal, "with predisposing bent toward innate criminal wrongdoing"; (2) the Habitual Criminal, "verging closely upon the instinctive offender in general description, differing from him chiefly in origin, possibly degree rather than kind, since he draws his inspirational forces from subsequent environment rather than parental fountains"; and (3) the Single Offender, "the legal defalcator and essentially social misdemeanant, accredited with a single isolated act of overt wrongdoing." Drähms also argued that "the American criminal differs in physiognomical type from his European contemporary." To this, Lombroso, in the introduction to Drähms's book, while in agreement with the remainder of the treatise, took exception:

> Now, while it is true that the majority of criminals retain the type
> of their native country, nevertheless, this is so only of the
> "criminal by occasion"; that is, criminals made so by environment
> or circumstances, and in whom degeneration is not so universal
> and pronounced as in the congenital criminal.[48]

Despite the biological orientation, however, Drähms regarded criminology as a social science: "Criminology is that department of social science that relates to the causes, nature, and treatment of crime with special reference to its individual exponents regarded from a psychological, physiological, and socialistic standpoint."[49]

The Italian criminologists also had direct effect on a number of other criminological works in the United States. In *Crime and the Criminal*, Philip A. Parsons, a professor of social work and applied sociology at the University of Oregon, gave considerable attention to criminal classification.[50] Parsons offered a classification that reflected the influence of the Italian criminologists. The classification consisted of six types: (1) insane criminal, (2) born criminal, (3) habitual criminal, (4) professional criminal, (5) occasional criminal, and (6) criminal by passion or accident. In regard to causation, Parsons suggested that "internal causation" operates in the first five types of criminals and "external causation" operates in types three through six.

The continuing influence of Lombroso's substantive theory can be seen in a number of fairly recent post-Lombrosian developments in the United States. Notable are E. A. Hooton's revival of Lombrosian criminal anthropology in his research on the assumed biological inferiority of criminals, published as *The American Criminal*; William H. Sheldon's writings, especially *Varieties of Delinquent Youth,* on somatotypes and constitutional inferiority; and some of Sheldon and Eleanor Glueck's work, especially *Physique and Delinquency*, on the physical characteristics of delinquents.[51] Earlier there had been an attempt to explain criminal behavior in terms of the biological functioning of endocrine glands. For example, in *The New Criminology*, Max G. Schlapp and Edward H. Smith, primarily through reasoning by analogy, claimed that individuals suffering from endocrine disturbances were typical born criminals.[52]

Another post-Lombrosian development can be seen in the research that has attempted to relate criminal behavior to heredity. As noted by Edwin H. Sutherland and Donald R. Cressey, at least five types of methods have been used to reach the conclusion that criminality is hereditary: (1) comparison of criminals with the "savage," as in the work of Hooton; (2) family trees, as in A. H. Estabrook's *The Jukes in 1915*; (3) Mendelian ratios in family trees, as in the study of family histories of German prisoners by Carl Rath; (4) statistical associations between crimes of parents and of offspring, as found in Charles Goring's *The English Convict*; and (5) comparison of identical and fraternal twins, as found especially in Johannes Lange's *Crime and Destiny*.[53] Post-Lombrosian criminal anthropology also appears in the numerous multiple-factor approaches to criminality that include biological factors among the many other diverse factors.

For the most part, however, as criminology developed in the United

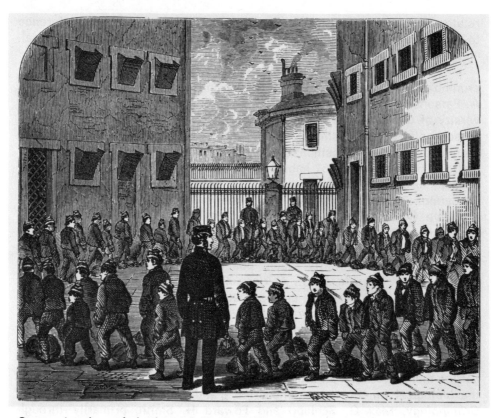

States, Lombroso's biological emphasis was discarded, although his positivism was accepted as essential to modern criminology. The translation of Gustav Aschaffenburg's *Crime and Its Repression* in 1913 presented to American criminologists a severe criticism of Lombroso's biological theory.[54] Using data from Germany, Aschaffenburg considered many individual and social factors as causes of crime.

But perhaps the most crucial blow to Lombrosian theory was the evidence presented by Charles Goring in his statistical study of three thousand male convicts, published as *The English Convict*. From the data collected as medical officer at Parkhurst Prison, Goring sought, as he conceived it, "to clear from the ground the remains of the old criminology, based upon conjecture, prejudice, and questionable observations," and "to found a new knowledge of the criminal upon facts scientifically acquired, and upon inferences scientifically verified: such facts and inferences yielding, by virtue of their own established accuracy, unimpeachable conclusions."[55]

Goring did not intend to refute Lombroso's theory but, through the newly developed statistical techniques, to rigorously test its validity: "It must, however, be remembered that in this inquiry, our first object is not to disprove the Lombrosian doctrine, nor is it to prove the falsity of the conclusions of criminal anthropology, upon which this doctrine is based. Our attack, insofar as it is an attack at all, is directed not against *conclusions*, but against the *methods* by which they were reached." In further statement of his purpose, Goring continued, "We cannot presuppose, at the onset, the invalidity of these dogmas, nor make any judgment upon the extent of their falsity or their truth: we can only assert that, since they were arrived at by unscientific means, they must not be accepted without further investigation."[56] Goring concluded that there was not a born criminal type, as Lombroso has assumed, but that criminals are nevertheless distinguishable from noncriminals.

> *The preliminary conclusion reached by our inquiry is that this anthropological monster has no existence in fact. The physical and mental constitution of both criminal and law-abiding persons, of the same age, stature, class, and intelligence, are identical. There is no such thing as an anthropological criminal type. But despite this negation, and upon the evidence of our statistics, it appears to be an equally indisputable fact that there is a physical, mental, and moral type of normal person who tends to be convicted of crime: that is to say, our evidence conclusively shows that, on the average, the criminal of English prisons is markedly differentiated by defective physique—as measured by stature and body weight; by defective mental capacity—as measured by general intelligence; and by increased possession of willful anti-social proclivities—as measured, apart from intelligence, by length of sentence to imprisonment.*[57]

In rejecting the inheritance of crime, Goring turned the attention of criminologists to the study of psychological characteristics, especially defective intelligence, as a cause of criminal behavior.

As intelligence testing came into vogue immediately before and after World War I, an increasing number of scholars began to apply intelligence tests to delinquents and criminals in the attempt to prove a causal relationship between crime and feeblemindedness. Henry H. Goddard, an enthusiastic supporter of feeblemindedness as a cause of criminality, estimated in his book on feeblemindedness that over 50 percent of criminals were feebleminded.[58] Later, in another book on the subject, Goddard concluded: "It is no longer to be denied that the greatest single cause of delinquency and crime is low-grade mentality, much of it is within limits of feeblemindedness."[59] With the publication of army data on intelligence testing and with a revision of the tests and their standards, the relationship between crime and intelligence was critically evaluated. A critical review by L. D. Zeleny and studies by H. M. Adler and M. R. Worthington, Carl Murchison, and Simon H. Tulchin led to the retraction of low intelligence as a causal explanation of criminal behavior.[60]

Nevertheless, through the use of other tests and measures, attempts to differentiate criminals from noncriminals continued. There were numerous efforts to differentiate criminals according to such psychological traits as emotional instability, aggressiveness, character, mechanical aptitude, immaturity, excitability, and so forth. For the sociologically oriented criminologist, the summary and critique by Karl F. Schuessler and Cressy of 113 studies in which personality scores of delinquents and criminals were compared to scores of control groups provided the necessary evidence for the conclusion that criminality and personality are not causally related.[61] A notable recent effort to establish such a relation to delinquency, nevertheless, is found in the use of the Minnesota Personality Inventory by S. R. Hathaway and Elio D. Monachesi.[62] However, as cautioned by Cressey, whatever relationships may be found in such studies, "establishing statistically significant differences between criminals and non-criminals, even when the statistical techniques are adequate and the sample groups are truly representative, does not in itself lead to conclusions about crime causation."[63]

Emphasis on a multitude of factors in the causation of crime was a reaction by criminologists to the practice of explaining crime in terms of one particular class of phenomena. The search for factors or variables, their measurement, and correlation to criminal behavior also reflected the growing trend toward empiricism and quantification in the social sciences. The multiple-factor approach to theories of crime causation had, of course, been present in many of the writings before the beginning of this century. However, it was in reaction to particularistic, that is, reductionist, theories, especially the biological theories, that many research scholars in the first half of the century insisted that criminal behavior was a product of a large variety of factors and that the many factors could never be organized into general propositions, that each criminal act was caused by a different set of factors.

One of the first empirical studies to employ the multiple-factor approach was William Healy's *The Individual Delinquent* in which a large variety and combination of factors were considered.[64] The multiple-factor approach was also used in Cyril Burt's *The Young Delinquent*, with the percentage of causative importance attributed to each of the factors considered. Burt's comment on crime causation was typical of the underlying assumption of the approach: "Crime is assignable to no single universal source, nor yet to two or three: it springs from a wide variety, and usually from a multiplicity, of alternative and converging influences."[65] The multiple-factor strategy is found today in the work of Sheldon and Eleanor Glueck. Reported in the Gluecks' *Unraveling Juvenile Delinquency* are the results from a controlled comparison of five hundred delinquent boys and five hundred nondelinquent boys on a host of factors.[66]

The most recent individualistic emphasis in the study of criminal behavior is found in the field of psychiatry. While various branches of psychiatry are concerned with the relation of mental illness to deviant social behavior, psychoanalytic psychiatry has developed the most elaborate explanations of criminal behavior. Following from the work of Freud, psychoanalytic psychiatrists in their study of criminal cases, have related the criminal act to such concepts as innate impulse, mental conflict, and repression. Crime, in most of the psychoanalytic theories, has represented a form of substitute behavior. In an early study, *New Light on Delinquency and Its Treatment*, William Healy and Augusta F. Bronner summarized their theory as follows: "Unsatisfying human relationships form obstructions to the flow of normal urges, desires, and wishes in the channels of socially acceptable activities. The deflected current of feelings of being inadequate, deprived or thwarted in ego or love satisfactions turns strongly into urges for substitutive satisfactions."[67]

Other well-known psychoanalytic works on criminal behavior as substitute behavior include Ben Karpman's *The Individual Criminal*, Robert Lindner's *Rebel Without a Cause*, Kate Friedlander's *The Psychoanalytic Approach to Juvenile Delinquency*, David Abramson's *Who Are the Guilty?*, and Franz Alexander and Hugo Staub's *The Criminal, the Judge, and the Public*.[68] All of the works, from the sociologist's point of view, rest on questionable research procedures and a theory that is not subject to verification.[69] There is also the problem of circularity in the psychoanalytic approach, psychopathy being suggested as a cause of criminal behavior, with criminal behavior, in turn, being used as an indicator of psychopathy. The pertinent question remains, however, in regard to the radical differences between psychiatry and sociology, of whether the two approaches to the explanation of crime are in reference to two different and distinct classes of phenomena.

TWENTIETH-CENTURY
SOCIOLOGICAL CRIMINOLOGY

With the turn of the century, the study of crime as a social phenomenon became centered in the United States. The rapid changes taking place in American society provided the background for a social perspective on crime. As the history of criminology indicates, crime is one of those behaviors that scholars have had difficulty accepting as social. It has always been more convenient to view crime as an individual phenomenon, more convenient for purposes of study as well as for programs of treatment. To conceive of the criminal as a personal failure rather than in relation to societal conditions also supports the status quo. A critical criminology in fact asks the question, Why is this so? Why is it that criminology, especially in its formative stages and still to a great extent today, views crime as an individual phenomenon? Why does it gravitate toward the "criminal as flawed person" rather than toward "crime rates as spin-offs of flawed social structures"? It is questions such as these that critical criminology seeks to ask of any history of criminological theory. That is, what are the social sources and the social consequences of any criminological theory or general paradigm? In any case, twentieth-century sociological criminology remedied the individual orientation to the extent that in the study of crime attention was now directed toward social conditions, if not toward social structures and master institutions such as the political economy and wealth-distributing mechanisms.

Perhaps because of the dynamics of American society, the relation between social conditions and crime seems obvious to American scholars. Urbanization, immigration, population growth, and social and geographical mobility were some of the dynamics scholars faced at the beginning of the twentieth century. Since much of criminal behavior occurred among groups most affected by these changes, it was reasonable to investigate the social sources of crime. In addition, as Radzinowicz suggests, American criminology came to display a strong sociological emphasis because such a view "accords with the fundamentally optimistic American outlook on life in general, into which the thesis that crime is a product of remediable social forces would fit more naturally than insistence on the part played by endogenous factors."[70] Also important to the social conception of crime was the fact that crime was included in the sociological study of social problems. The study of crime has since shared in the general growth of sociology.

While it is significant that the study of crime became located primarily within the sociological tradition, the social conception of crime was part of a new thought system that was developing at the beginning of the century in the United States. In what Morton White has documented as "the revolt against formalism," it was a style of thinking (a liberal social philosophy) compounded of pragmatism, institutionalism, behaviorism, legal realism, economic determinism, and the "new history."[71] Instrumental in the new intellectual pattern were John Dewey, holding that ideas are plans of action; Thorstein Veblen, insisting upon the importance of studying the connections between economic institutions and other aspects of culture; Justice Oliver Wendell Holmes, rejecting the view that law is an abstract entity; Charles A. Beard, looking for the underlying economic forces that determine the acceleration of social life; and James Harvey Robinson, representing the view that an understanding of history is essential for explaining the present and controlling the future.

All of these emerging ideas had in common a *relativism* that suggested that ideas and events have meaning only in relation to context. It was this same relativism that made the study of crime in the United States different from previous and other contemporary efforts. In being removed from an absolute conception of the world, the student of crime could perceive crime as a violation of one of a number of possible codes, with the behavior of the offender viewed as a consequence of participation in one of several social worlds. Although the ideas of the social philosophers who reacted against nineteenth-century formalism no longer serve as reference points, relativism continues in the study of crime. Recent developments and current trends in criminology reflect the extension of modern relativism.

AN EMERGING SOCIOLOGICAL CRIMINOLOGY

The sociological study of crime, nevertheless, proceeded at a painstaking pace in the United States during the first part of the century. Given the hindsight of today, the study of crime by early sociologists was filled with questionable assumptions and was not specifically concerned with sociological phenomena. For example, one of the first works on crime that was supposed to be sociological, Frances A. Kellor's *Experimental Sociology*, was actually a study of the physical differences (according to length of ears, average month width, height of forehead, weight, nasal index, etc.) between women criminals and women students. Enlightening also is the introduction to the book by C. R. Henderson, one of the first members of the Sociology Department at the University of Chicago. Henderson gave expression to a social moralism that had not yet been tempered by relativism, while also showing the adventure the early sociologists must have felt in the new social science: "The university cannot neglect any phase of social life. As in astronomy the study of perturbations in the movements of known bodies leads to the discovery of new worlds, so in social science the investigation of evil brings us nearer to an understanding of the good and helps us on the path upward."[72]

Earlier, in 1893, Henderson himself in *An Introduction to the Study of Dependent, Defective, and Delinquent Classes* had written on crime and the related topics of the time. Much of the book was devoted to the organization of care for dependents: "We seek the ethical basis of charity, the ideals of philanthropy, and the social mechanism for attaining in larger measure what ought to be done."[73] Outside of the programmatic aspect of the book, Henderson suggested an early social psychology of crime that stressed the reaction of the person possessing inherited tendencies:

> *The causes of crime are factors of personality and of environment, and of the reaction of personality upon environment in the formation of habits and new nature. Personal nature is, at a given moment, the product of inherited tendencies, of acquired habits and character, and of the response to external circumstances.*[74]

Criminology at the beginning of the twentieth century in the United States, similar to other areas of study, was affected by evolutionary theory, particularly Social Darwinism. This theoretical orientation to crime is perhaps best displayed in Arthur C. Hall's *Crime and Its Relation to Social Progress.* In the introduction to the book, Franklin H. Giddings, first professor of sociology at Columbia University, set the tone by arguing that as civilization evolves it is necessary to define, through the criminal law, certain behaviors as criminal and that "this process of connecting immoralities into positive crimes is one of the most powerful means by which society in the long run eliminates the socially unfit, and gives an advantage in the struggles for existence to the thoughtful, the considerate, the far-seeing, the compassionate; so lifting its members to higher planes of character and conduct."[75] Hall, a fellow in sociology at Columbia University, in viewing crime in relation to social progress, considered the criminal law itself as well as the behavior of the offender. To Hall, crime was "the branding by society of some forms of conduct as criminal." Crime was viewed as inevitable to social progress. Using a natural-law conception as well as evolutionary theory, Hall wrote:

> *Out of the teachings of natural law, which, whether we like it or not, whether we aid it or oppose it, is driving the world forward to higher and higher planes of life, of intelligence and mutual helpfulness, comes the idea of crime, and the necessity for the appearance of the criminal in every human community. Crime is an inevitable social evil, the dark side of the shield of human progress. The shifting processes of natural selection continue within the domain of social life, rejecting, through social pressure, both*

weaklings and workers of iniquity. Anti-social individuals, or malefactors, result from the persistent tendency to variation, manifest in all life. They become criminals through processes of social selection, during which individuals refusing to live up to the social standard of right action are punished by the community, and their actions become known as crime.[76]

One of the most significant events in the development of criminology during the first decade of this century was the establishment of the American Institute of Criminal Law and Criminology by the Faculty of Law at Northwestern University, in June 1908, to celebrate the first fifty years of the university. The institute represents the formal recognition of American criminology. In addition to the founding in May 1910 of a journal for the communication of ideas in criminology, known for years as the *Journal of Criminal Law, Criminology and Police Science*, and known since 1973 as the *Journal of Criminal Law and Criminology*, the institute initiated the Modern Criminal Science series. In the course of the series, the writings of European criminologists were translated and introduced to American readers. Included in the series were the writings of Gross, Quirós, Ferri, Saleilles, Lombroso, Tarde, Bonger, Garofalo, and Aschaffenburg. An international bibliography under the editorship of John H. Wigmore of Northwestern University Law School was published in 1909, introducing American criminologists to an extensive list of writings in criminology and criminal law.[77]

Extremely important in the development of sociological criminology were the translations of Gabriel Tarde's *Penal Philosophy* and Willem A. Bonger's *Criminality and Economic Conditions*.[78] Tarde, in setting forth a sociological conception of crime, as well as attempting to reconcile moral responsibility with determinism, attacked Lombroso's theory of the anthropological criminal type. Bonger's use of statistics and his analysis according to the economic structure of society also contributed to sociological criminology, although his economic determinism found few adherents in the United States.

Maurice Parmelee, perhaps more than any other person at the beginning of the century, brought about the union of sociology and criminology. Parmelee, in *The Principles of Anthropology and Sociology in Their Relations to Criminal Procedure*, while at places drawing favorably upon Lombroso's theory, suggested a sociological criminology.[79] Later, in the first American attempt at a comprehensive exposition of criminological knowledge, Parmelee in his *Criminology* discussed the social sources of crime.[80] Yet, he found it necessary to devote attention to evolution, to the physical environment, to "criminal traits," and to the "organic basis of criminality." Parmelee's work, nevertheless, marks the beginning in the United States of a transition from a general, eclectic study of crime to a sociological level of explanation.

UNIVERSITY OF CHICAGO SOCIOLOGY AND CRIMINOLOGY

A truly sociological criminology was achieved during the 1920s and 1930s at the University of Chicago. Albion W. Small, as founder and head of the first sociology department to be established as an independent unit anywhere in the world, gathered a distinguished group of colleagues at the University of Chicago. Persons with considerable ability and scope established a sociological tradition that had as one of its principal concerns the study of crime. The distinctly sociological orientation to the study of crime that developed at the University of Chicago is implied in the following summary of the sociologist's conception of crime:

> They are increasingly interested in the conflicting values present in our culture, in the extent of a criminal's membership in social groups with deviant values, the role the person plays in such deviant groups, his conception of himself arising out of such group participation, the conduct norms in the neighborhood from which he comes, the extent of his mobility and association with other deviant norms, his attitude toward law and society, and his degree of criminal association.[81]

That criminal behavior is similar to any other social behavior became the underlying theme in the sociological study of crime.

Two early concepts derived from the Chicago school were "social disorganization" and "the four wishes." W. I. Thomas and Florian Znaniecki, in what is regarded as the first American empirical study in sociology, *The Polish Peasant in Europe and America*, defined the concept of social disorganization as a "decrease of the influence of existing social rules of behavior upon individual members of the group."[82] As employed by Thomas and Znaniecki, the concept was a useful tool to describe the condition of the groups they were studying. But the concept became unwieldly when it was used by subsequent criminologists to explain crime. Crime, as seen in terms of the concept of social disorganization, became an indicator of the condition of social disorganization and, in a circular fashion, disorganization became an explanation of crime. Also, as used in the hands of others, social disorganization implied a social absolutism that regarded only one system as being the standard from which all behavior was evaluated. Thomas and Znaniecki were to a certain extent relativistic, as can be seen in their concept of the four wishes: response, recognition, security, and new experience. Thomas, utilizing the four wishes in *The Unadjusted Girl*, indicated that the wishes as the basis of motivation and behavior can be satisfied in any number of ways. Whether the result is regarded as moral or not depends upon the meaning attached by others to the activity.

> *From the foregoing description it will be seen that wishes of the same general class—those which tend to arise from the same emotional background—may be totally different in moral quality. The moral good or evil of a wish depends on the social meaning or value of the activity which results from it. Thus the vagabond, the adventurer, the spendthrift, the bohemian are dominated by the desire for new experience, but so are the inventor and the scientist; adventurers with women and the tendency to domesticity are both expressions of the desire for response; vain ostentation and creative artistic worth both are designed to provoke recognition; avarice and business enterprise are actuated by the desire for security.*[83]

To Thomas, the means of satisfying the wishes were merely functional alternatives.

The influence of Robert E. Park at the University of Chicago on early students of crime was considerable. Park, in collaboration with a colleague, E. W. Burgess, suggested the possibilities of the study of the spatial distribution of social phenomena within the city.[84] Students of Park and Burgess examined the proposition that various deviant behaviors may be associated with urban growth and ecological patterns. Frederick M. Thrasher, in his study of 1313 gangs in Chicago, argued that groups of boys located in "interstitial areas" of the city, through participation in a particular way of life, would become transformed from slum groups into unified delinquent groups.[85]

Clifford R. Shaw and his collaborators in a study of the distribution of delinquency rates found, among other things, that delinquency was concentrated in deteriorated areas of the city, and that the areas of high delinquency rates consistently have high rates in spite of population changes.[86] Through a number of case studies, including *The Jack-Roller, Natural History of a Delinquent Career*, and *Brothers in Crime*, Shaw shifted his attention from physical factors in the environment to a consideration of the relationships of offenders with others.[87] Slum youth were seen as participating in a culture in which delinquent behavior was prescribed. Thus, the distinctly sociological view that crime is acquired in a social and cultural setting was an eventual product of the Chicago school.

THE PERSON IN SOCIETY

In an early article entitled "The Delinquent as a Person," E. W. Burgess suggested that the individual delinquent could be studied sociologically as a "person" who is the product of social interaction with his fellows.

> *Not only criminology, but all social problems, indeed the entire area of group behavior and social life, is being subjected to sociological description and analysis. The person is concerned in his interrelations with the social organization, with the family, the neighborhood, the community, and society. Explanations of his behavior are found in terms of human wishes and social attitudes, mobility and unrest, intimacy and status, social contacts and social interaction, conflict, accommodation and assimilation.*[88]

In the hands of Burgess, the concept of the relation of the person to society was a sound statement of the social-psychological explanation of the offender and his or her behavior. As used by others, however, the social psychology of crime became a social psychology cluttered by factors *outside* interpersonal relations, as well as a perspective that included unwarranted value assumptions.

In part because of the failure to understand the construction of theory, numerous students of crime have suggested that crime is a consequence of various factors interacting on the individual. All the early criminology textbooks were organized according to various factors that were supposedly associated with criminal behavior. Clayton J. Ettinger's *The Problem of Crime* is typical with Part I on "the criminal" being divided into chapters on the sociological, psychiatric, economic, and political factors.[89] Otto Pollak's selected bibliography on studies between 1939 and 1949 of crime causation was similarly arranged according to the types of factors with which the various studies were concerned.[90]

The solution to the realization that crime is a complex phenomenon often has been the multiple-factor approach, rather than theory construction in terms of a particular level of explanation. The comment by Albert Morris that "it must be held in mind that we are dealing with the interaction of multiple factors and that the particular factors in each situation are unique" is representative of the acceptance of the multiple-factor approach by many sociologists who study crime.[91]

The multiple-factor approach, thus, was often pursued as an unsophisticated form of social psychology. For example, in the course of a survey of research in criminology, Morris Ploscowe concluded: "The soundest approach to the problem of causation of crime therefore lies through a study of the individual criminal in relation to all the social and environmental factors which have an influence on his personality."[92] Robert H. Gault, professor of psychology at Northwestern University and editor of the *Journal of Criminal Law and Criminology*, also developed a partial social psychological explanation. Referring to his criminology textbook as "from first to last, an attempt at a psychologic approach," Gault wrote that personality is in part a product of social contacts, that attitudes are acquired, and that "these attitudes develop out of infinitely numerous reactions that are facilitated or retarded by reason of our capacities, our prepotent reflexes, etc."[93]

While still pursuing an early form of social psychology of the interaction of the person with factors in the environment, a number of criminologists offered theories of crime that included the assumption that the organization of society is not appropriate for the functioning of the individual. For example, one of the first statements of the interaction between the individual and an improper environment is found in John L. Gillin's *Criminology and Penology*. In a well-written, erudite criminology textbook, Gillin conceived of a social psychological explanation of the criminal in the following way:

> *Hence there is a conspiracy of conditions which account for his becoming a criminal—conditions in his own constitutional make-up, in his early social development, in his lack of training, in his poverty and in the surrounding social atmosphere, including habits, customs, ideals, beliefs, and practices. The social conditions around him set the stage on which each of these factors plays its part and release in his conduct the good or the evil in his nature. Thus, is the criminal made.*[94]

In a not too different explanation of crime, Boris Brasol suggested a "psycho-social interpretation" of crime. In noting that "social friction is the prime cause of crime," Brasol wrote that "between society as a whole and its individual member, there develops friction promoting the latter to violate certain traditions which have been produced and sanctioned by the community."[95]

The thesis that crime results from problems in the interaction of the individual with society is found in Nathaniel F. Cantor's *Crime and Society*, a popular textbook of its time. Cantor wrote: "Criminal behavior, then, is in part symptomatic of the needs of the individuals which have been frustrated by their culture."[96] He argued, further, that when the emotional stresses become too intense some individuals are unable to make "normal adjustments" and that this social maladjustment may take the form of criminal behavior. Similarly, noting that the criminal must be understood in reference to the community, associates, and culture, Arthur E. Wood and John B. Waite observed: "From this sociological view of things the criminal may be said to be *maladjusted* to his social environment."[97] More recently, in the preface to his *Crime: Causes and Conditions*, Hans von Hentig noted: "Crime, being a pattern of social disorganization, has a multiplicity of causations that rest on defects and obstructions in the working order of society."[98]

The conception of crime as a result of interaction between the person and society has thus taken several forms. The forms have differed from the social psychology that was developing among sociologists at the University of Chicago. Criminologists who utilized the person-in-society perspective to crime either resorted to a multiple-factor approach, often employing factors such as heredity or physical characteristics, that stand outside the interaction between person and society or formulated their conceptions on questionable assumptions about the relation of the person to society and the nature of society. Often, in addition, there were values implied in what the observers believed should be appropriate behavior. Regardless of the direction taken in this perspective, however, no integral, coherent body of theory was developed.

CRITICISM OF THEORETICAL CRIMINOLOGY

The 1930s mark a period of turmoil and assessment in the development of criminology. A number of students of crime, as we have already seen, dissatisfied with the various particularisms, turned to the multiple-factor approach. Other criminologists, such as Sutherland, sought to integrate the diverse facts associated with crime. Still others, such as Nathaniel F. Cantor, in *Crime, Criminals and Criminal Justice*, attempted to examine the state of criminology and add "sound methods of inquiry."[99] Others summarized the findings of criminology in little more than a descriptive form, as in Fred E. Haynes's *Criminology*.[100] Some criminologists, such as Harry Best in *Crime and the Criminal Law in the United States*, unabashedly presented the findings of criminology without any theoretical perspective whatsoever, in the name of objectivity.

> *It [the book] is designedly of the objective character, based simply upon what has been revealed in studies upon it [crime and criminal law in the United States]. There is no thesis to be propounded, and no particular set of views or system of criminological doctrine to be enunciated. Practical matters and issues of today are what receive the substance of attention and regard. . . .*[101]

The beginning of the 1930s was characterized by an optimism brought about, in part at least, by the acceptance of positivism in the United States, an acceptance inspired by the belief that the causes of criminal behavior could be discovered if enough effort was devoted to the empirical study of crime. The validity of such optimism in criminology was soon questioned on

the basis of a single report. In the early 1930s criminologists became more and more interested in establishing an institute of crime. Two Columbia University professors, Jerome Michael of the law school and Mortimer J. Adler of the philosophy department, were commissioned to examine the state of knowledge in criminology. Their report, published as *Crime, Law and Social Science*, was highly critical. The conclusion reached by Michael and Adler in their review of past research on crime was typical of the tone of the entire book: "The absurdity of any attempt to draw etiological conclusions from the findings of criminological research is so patent as not to warrant further discussion."[102]

Despite the severity of their criticism, however, Michael and Adler recommended that an institute of criminology and criminal justice be established. But their report had been so devastating that there was little hope left that such an institute could improve criminology.

Fortunately, few criminologists agreed with the diagnosis Michael and Adler had presented. A committee, consisting of a number of sociologists appointed by the Social Science Research Council to review the report, submitted a contradictory conclusion on the status of criminology.[103]

Nevertheless, the Michael and Adler report did provide a sort of negative point of reference for criminologists in that it made them aware of the importance of the criminal law in defining the scope and boundaries of criminology, a consideration that had been neglected up to that time and one that is being rediscovered today in current criminology and sociology of law. The report also made some criminologists recognize that the criteria used by Michael and Adler to judge criminology represented only one view of the science. Michael and Adler, in stating that "there is no scientific knowledge in the field of criminology," could only reach such a dogmatic conclusion by basing their survey on (1) a misconception of the methodological theory of causation, (2) a natural science model of social science, and (3) a restricted sampling of research and writing in criminology. Given the assumptions, criteria, and sources of the report, these are accurate conclusions. But if Michael and Adler had made use of other assumptions and criteria and examined other research in criminology, their report on criminology could have been altogether different. Nevertheless, *Crime, Law and Social Science* provided criminologists with a guide that would serve as a basis for the further development of criminology.

CULTURE CONFLICT

Michael and Adler forcefully argued that the most precise and least ambiguous definition of crime is based on conduct that is defined as criminal in the criminal code, a legalist and relativist definition of crime. The formulation and administration of criminal law would conceivably provide a level of criminological explanation and an object of study for criminology. A number of criminologists, sociologists, and anthropologists in the 1920s and 1930s presented evidence on the existence of norms in conflict with one another. The delinquency area studies by Shaw indicated that urban areas with certain characteristics give rise to social attitudes that conflict with the norms of the law. Sutherland, in an early article, wrote on the relation of crime to culture conflict. Criminal behavior, he noted, is itself "a part of the process of conflict, of which law and punishment are other parts." Sutherland continued:

> *This process begins in the community before the law is enacted, and continues in the community and in the behavior of particular offenders after punishment is inflicted. This process seems to go on somewhat as follows: A certain group of people feel that one of their values—life, property, beauty of landscape, theological doctrine—is endangered by the behavior of others. If the group is politically influential, the value important, and the danger serious, they secure the enactment of a law and thus win the cooperation of the State in the effort to protect their value.*[104]

Thus, to carry the argument further, those persons who follow the norms of a culture that prescribes ways of behaving that are in opposition to the norms embodied in the criminal law share the high probability of being defined as criminal.

The case for the analysis of crime according to culture conflict was most strongly presented in a monograph by Thorstein Sellin, *Culture Conflict and Crime.* Noting the importance of criminal law to the study of crime, Sellin observed the operation of the law as follows:

> *Among the various instrumentalities which social groups have evolved to secure conformity in the conduct of their members, the criminal law occupies an important place, for its norms are binding upon all who live within the political boundaries of a state and are enforced through the coercive power of the state. The criminal law may be regarded as a part of the body of rules, which prohibit specific forms of conduct and indicate punishments for violations. The characteristic of these rules, the kind or type of conduct they prohibit, the nature of the sanction attached to their violation, etc., depend upon the character and interests of those groups in the population which influence legislation. In some states, these groups may comprise the majority, in others a minority, but the social values which receive the protection of the criminal law are ultimately those which are treasured by dominant interest groups.*[105]

For Sellin, culture conflict could arise in several different ways, with each form of conflict being potentially related to crime. In general terms there is the conflict that develops in the growth of a civilization and the conflict that results from the contact between the norms of divergent cultural codes. The latter form of conflict may arise "(1) when these codes clash on the border of contiguous culture areas; (2) when, as may be the case with legal norms, the law of one cultural group is extended to cover the territory of another; or (3) when members of one cultural group migrate to another."[106] Sellin gave support to this thesis by reviewing the research on criminal behavior among immigrants, the foreign-born, and second-generation immigrants. In all cases, crime was viewed as a matter of conflict between conduct norms, with legal norms being one form of conduct norms.

The importance of conflict in the making of the individual offender was vividly presented in 1938 in a popular criminology textbook, *Crime and the Community*, by Frank Tannenbuam, professor of Latin-American history at Columbia University. Tannenbaum viewed crime as a matter of definition by the community, the offender as a person in conflict with the community, and the offender as continuing in crime with his or her acceptance of this definition by the community. Tannenbaum referred to the process by which the person becomes a criminal in the course of community reaction as "the dramatization of evil." As a result of forms of community reaction, the offender's self-image becomes that of a criminal or delinquent and he or she carries out the corresponding behavior.

> *The process of making the criminal, therefore, is a process of tagging, defining, identifying, segregating, describing, emphasizing, making conscious and self-conscious; it becomes a way of stimulating, suggesting, emphasizing, and evoking the very traits that are complained of. If the theory of relation of response to stimulus has any meaning, the entire process of dealing with the young delinquent is mischievous insofar as it identifies him to the environment as a delinquent person.*[107]

The cultural-conflict perspective thus provided a framework for the analysis of both the creation of criminal law and the response of the individual to the application of the law. Some recent developments in criminology are a continuation of the ideas presented in the cultural-conflict approach.

DIFFERENTIAL ASSOCIATION

As a prelude to his theory of differential association, in a study of the professional thief published in 1937, Sutherland presented the view that criminals gradually learn the knowledge, skills, and motivation for engaging in criminal behavior.[108] Two years later, in the revision of his popular criminology textbook, Sutherland, in attempting to offer an explanation of crime that would replace the multiple-factor approach and go beyond the simple enculturation explanation of crime, offered his theory of differential association.[109]

The theory of differential association as finally developed has since become well known. It contains the following propositions: (1) Criminal behavior is learned, and (2) it is learned in interaction with other persons in a process of communication. (3) The principal part of the learning of criminal behavior occurs within intimate personal groups. (4) When criminal behavior is learned, the learning includes (a) techniques of committing the crime, which are sometimes very complicated, sometimes very simple, and (b) the specific direction of motives, drives, rationalizations, and attitudes. (5) The specific direction of motives and drives is learned from definitions of the legal codes as favorable or unfavorable. (6) A person becomes delinquent because of an excess of definitions favorable to violation of law over definitions unfavorable to violation of law. (7) Differential associations may vary in frequency, duration, priority, and intensity. (8) The process of learning criminal behavior by association with criminal and anticriminal patterns involves all of the mechanisms that are involved in any other learning. (9) While criminal behavior is an expression of general needs and values, it is not explained by those general needs and values since noncriminal behavior is an expression of the same needs and values.[110]

Sutherland thus provided an integrative theory for criminology, a theory that assumed that the many diverse factors and correlates of crime were important to the extent that they affected an individual's associations and learning experiences. The theory, in postulating that criminal behavior is learned in primary association with others, in relative isolation from opposing values, continues to serve as one of the major theoretical perspectives in criminology.

SOCIAL STRUCTURE AND ANOMIE

At the end of the 1930s Robert K. Merton published his now famous article, "Social Structure and Anomie."[111] Elaborating on Emile Durkheim's description of the emergence of aspiration and the breakdown in regulatory norms, Merton sought to explain the kinds and amounts of deviation in a society. The theory, nevertheless, was similar in some ways to criminological theories that had preceded it. Merton's emphasis on the breakdown of cultural structure, occurring particularly when there is a disjunction between the goals and the norms, is similar to the social disorganization theory in analyzing deviation from what is assumed to be a fairly homogenous culture. The social structure and anomie theory is, also, a sophisticated version of the criminological theories that stated that crime was in some way a

result of problems in the relation of the person to society, without the explicit assumption that persons violating the law are maladjusted. According to Merton's middle-range theory, explanations of crime are to be sought in the social and cultural structure of society rather than in the individual. Merton's theory goes beyond the others in suggesting that there are different "modes of adaptation" to society. The theory attempts to explain both the behavior of individuals and the rates of crime.

At least one criminologist has recently been critical of the policy implications of Merton's anomie theory. Keenly aware that the social consequences of a theory, consequences expressed as social policy, are of equal if not greater importance than the substance of the theory, Elliott Currie writes:

> From [Merton's] basic idea that "disadvantaged" people turn to deviance because they are blocked from achieving social goals, it is easy to derive a policy that involves using the penal system to reconcile people to lowered aspirations and the acceptance of the restrictions of working-class life.[112]

A CRITICAL CRIMINOLOGY

Theoretical developments in criminology during the post-World War II period, at least up to the mid-1960s, consisted primarily of an extension of the theoretical perspectives that were formulated at the end of the 1930s.[113] Gradually, criminological research began to focus on the legal system, giving attention to the process by which definitions of crime are constructed and applied.[114] Eventually, the conflict approach, combined with the political nature of crime control and criminality, developed as a major theory in criminology.[115] Underlying the current study of such subjects as criminal law, law enforcement, administration of justice, criminal behavior patterns, and social reaction to crime is the thesis that crime is a socially and historically defined phenomenon and problem.

The most significant development in recent years, however, as discussed in the first chapter, is the emergence of a critical-Marxian criminology. This development has broadened the subject matter of criminology and led to the growth of a critical criminology.

NOTES

1. See Sawyer F. Sylvester, Jr., ed., *The Heritage of Modern Criminology* (Cambridge: Schenkman, 1972).
2. See Herbert Marcuse, *Reason and Revolution* (Boston: Beacon Press, 1960); Irving M. Zeitlin, *Ideology and the Development of Sociology* (Englewood Cliffs, N.J.: Prentice-Hall, 1968).
3. Similar observations on the development of physical science are found in Thomas S. Kuhn, *The Structure of Scientific Revolutions* (University of Chicago Press, 1962), chap. 11.
4. See Willem A. Bonger, *Introduction to Criminology,* trans. Emil van Loo (London: Methuen, 1936), chap. 2.
5. George B. Vold, *Theoretical Criminology* (New York: Oxford University Press, 1958), pp. 5–6.
6. Among his many works on this theme, see especially, Thomas Szaz, *The Manufacture of Madness* (New York: Dell (Delta Books), 1970), especially part I.
7. See Coleman Phillipson, *Three Criminal Law Reformers: Beccaria, Bentham, Romilly* (London: J. M. Dent and Sons, 1923); Cesare Beccaria, *Essays on Crimes and Punishment,* 1st American ed. (New York: Stephen Gould, 1809); Jeremy Bentham, *An Introduction to the Principles of Morals and Legislation,* corrected ed. (Oxford: Claredon Press, 1823).
8. Elio Monachesi, "Cesare Beccaria," in Hermann Mannheim, ed., *Pioneers in Criminology* (London: Stevens, 1960), pp. 36–50.
9. Ian Taylor, Paul Walton, and Jock Young, *The New Criminology* (Boston: Routledge & Kegan Paul, 1973), p. 2.
10. Bonger, *Introduction to Criminology,* p. 47.
11. See Pitirim Sorokin, *Contemporary Sociological Theories* (New York: Harper & Row, 1928), pp. 557–561.
12. See C. Bernaldo de Quirós, *Modern Theories of Criminality,* trans. Alfonso de Salvio (Boston: Little, Brown, 1911), pp. 66–79.
13. Yale Levin and Alfred R. Lindesmith, "English Ecology and Criminology of the Past Century," *Journal of Criminal Law and Criminology,* 27 (March–April 1937), pp. 801–

816; Alfred R. Lindesmith and Yale Levin, "The Lombrosian Myth in Criminology," *American Journal of Sociology*, 42 (March 1937), pp. 653–671.

14. Terence Morris, *The Criminal Area: A Study in Social Ecology* (Boston: Routledge & Kegan Paul, 1958), chap. 3.

15. Patrick Colquohoun, *Treatise on the Police of the Metropolis*, 7th ed. (London: J. Mawman, 1806).

16. Luke O. Pike, *A History of Crime in England*, 2 vols. (London: Smith, Elder, 1873–1876).

17. Charles Booth, *Life and Labour of the People of London*, 2d ed., 9 vols. (New York: Macmillan, 1892–1897).

18. T. S. Simey and M. B. Simey, *Charles Booth, Social Scientist* (New York: Oxford University Press, 1960), p. 4.

19. Ibid., p. 3.

20. See Floyd N. House, *The Development of Sociology* (New York: McGraw-Hill, 1936), pp. 331–337.

21. Ellen Elizabeth Guillot, *Social Factors in Crime: As Explained by American Writers of the Civil War and Post Civil War Period*, published PhD dissertation (University of Pennsylvania, 1943), p. 21.

22. Guillot, *Social Factors in Crime*, p. 172.

23. Charles Loring Brace, *The Dangerous Classes of New York* (New York: WynKoop and Hallenbeck, 1872).

24. Edward Crapsey, *The Nether Side of New York* (New York: Sheldon and Co., 1872), p. 9.

25. See Eric F. Goldman, *Rendezvous with Destiny* (New York: Random House, 1952), pp. 90–96.

26. Quoted in Goldman, *Rendezvous with Destiny*, p. 96. For the entire speech, see Arnold, Ehninger, and Gerber, *Speakers' Resource Book* (New York: Scott, Foresman, 1961), p. 136ff.

27. Harry Elmer Barnes, "Criminology," in *Encyclopedia of the Social Sciences* (New York: Macmillan, 1931), p. 585.

28. Leon Radzinowicz, *In Search of Criminology* (Cambridge: Harvard University Press, 1962), p. 3. A similar statement is found in Olof Kinberg, *Basic Problems of Criminology* (Copenhagen: Levin and Munkgaard, 1935), p. 70.

29. Lindesmith and Levin, "The Lombrosian Myth in Criminology," p. 664.

30. See C. H. S. Jayewardene, "The English Precursors of Lombroso," *British Journal of Criminology*, 4 (October 1963), pp. 164–170.

31. Quoted in Charles Goring, *The English Convict: A Statistical Study* (London: His Majesty's Stationery Office, 1913), p. 13.

32. Cesare Lombroso, *Crime, Its Causes and Remedies*, trans. H. P. Horton (Boston: Little, Brown, 1911).

33. Quoted in Quirós, *Modern Theories of Criminality*, p. 20.

34. Enrico Ferri, *Criminal Sociology*, (New York and London: D. Appleton & Company) Authorized Limited Edition, no. 422, pp. XV and XVI.

35. Radzinowicz, *In Search of Criminology*, p. 15.

36. Quoted in Quirós, *Modern Theories of Criminality*, p. 16.

37. Vold, *Theoretical Criminology*, pp. 35–36.

38. Herbert Bloch and Gilbert Geis, *Man, Crime and Society*, 2d ed., (New York: Random House, 1970), p. 89. They cite Tarde's *Penal Philosophy*, p. 220, as the source of the incident.

39. See Quirós, *Modern Theories of Criminality*, pp. 79–100.

40. Cf. Lindesmith and Levin, "The Lombrosian Myth in Criminology," pp. 667–670.

41. Herbert A. Bloch and Gilbert Geis, *Man, Crime, and Society* (New York: Random House, 1962), p. 92.

42. Arthur E. Fink, *Causes of Crime: Biological Theories in the United States*, 1800–1915 (University of Pennsylvania Press, 1938).

43. Richard L. Dugdale, *The Jukes: A Study in Crime, Pauperism, Disease and Heredity* (New York: Putnam, 1877).
44. Lombroso, *Crime, Its Causes and Remedies;* Raffaele Garofalo, *Criminology,* trans. Robert Wyness (Boston: Little Brown, 1914); Enrico Ferri, *Criminal Sociology,* trans. J. I. Kelly and John Lisle (Boston: Little, Brown, 1917).
45. Havelock Ellis, *The Criminal* (New York: Scribner, 1892).
46. Arthur MacDonald, *Criminology* (New York: Funk and Wagnalls, 1892).
47. August Drähms, *The Criminal, His Personnel and Environment: A Scientific Study* (New York: Macmillan, 1900).
48. Lombroso, in introduction to Drähms, *The Criminal, His Personnel and Environment,* p. xiii.
49. Drähms, *The Criminal, is Personnel and Environment,* p. 1.
50. Philip A. Parsons, *Crime and the Criminal* (New York: Knopf, 1926).
51. E. A. Hooton, *The American Criminal: An Anthropological Study* (Cambridge: Harvard University Press, 1939); William H. Sheldon, *Varieties of Delinquent Youth* (New York: Harper & Row, 1949); Sheldon and Eleanor Glueck, *Physique and Delinquency* (New York: Harper & Row, 1956). For a recent discussion of these works, see Hermann Mannheim, *Comparative Criminologies* (Boston: Houghton Mifflin, 1965), chap. 13.
52. Max G. Schlapp and Edward H. Smith, *The New Criminology* (New York: Liveright, 1928).
53. See Edwin H. Sutherland and Donald R. Cressey, *Principles of Criminology,* 9th ed. (Philadelphia: Lippincott, 1974), pp. 112–118. The notable studies on crime and heredity are A. H. Estabrook, *The Jukes, in 1915* (Washington, D.C.: Carnegie Institute, 1916); Johannes Lange, *Crime and Destiny,* trans. Charlotte Haldane (New York: Liveright, 1930).
54. Gustav Aschaffenburg, *Crime and Its Repression,* trans. Adalbert Albrecht (Boston: Little, Brown, 1913).
55. Goring, *The English Convict,* p. 18.
56. Ibid., p. 19.
57. Ibid., p. 370.
58. Henry H. Goddard, *Feeblemindedness: Its Causes and Consequences* (New York: Macmillan, 1914).
59. Henry H. Goddard, *Human Efficiency and Levels of Intelligence* (Princeton University Press, 1920), p. 74.
60. L. D. Zeleny, "Feeblemindedness and Criminal Conduct," *American Journal of Sociology,* 38 (January 1933), pp. 564–576; Herman M. Adler and Myrtle R. Worthington, "The Scope of the Problem of Delinquency and Crime as Related to Mental Deficiency," *Journal of Psycho-Asthenics,* 30 (1925), pp. 47–57; Carl Murchison, *Criminal Intelligence* (Worcester, Mass.: Clark University Press, 1926); Simon H. Tulchin, *Intelligence and Crime* (University of Chicago Press, 1939).
61. Karl F. Schuessler and Donald R. Cressey, "Personality Characteristics of Criminals," *American Journal of Sociology,* 55 (March 1950), pp. 476–484.
62. S. A. Hathaway and Elio D. Monachesi, *Analyzing and Predicting Delinquency with the MMPI* (Minneapolis: University of Minnesota Press, 1953). A recent application of the MMPI is found in John C. Ball, *Social Deviancy and Adolescent Personality: An Analytical Study with the MMPI* (University of Kentucky Press, 1962).
63. Donald R. Cressey, "Crime," in Robert K. Merton and Robert A. Nisbet, eds., *Contemporary Social Problems,* 2d ed. (New York: Harcourt Brace Jovanovich, 1955), p. 167.
64. William Healy, *The Individual Delinquent* (Boston: Little, Brown, 1915).
65. Cyril Burt, *The Young Delinquent* (New York: D. Appleton & Company, 1925).
66. Sheldon and Eleanor Glueck, *Unraveling Juvenile Delinquency* (New York: Commonwealth Fund, 1950).

67. William Healy and Augusta F. Bronner, *New Light on Delinquency and Its Treatment* (New Haven: Yale University Press, 1936), p. 5.
68. Ben Karpman, *The Individual Criminal* (Washington, D.C., Nervous and Mental Disease Publication, 1935); Robert Lindner, *Rebel Without a Cause* (New York: Grune & Stratton, 1944); Kate Friedlander, *The Psychoanalytic Approach to Juvenile Delinquency* (Boston: Routledge & Kegan Paul, 1947); David Abrahamsen, *Who are the Guilty?* (New York: Holt, Rinehart and Winston, 1952); Franz Alexander and Hugo Staub, *The Criminal, the Judge, and the Public,* rev. ed. (New York: Free Press, 1956).
69. Michael Hakeem, "A Critique of the Psychiatric Approach to Crime and Correction," *Law and Contemporary Problems,* 23 (Autumn 1958), pp. 650–682.
70. Radzinowicz, *In Search of Criminology,* p. 119.
71. Morton White, *Social Thought in America: The Revolt Against Formalism* (New York: Viking Press, 1949).
72. Frances A. Kellor, *Experimental Sociology* (New York: Macmillan, 1901), pp. ix–x.
73. Charles R. Henderson, *An Introduction to the Study of Dependent, Defective, and Delinquent Classes,* 2d ed. (Lexington, Mass.: Heath, 1901), preface.
74. Ibid., p. 238.
75. Arthur C. Hall, *Crime In Its Relation to Social Progress* (New York: Columbia University Press, 1902), p. xi.
76. Hall, *Crime and Its Relation to Social Progress,* p. 376.
77. John H. Wigmore, *A Preliminary Bibliography of Modern Criminal Law and Criminology* (Chicago: Northwestern University Law School, 1909), Bulletin No. 1.
78. Gabriel Tarde, *Penal Philosophy,* trans. Rapelje Howell (Boston: Little, Brown, 1912); Willem A. Bonger, *Criminality and Economic Conditions,* trans. Henry P. Horton (Boston: Little, Brown, 1916).
79. Maurice Parmelee, *The Principles of Anthropology and Sociology in Their Relations to Criminal Procedure* (New York: Macmillan, 1908).
80. Maurice Parmelee, *Criminology* (New York: Macmillan, 1918).
81. Marshall B. Clinard, "Sociologists and American Criminology," *Journal of Criminal Law, Criminology and Police Science,* 41 (January–February 1951), p. 551.
82. W. I. Thomas and Florian Znaniecki, *The Polish Peasant in Europe and America,* 2 vols., 2d ed. (New York: Knopf, 1927).
83. W. I. Thomas, *The Unadjusted Girl* (Boston: Little, Brown, 1923), p. 38.
84. Cf. Robert E. Park, ed., *The City* (University of Chicago Press, 1925).
85. Frederick M. Thrasher, *The Gang: A Study of 1,313 Gangs in Chicago* (University of Chicago Press, 1927).
86. Clifford R. Shaw, *Delinquency Areas,* with the collaboration of Frederick M. Zorbaugh, Henry D. McKay, and Leonard S. Cottrell (University of Chicago Press, 1929).
87. Clifford R. Shaw, *The Jack-Roller* (University of Chicago Press, 1930); Shaw, *Natural History of a Delinquent Career* (University of Chicago Press, 1931); Shaw, *Brothers in Crime* (University of Chicago Press, 1938).
88. Ernest W. Burgess, "The Study of the Delinquent as a Person," *American Journal of Sociology,* 28 (May 1923), p. 679.
89. Clayton J. Ettinger, *The Problem of Crime* (New York: Ray Long and Richard R. Smith, 1932).
90. Otto Pollak, *Crime Causation: Selected Bibliography of Studies in the United States, 1939–1949* (University of Pennsylvania Press, 1950).
91. Albert Morris, *Criminals and the Community* (Melbourne University Press, 1953), p. 30.
92. Morris Ploscowe, "Some Causative Factors in Criminality: A Critical Analysis of the Literature," in *Report on the Causes of Crime,* vol. 1 (Washington, D.C.: National Commission on Law Observance and Enforcement, 1931), p. 17.
93. Robert H. Gault, *Criminology* (Lexington, Mass.: Heath, 1932).
94. John L. Gillin, *Criminology and Penology* (Englewood Cliffs, N.J.: Prentice-Hall, 1926), pp. 250–251.

95. Boris Brasol, *The Elements of Crime* (New York: Oxford University Press, 1927), p. 28.
96. Nathaniel F. Cantor, *Crime and Society* (New York: Holt, Rinehart and Winston, 1939), p. 399.
97. Arthur E. Wood and John B. Waite, *Crime and Its Treatment* (New York: American Book, 1941). p. 5.
98. Hans Von Hentig, *Crime: Causes and Conditions* (New York: McGraw-Hill, 1947).
99. Nathaniel F. Cantor, *Crime, Criminals and Criminal Justice* (New York: Holt, Rinehart and Winston, 1932).
100. Fred Haynes, *Criminology* (New York: McGraw-Hill, 1930).
101. Harry Best, *Crime and the Criminal Law in the United States* (New York: Macmillan, 1930), p. vii.
102. Jerome Michael and Mortimer J. Adler, *Crime, Law and Social Science* (New York: Harcourt Brace Jovanovich, 1933), p. 169.
103. See Albert K. Cohen, Alfred Lindesmith, and Karl F. Schuessler, eds., *The Sutherland Papers* (Indiana University Press, 1956), p. 290.
104. Edwin H. Sutherland, "Crime and the Conflict Process," *Journal of Juvenile Research*, 13 (January 1929), p. 41.
105. Thorstein Sellin, *Culture Conflict and Crime* (New York: Social Science Research Council, 1938), p. 21.
106. Ibid., p. 63.
107. Frank Tannenbaum, *Crime and the Community* (Boston: Ginn, 1938), pp. 17–18.
108. Edwin H. Sutherland, *The Professional Thief* (University of Chicago Press), 1937.
109. Edwin H. Sutherland, *Principles of Criminology*, 3d ed. (Philadelphia: Lippincott, 1939), pp. 5–7.
110. Edwin H. Sutherland, *Principles of Criminology*, 4th ed. (Philadelphia: Lippincott, 1947), pp. 6–7.
111. Robert K. Merton, "Social Structure and Anomie," *American Sociological Review*, 3 (October 1938), pp. 672–682.
112. Elliott Currie's review of Taylor, Walton, and Young, *The New Criminology* in *Issues in Criminology*, 9:1 (Spring, 1974), p. 13.
113. See, for example, George B. Vold, *Theoretical Criminology* (New York: Oxford University Press, 1958); Melvin L. De Fleur and Richard Quinney, "A Reformulation of Sutherland's Differential Association Theory and a Strategy for Empirical Verification," *Journal of Research in Crime and Delinquency*, 3 (January 1966), pp. 1–22; Daniel Glaser, "Criminality Theories and Behavioral Images," *American Journal of Sociology*, 61 (March 1956), pp. 433–444; Walter C. Reckless, Simon Dinitz, and Barbara Kay, "The Self Component in Potential Delinquency and Potential Non-Delinquency," *American Sociological Review*, 22 (October 1957), pp. 566–570; Marshall B. Clinard, ed., *Anomie and Deviant Behavior* (New York: Free Press, 1964); Richard A. Cloward and Lloyd E. Ohlin, *Delinquency and Opportunity* (New York: Free Press, 1960); Albert K. Cohen, *Delinquent Boys* (New York: Free Press, 1955).
114. For example, see Abraham S. Blumberg, *Criminal Justice* (New York: Quadrangle, 1967); Marshall B. Clinard and Richard Quinney, *Criminal Behavior Systems: A Typology*, 2d ed. (New York: Holt, Rinehart and Winston, 1973); Donald R. Cressey, *Theft of the Nation* (New York: Harper & Row, 1969); Don C. Gibbons, *Changing the Lawbreaker* (Englewood Cliffs, N.J.: Prentice-Hall, 1965); Daniel Claser, *The Effectiveness of a Prison and Parole System* (Indianapolis: Bobbs-Merrill, 1964); Edwin M. Lemert, *Human Deviance, Social Problems, and Social Control* (Englewood Cliffs, N.J.: Prentice-Hall, 1964); Arthur Niederhoffer, *Behind the Shield* (Garden City, N.Y.: Doubleday, 1967); Jerome H. Skolnick, *Justice Without Trial* (New York: Wiley, 1966); Richard Quinney, ed., *Crime and Justice in Society* (Boston: Little, Brown, 1969).
115. Richard Quinney, *The Social Reality of Crime* (Boston: Little, Brown, 1970); and Austin T. Turk, *Criminality and Legal Order* (Skokie, Ill.: Rand McNally, 1969)

CONTEMPORARY ISSUES IN THE STUDY OF CRIME

With the increasing emphasis on crime as a legally and, more recently, a socially defined phenomenon, a common core of concerns is forming in the study of crime and crime control. A number of contemporary issues underlie the study of crime and societal attempts to control it. These issues can be grouped into a discussion of (1) the substance of contemporary criminology, (2) the meaning of criminal statistics, (3) the methodology of explanation, and (4) theorizing in criminology.

THE SUBSTANCE OF CONTEMPORARY CRIMINOLOGY

The diversity of today's criminology is to a great extent a reflection not only of the different intellectual and practical backgrounds of those who focus their attention on crime, but also of their immediate, concrete *reasons* for studying it. The selection of subject matter, the development of theoretical perspectives, and the particular methodology chosen in criminology have been dependent upon the location of the observer in reference to the possible objects of study. The study of crime is thus not unlike the quest of the six blind men of Indostan, "to learning much inclined, who went to see the elephant," and thereupon discovered its different parts, in separate ways. The phenomenon of crime likewise may be approached in a number of ways.

What, then, is criminology? One conception of criminology is that of a discipline consisting of a cluster of fields that bear some relation to crime. These fields may embody diverse theoretical points of view or they may constitute a synthesis of perspectives. In addition, some of the fields may be devoted to the practical application of knowledge about crime. Such a conception of criminology as a unitary and autonomous science was advocated in the late 1950s in a report prepared by members of the International Society of Criminology for UNESCO.[1]

However, a unified field of criminology will probably never be achieved because of the fact that several quite different intellectual and occupational enterprises are engaged in the study and control of crime. In noting this diverse nature of criminology, Stanton Wheeler has listed five types of contributors to criminology:

1. Those persons who are directly involved in daily programs of crime control—a police commissioner, the director of a parole agency, a prison administrator, etc.
2. Those who train persons for professional roles in crime processing or control—faculty of schools of police or correctional administration, etc.
3. Those who are involved in policy research within a correctional or crime control system—the research staff of a state or federal agency, etc.
4. Those whose primary allegiance is to a particular academic discipline such as sociology, but who typically apply the knowledge of the discipline to problems of crime and its control.
5. Those whose contributions to criminology came essentially as side products of their primary pursuits within an academic discipline—a psychologist who studies delinquents in order to learn about conscience developments or aggression, a sociologist who finds prisons interesting because of what they can reveal for a sociology of power, etc.[2]

Rather than the development of a *single* discipline, then, the situation in criminology is one in which there are several different interrelated fields of academic and vocational interest. In one of the more comprehensive discussions to be found in the textbook literature of the question of what criminology is, Walter Reckless has listed ten "focal concerns" of criminology (1) compilation of crime statistics, (2) crosscultural, comparative studies of criminal law, (3) study of demographic characteristics of criminals, (4) hypothesis testing of etiological theories of crime, (5) formulation of typologies of criminal behavior systems, (6) study of recidivism patterns and rates, (7) study and control of crimes without victims types of deviant behaviors, (8) research on law-enforcement organizations and operations, (9) measuring "treatment" success, and (10) formulation and evaluation of crime prevention programs.[3]

If criminology should ever achieve any unity it will be through a concern for a concrete problem rather than through the development of a single theoretical perspective. While it would be untenable to defend the proposition that criminology as a single discipline *has* achieved any unity, a quite defensible argument could be constructed to the effect that there is a clearly identifiable dominant *current* in the history of criminology in Western society. This dominant current in the history of Western criminology has been its commitment to positivism as a methodology. "In spite of the tremendous variety of its theories and research efforts, in spite of a proliferation of its conflicting schools, and, finally, in spite of its relatively limited success in building a cumulative body of knowledge, the history of criminology in Western societies has been until recently unified by the positivist assumption that crime exists as a reality independent of the reactions of others to the behavior called criminal."[4] Thus, we could argue for a sort of methodological unity in criminology, a unity that will be discussed later in this chapter.

Another unifying theme in criminology can be found in the common concern that is shared by virtually all professionals in the field, a concern with order and control. In other words, criminologists are rarely found who identify themselves as libertarians. Thus, the organization of the field revolves about a felt need of those identifying with it for finding, by way of discovery or invention, methods of controlling human beings in such a manner that they either are not motivated or do not have the opportunity to violate the law of the state. So it is that, fragmented, as it may be, criminology as we know it in this country is itself rent with a *common* internal contradiction: Crime limits the freedom of the victim, but rigorous and effective crime control policies and methods limit the freedom of us all. The contradiction is obvious: That common problem that unifies criminology, the problem of freedom versus order, is the very same force that fragments the discipline. Thus, academic criminology has been and remains united in its contradictions.

Whatever the organization of criminology, there is the conventional, positivist view that criminology designates a body of scientific knowledge about crime, in particular, "the use of scientific methods in the study and analysis of regularities, uniformities, patterns, and causal relationships concerned with crime, criminals, or criminal behavior."[5] Even if criminology is restricted to the scientific study of crime, there is still the problem that crime may be studied from a number of theoretical and substantive perspec-

tives. There may be, for example, a biological study of crime, a psychological study of crime, an anthropological study of crime, a sociological study of crime, and other possible variations. Is the term "criminology" to be limited to any one of these perspectives, or is it to include all of them?

There is a specialized criminology from the standpoint of the sociological study of crime. According to this "sociological criminology," crime is of interest when studied as a social phenomenon. Such a criminology is the principal concern of a considerable number of sociologists in the United States. Evidence of this is found in a 1970 survey of the members of the American Sociological Association (A.S.A.).[6] Members were asked to report their special fields of expertise. Of the 33 fields of specialization within sociology, the study of crime and delinquency ranked eighth as the field selected for specialization by sociologists. Curiously enough, however, the 1975 pamphlet, "Subscription Coupons for Journals Offering Special Rates to American Sociological Association Members," sent to all A.S.A. members, lists only *one* journal, *Acta Criminologica*, that is related to the study of crime and delinquency. The pamphlet lists 67 journals! Of the 58 fields of specialty recognized by *Sociological Abstracts* in 1972, four of them related to crime (sociology of law, social disorganization, delinquency, and penology) accounted for 4.15 percent of all articles appearing in the *Abstracts* that year.

Once the sociologist selects criminology as a specialized field within sociology, his or her activities must necessarily focus at any one time on a particular subject area within criminology. There is, however, a lack of agreement among sociologists concerning the appropriate subject matter of criminology.[7] In fact, the selection of subject matter is at times a controversial issue in criminology.

One suspects that not a small amount of confusion and disagreement over what actually constitutes the proper subject matter of criminology is due to the catalogs issued by the publishing industry. For example, one of the largest publishing houses in this country, McGraw-Hill, in its 1975 Sociology and Anthropology catalog grouped "Social Problems, Criminology, and Deviant Behavior" together under one heading. Books dealing with such diverse subject matters as the history of labor's struggles, black self-concepts, drug addiction, suicide, women's liberation, alcoholism, crime, criminal law, the police, and the American Indian liberation movement were thus lumped together.

In recent times, in particular, there is increasing awareness that the emphasis in criminology has in the past been overwhelmingly on the study of "the criminal." George B. Vold has noted, however, that the study of crime has a dual nature:

> *Crime always involves both human behavior (acts) and the judgment or definitions (laws, customs, mores) of fellow human beings as to whether specific behavior is appropriate and permissible, or is improper and forbidden. Crime and criminality*

*lie in the area of behavior that is considered improper and forbidden.
There is, therefore, always a dual problem of explanation—
that of accounting for the behavior as behavior, and equally
important, accounting for the definitions by which specific behavior
comes to be considered as crime or noncrime.*[8]

The criminal law and its administration, or the processes by which
behavior is labeled as criminal, have been seriously neglected as subjects
of study in criminology in the past. Emphasis on the offender as the principal subject matter of criminology has been to a great extent due to the
acceptance of the positivistic position.[9] Following the work of Lombroso,
criminologists have assumed that there is a sharp distinction between the
criminal and noncriminal. Subsequent research has thus been devoted to
discovering why and how the offender behaves as he or she does and
how he or she differs from the nonoffender. The explanation of crime has
been sought in the makeup and behavior of the person. Emphasis on the
individual offender to the neglect of the criminal law was sharply criticized
by C. Ray Jeffery as far back as 1959:

> *The importance of the Positive School is that it focussed attention
> on motivation and on the individual criminal. It sought an
> explanation of crime in the criminal, not in the criminal law. This
> is true of every theory of criminal behavior which is discussed
> in the textbooks today, even though the explanation is in terms of
> social and group factors rather than in terms of biological
> factors. The shift in criminological thinking has been from a biological
> to a sociological and psychological explanation of behavior, not
> in terms of a shift in interest from the criminal to crime. The emphasis
> is still upon the individual offender, not crime.*[10]

Criminologists have until recently avoided studying the criminal
law for a variety of reasons. The reasons include a fear of being legalistic,
a lack of knowledge about the law, adherence to a status quo position,
that is, accepting law and society as they exist, and the belief that the
study of criminal law and its operation is unrelated to an explanation of
crime. In recent times, however, criminologists have turned their attention
to the criminal law as a result of such forces as the development of a
sociology of law within sociology, which development was reviewed in the
previous chapter; the social-science emphasis in the more progressive
schools of law; the availability of research funds for the study of law in
a social context; and a questioning of the existing system of law and justice,

brought about in part by a developing social consciousness among students of crime. In addition, the sociological study of criminal law provides criminology with a stronger identity within sociology. As has been suggested by Austin T. Turk, the criminology of the future must focus on the explanation of the "criminality" of behavior, that is, on the labeling of behavior as criminal:

> *If the primary aim of "criminological" research per se is not to*
> *develop theories of criminal behavior—if, indeed, any attempt to do*
> *so is doomed to failure—it follows that the traditional image*
> *of criminology as the scientific discipline that seeks to do just that*
> *is not an image which can be accepted by those who are*
> *interested in the distinctive problems of explaining* criminality.[11]

There has been in recent years a marked increase in the literature being published on the structure and process of criminal law and its interaction over time with the behavior patterns of people differentially located in the social structure. Perhaps the most spectacular development of all in this area is the publication by Arno Press of 28 volumes on the history of American law, volumes written as early as 1622 and as recently as 1972.[12] This literature zeroes in on the complex of political and social forces impinging on the various role incumbents in law enforcement, the administration of justice, and the administration of corrections. It examines the reverse process as well, how the social organization of the legal system labels persons as criminal, generating crime rate differentials in our segmentally organized society.

By the early and mid-1970s, this trend reached maturity and criminology definitely included the established field of criminal justice. This field is variously identified as an area of research, employment, teaching specialization, or some combination of these, that revolves around and focuses on the United States criminal justice system. This work is currently richly rewarded with grant money coming chiefly from the Law Enforcement Administration (LEAA). The ideology here is that of mainstream criminology in this country: liberal. The current liberal response to the problem of crime is a call for studies of the established criminal justice system in order to make policy recommendations based on so-called "hard" data. Thus, the rise of the criminal justice field. The liberal myth is that those in authority will in fact make policy on the basis of consultation with the experts, thus moving the country toward a more humane way of dealing with law violators.

Rather than restrict the sociology of crime to one particular subject, we may suggest that a number of sociologically relevant topics can be subsumed under three interrelated subject areas of study: (1) the formulation and administration of criminal law, (2) the development of persons and behaviors that become defined as criminal, and (3) the social reactions to crime. In regard to the first subject area, attention is today being focused on crime as a legal definition that is imposed upon human activity by agents of the society charged with the formulation and administration of criminal law.[13] In the second area, the interest is in the process by which persons who become defined as criminal acquire their values and self-conceptions through their associations with others in social and cultural contexts.[14] Important in the sociological study of criminally defined behavior is the relation of the forms and amounts of such conduct to the social arrangements in the society.[15] More recently the Marxian analysis of social structure and crime has become important in critical or radical criminology as opposed to conservative and liberal criminology, a distinction to be dealt with shortly.

The third subject area, social reactions to crime, has always been of interest to the sociologist. Criminology textbooks have tended to devote at least half of their contents to such matters as crime control, prevention, and treatment.[16] As far as criminological research is concerned, students of crime have investigated such correctional topics as the social organization of the prison, rehabilitation, and probation and parole, and have on occasion engaged in community programs for the prevention of crime and delinquency.[17] More recently some sociologists have begun to study the informal reactions to crime as found in the public attitudes toward crime.[18] Such study may eventually lead to an understanding of the subjective realities that people construct in regard to crime. With the construction and diffusion of these realities, crime becomes a part of the social reality of the society.

Some sociologists, however, have begun to write about the exhaustion of what has come to be called labeling theory and deviance theory in academic criminology. For instance, Peter Manning's "Survey Essay" in the influential journal of reviews published by the American Sociological Association, *Contemporary Sociology*, argues in part that:

> *Although a new vision attracts some to pursue an existential or critical sociology, the present exhaustion of deviance (labeling) theory reflects perhaps the exhaustion of large segments of sociology in the early seventies.*[19]

Another theme, albeit a minor one, that seems to be developing in the substance of contemporary criminology has to do with the conceptualization of work and career as criminally defined behavior in capitalist society.[20] Thus, under the proper socioeconomic conditions and structures, even work may become criminalized. This theme grows out of a blend of the concerns of those in the sociology of work and occupations with the concerns of those criminologists who study criminal career patterns. Accordingly, research in this line of development in criminology frequently and commonly reads like a sociological analysis of the "straight" world of work: relative skills required, job status, work satisfaction, self-image, technical dimension of job, categories of different professions, professional world views, and stealing as a business. This theme is particularly useful in that it highlights the extent and degree of alienation in a society that produces such a high rate of criminally defined careers in economic survival. It accentuates the internal contradictions in our economic structure, a structure that is incapable of absorbing all the people into meaningful, productive, and legitimate jobs.

Finally, the sociology of crime consists of the study of the interrelationships between the three subject areas of criminal law, criminally defined behavior, and social reaction. For example, the defining of persons as criminal is influenced by the nature and extent of criminally defined behavior. The development of careers in crime is affected by the social reactions to crime. And to mention another of several possibilities, social reactions to crime influence the defining of persons and behaviors as criminal. Criminology as delimited by the above subject areas and their interrelations provides considerable scope for the development of significant sociological theory and research.

However, no matter what the substance of criminology, future developments in the study of crime will be influenced by the larger assumptions that underlie criminology. That is, the future of criminology will be closely tied to notions about the scientific enterprise and ideological assumptions about the state and the relation of the sociologist to the state.

The two ideologies that have dominated most research and theory in academic criminology have been those of liberalism and, to a lesser extent, conservatism. Although the liberal ideology is by no means monolithic nor consistent, as Anthony Platt has observed, most of its domain assumptions are shared by criminologists.[21] Following this liberal ideology, criminologists have tended (1) to follow a legalistic definition of crime, accepting the definitions of the state, (2) to support reformist measures in the rehabilitation of "criminals" and amelioristic reforms of society, (3) to reject general theory and macroscopic historical analysis, favoring pragmatism and social behaviorism, and (4) to be susceptible to cynicism and a lack of passion, ignoring the possibility of far-ranging changes in society. These liberal values are translated into the kinds of research criminologists conduct, the theories they construct, and the way in which they are ideologically tied to the state.

Moreover, by pursuing a narrow scientific model, also supported by the liberal ideology, criminologists tend to find their interests tied to those of the state. The conventional scientific model eliminates the possibility of dealing with values on an explicit basis. This means that the state is only superficially criticized for relatively minor failings; it is presumed right merely because it exists and has the authority to do so. The only time that a policy might be questioned is when "scientific evidence" appears to make that policy unsound, that is, when a policy is either inefficient or uneconomical. At any rate, a narrow conception of science prevents criminologists from making moral judgments beyond the scientific-technocratic control ethos of the state.

The conservative ideology, on the other hand, tends more toward an involvement in descriptive work, descriptive principally of criminal behavior patterns, organized crime structures, delinquent behavior, etc. This "inside" information, very useful from a practical viewpoint, is then transmitted to the authorities, and implemented through mechanisms of stronger social control to maintain the existing order. Such an ideology, consistent with the classical conservatism of an Edmund Burke, assumes an image of human beings as creatures in need of external control, incapable of self-control. Hence, principles of hierarchy, dominance, and voluntary consensus characterize the conservative view of society:

> Much of the "police college" criminology on systems of policing in
> the United States, for example, adjudicating on the merits of
> "beat versus car" police in various types of neighborhoods to
> encourage favorable community response to the police, is conserv-
> ative work of the kind we have in mind.[22]

Critical criminology seeks to break the hold of the past, mainly the hold of liberal-scientific criminology. The objectives of liberal-scientific criminology are noted in the first newsletter of the Union of Radical Criminologists:

> In this time of domestic and international repression, the activities
> of the police, the courts, the prison system, and other institutions
> of "social control" have become an increasingly pervasive and
> significant factor of life in the United States. At the same time, the
> conventional approach to these institutions in the academic
> fields of criminology and sociology has served to both mystify their

> *resistance to change. Criminology, in particular, has functioned*
> *in the United States and elsewhere as an integral part of the*
> *apparatus of state repression.*[23]

The Union of Radical Criminologists "welcomes any contribution that exposes the fundamental political and economic causes of crime and delinquency; that constructs definitions of crime that are in the interests of oppressed peoples and exploited classes; that critically analyzes the legal and extra-legal strategies of coercion employed by the state and its supportive institutions and that generally contributes to the development of a people's criminology."[24]

The radical criminology that is emerging in both the United States and England tries to combine its theory with practice. The important problem is not to "scientifically" understand the laws of the objective world, for the sole purpose of description and at best explanation, but to apply the knowledge of investigation in changing the world. Rejecting as false the distinction between theory and praxis, this emergent criminology seeks to change the social world *while* investigating it. Theory without practice is false theory; and practice without theory can only lead to irrational action and cynicism. This is a criminology that is a force in transforming society.

THE MEANING OF CRIMINAL STATISTICS

A serious problem for criminology is the meaning and use of criminal statistics. In bourgeois society criminal statistics are ultimately used for political purposes. There seems to be an innate compulsion in the bureaucratic mind to count things and to keep a record of the counts, thus rendering that which is counted more amenable to strict control. Moreover, criminal statistics collected by various government agencies serve as the primary forms of data for much criminological research and as indicators of the actual amount of crime in society. The use of these statistics is, at the same time, a cause of considerable controversy among criminologists. Much of the controversy revolves around the issue of the collection of criminal statistics, but as pertinent as the collection of criminal statistics is the issue of the meaning and use of criminal statistics.

The meaning and use of crime statistics depends to a great extent upon the prior ideological assumptions of the person using them. Thus, we may distinguish at least three different approaches to the meaning and use of such statistics: the conservative, the liberal, and the critical.[25] The conservative's approach to criminal statistics is grounded in a classical, Beccarian, set of assumptions about human behavior: Statistics on crime reflect willful and willing conscious human choices to violate the social contract. Crime is freely chosen behavior, the result of the victory of passion over reason. Criminal statistics, therefore, are thought of as *actual* measures of offense against a reified social contract. Politically, such a use of statistics of crime boils down to an expectation that criminal behavior is all but randomly distributed throughout the social structure and that all have an equal need to be controlled. But the lower classes have more need of external control, for the concentration of crime in this segment of society reflects a weaker, more tenuous, commitment to the social contract.

The liberal's approach to criminal statistics incorporates a greater readiness to excuse. That is, the liberal conceptualizes all behavior as determined to a great extent by a complex of social and psychological forces beyond the control and sometimes even recognition of the individual. This is a world view that embraces positivist as opposed to classical assumptions about human nature and behavior, and the important question for liberal criminology is, therefore, What can empirical research reveal to us by way of statistical measures about the determinants of criminal behavior? What causal factors should be selected out to investigate? This approach to the meaning and use of criminal statistics sees them as indicators of those variables that act as forces determining people to commit crime.

Finally, a critical criminology would employ statistics on crime in a manner that radically differs from either of the above approaches. Some critical theorists argue that:

> . . . the statistics, for all the criticisms that have been levelled at
> them . . . can fruitfully be used as evidence of the underlying
> trends occurring in the wider social structure. For example, criminal
> statistics over the years can be read and used as evidence of
> the enthusiasm with which the . . . . ruling class is prosecuting
> individuals and groups under different sets of laws and for
> different sets of social behaviors.[26]

Critical criminologists have also argued that crime statistics can be used fruitfully as indicators, not of how bad things are but of how *good* they are for the propertied classes. That is, they indicate the extent of compliance in industrial society. Thus, crime statistics indicate the degree to which the working-class accepts or rejects the current distribution of wealth and property.[27]

SOURCES OF CRIMINAL STATISTICS

Most of the available criminal statistics that criminologists have relied upon in their research and generalizations have been derived from official sources, that is, from the statistics gathered by agencies of government.[28] In fact, there is the tendency in criminology to equate criminal statistics with official statistics. With such statistics in mind, criminal statistics have been defined in the following way: "By criminal statistics we mean (a) uniform data on offenses or offenders expressed in numerical terms; (b) derived by official agencies (police, prosecutors, courts, penal institutions, etc.) from their records; (c) classified, tabulated, and analyzed in order to establish relationships between or among the classes of items tabulated; and (d) published—preferably annually—in a uniform manner."[29]

The regularized collection of official criminal statistics by governmental agencies in the United States has not had a noteworthy history. The state of New York started to collect judicial statistics in 1829. Eventually, during the nineteenth century, 24 other states adopted the practice. The statistics were derived from reports sent by state attorneys or clerks of criminal courts to state officials. The collection of official statistics up to 1908 in the United States has been summarized as follows:

> To sum up the situation existing at the end of the period 1829 to
> 1908, twenty-five states were collecting judicial statistics and
> twenty-three states statistics of prisoners, an impressive total were
> it not that with rare exceptions both kinds of statistics were of
> very doubtful value serving no scientific purpose. Police statistics
> were mentioned occasionally in laws but that is about as far
> as they got. The Federal Government had tried from time to time in
> a half-hearted way to collect judicial criminal statistics, also,
> police statistics, but failed in each attempt. Its efforts to collect
> statistics of prisoners had, however, met with reasonable
> success. In the 1904 report, the earlier mistakes of making the
> statistics relate solely to a point of time was rectified but the
> length of time intervening between the statistical inquiries was
> discouragingly long.[30]

The official statistics that are available for use in criminological research are collected by several levels of government: federal, state, and local. The sources may be further divided according to the administrative stages at which the statistics are compiled. The criminal statistics most commonly used by criminologists are based on local police department reports gathered by the federal government. In 1927, at a convention of the

International Association of Chiefs of Police, a Committee on Uniform Crime Reports was appointed. Two years later the committee published a guide for the collection of police statistics titled *Crime Reporting: A Complete Manual for Police.* In 1930, the Federal Bureau of Investigation took over the system of reporting police statistics and issued the first bulletin of the *Uniform Crime Reports.* The *Uniform Crime Reports* were published monthly at first, then quarterly until 1944, and semiannually until 1957. Since 1958 the *Uniform Crime Reports* have been issued annually, with preliminary reports being prepared on a quarterly basis.

Statistics on matters of prosecutions, dismissals, acquittals, convictions, prison sentences, fines, and probation are compiled and published as judicial statistics. In 1932, the United States Bureau of the Census began to publish such statistics for state courts, but discontinued the task in 1947. Some states continue to collect their own court statistics. However, because of great variations in collection procedures, state comparisons are nearly impossible. On the federal level, the Administrative Office of the United States Courts publishes an *Annual Report* that compiles the judicial statistics of the federal courts. In regard to juvenile delinquency, judicial statistics of youth who appear before selected local courts have been published since 1946, under the direction of the Children's Bureau of the United States Department of Health, Education and Welfare, in a series known as *Juvenile Court Statistics.*

Statistics on prisoners have been published annually since 1926 in *National Prisoner Statistics.* Presently under the direction of the Federal Bureau of Prisons of the United States Department of Justice, this report includes information on the number of commitments to state and federal penal institutions as well as information on prison populations and discharges. The Federal Bureau of Prisons also issues an annual report entitled *Federal Prisons* that provides statistical data on persons convicted of violations of federal laws. In addition to the federally gathered statistics, several state departments of correction issue periodic reports on prisoners within their jurisdictions.

Further sources of criminal statistics include the reports of a number of other governmental and private agencies. Included are such reports as the following: *Vital Statistics in the United States,* which incorporates the reports of homicide submitted by local coroners; special reports occasionally published by the United States Treasury Department; reports of special offenses against the Federal Deposit Insurance Corporation; information on certain federal violations reported in the *Annual Report of the Attorney General of the United States;* records of burglaries and robberies committed against member banks of the American Bankers Association; reports

of state departments of public welfare; and special surveys and reports of historical interest, such as *Criminal Justice in Cleveland* of 1922, *The Missouri Crime Survey* of 1926, *The Illinois Crime Survey* of 1929, the *Survey of the Administration of Justice in Oregon* of 1932, and the series of reports in the state of New York in the late twenties by the Commission on the Administration of Criminal Justice.[31]

Finally, the most recent—and probably most influential and important—source of criminal statistics is the National Crime Panel. The National Crime Panel is a newly devised empirical instrument, one with the enthusiastic official *imprimatur* of the state, for measuring crime not only nationwide but also locally in selected metropolitan centers across the country. Under the actual administration of the U.S. Bureau of Census and sponsored by the Law Enforcement Assistance Administration, the panel measures the extent to which individual adults (persons over 12), households, and commercial establishments have been victimized. It gathers nationwide data on victim characteristics, relationship between victim and perpetrator, time and location of offense, degree and amount of injury or loss suffered, and whether or not the incident was reported to the police: "Because the Panel measures victimizations not reported to the police, in addition to those that come to official attention, it is expected to produce rates of victimization higher than those previously documented."[32] The panel is a direct result of the recommendations made by the 1967 President's Commisssion on Law Enforcement entitled *The Challenge of Crime in a Free Society.*

CRIMINAL STATISTICS AS MEASURES OF THE AMOUNT OF CRIME

Since most collections of criminal statistics have been gathered for purposes other than those explicitly intended in any particular criminological research, the appropriate use of criminal statistics by the criminologist is an important issue. Basically, all criminal statistics represent the operations of agencies that are charged with the administration of criminal law. Most criminologists, and the general public for that matter, have attempted to use criminal statistics as measures of the "actual amount of criminality" in any given geographical area or in the country as a whole. There is indeed controversy over the issue of the appropriateness of criminologists (social scientists) using official criminal statistics as raw data in their scientific research. Thus, Austin Turk argues:

> It is genuinely puzzling that scientists have been so persistent in
> trying to carry on research using second-hand and, for their
> purposes, virtually useless data collected by non-scientists for

non-scientific purposes, and that they have for so long, in Sellin's words, "permitted non-scientists to define the basic terms of inquiry."[33]

When criminal statistics are used for the purpose of assessing the "true" incidence of criminality, a number of valid criticism may indeed be raised concerning the methods of collecting criminal statistics. Pessimistic appraisals such as the following have relevance *if* criminal statistics are used to indicate actual criminality:

> *Since around 1920, a great deal of effort has been put forth in different parts of the United States, and at various levels of government toward the production of useful criminal statistics. But despite all of this work, there has not been produced in the United States any systematic collection of information on crime which furnishes the factual information desired, or which is comparable to the criminal statistics of many other countries.*[34]
> *The statistics about crime and delinquency are probably the most unreliable and most difficult of all social statistics. It is impossible to determine with accuracy the amount of crime in any given jurisdiction at any particular time. Some behavior is labeled "delinquency" or "crime" by one observer but not by another. Obviously a large proportion of all law violations goes undetected. Other crimes are detected but not reported, and still others are reported but not officially recorded. Consequently any record of crimes, such as crimes known to the police, arrests, convictions, or commitments to prison, can at most be considered an "index" of the crimes committed. But these "indexes" of crime do not maintain a constant ratio with the true rate, whatever it may be. We measure the extent of crime with elastic rulers whose units of measurement are not defined.*[35]

On the basis of such criticisms, numerous suggestions and recommendations have been made to improve the collection of criminal statistics, especially to improve the procedures used in the *Uniform Crime Reports*.[36] A principal difficulty in the use of available criminal statistics as indexes of criminality in the United States results from the lack of uniform reporting in the United States. Because of the political organization of the United States, each of the fifty states represents a separate political jurisdiction. Each state has its own constitutional provisions, penal codes, courts, criminal procedures, and systems of law enforcement. Furthermore, the administration of criminal law in each state is not centralized but is, instead, a localized activity. These political facts create considerable variation in the recording of criminal offenses and thus prohibit the comparability of information on criminal offenses from state to state and from one locality to another within states.[37]

Sellin pointed out some time ago that "the value of a crime rate for index purposes decreases as the distance from the crime itself in terms of procedure increases."[38] That is, police records are more reliable measures of the actual incidence of criminal offenses than arrest statistics, arrest statistics are more reliable than court statistics, and court statistics are more reliable than prison statistics. The implication is that many offenses are "lost" between the records of police and prosecution. It is with an awareness of these facts that criminologists usually use the records of police rather than other records to make inferences about the extent of criminality. The principal source of such information is found in the statistics designated as "crimes known to the public." These statistics, as contained in the annual *Uniform Crime Reports,* consist of the offenses that are recorded by the police departments of approximately eight thousand jurisdictions in the United States. For purposes of the annual report, the offense records of the local police departments are grouped into 29 offense categories. Seven of the categories (murder and nonnegligent manslaughter, forcible rape, robbery, aggravated assault, burglary, larceny of fifty dollars and over, and motor vehicle theft) are combined and designated by the Federal Bureau of Investigation as the "Index of Crime." Shown in Table 1 is the "Index of Crime," from the *Uniform Crime Reports,* for the year 1974.

The reader of this and other tables in the *Uniform Crime Reports,* however, is cautioned lest he or she fail to recognize the limitations of these official statistics. We are warned that not only population, size, and density, but a series of other factors and conditions as well affect the volume and type of crime from one place to another. These are enumerated: population composition by age, sex and race; economic status and mores; stability; climate; educational, recreational, and religious parameters; strength of police force and standards of appointment; policies of prosecuting officials, the courts, and corrections; nature of police-community relations; administrative and investigative efficiency of law enforcement; and cooperation of adjoining police jurisdictions. Note that according to the Federal Bureau of Investigation at least five police-related factors affect the crime rate.

An example of the reduction of criminal statistics in the movement from one criminal procedure to another is found in the difference between "crimes known to the police" and "crimes cleared by arrest." Furthermore,

TABLE 1. INDEX OF CRIME IN THE UNITED STATES, 1974

Area	Population[1]	Total Crime Index	Violent[2] crime	Property[2] crime
United States Total	211,392,000	10,192,034	969,823	9,222,211
Rate per 100,000 inhabitants		4,821.4	458.8	4,362.6
Standard Metropolitan Statistical Area	154,095,271			
Area actually reporting[3]	97.1%	8,515,137	850,719	7,664,418
Estimated total	100.0%	8,662,603	860,470	7,802,133
Rate per 100,000 inhabitants		5,621.6	558.4	5,063.2
Other Cities	23,183,092			
Area actually reporting	91.3%	859,013	52,657	806,356
Estimated total	100.0%	933,625	57,772	875,853
Rate per 100,000 inhabitants		4,027.2	249.2	3,777.9
Rural	34,113,637			
Area actually reporting	81.2%	509,765	41,389	468,376
Estimated total	100.0%	595,806	51,581	544,225
Rate per 100,000 inhabitants		1,746.5	151.2	1,595.3

SOURCE: Federal Bureau of Investigation, *Uniform Crime Reports,* 1974 (Washington, D.C.: U.S. Government Printing Office, 1975), p. 55.
[1] Population is Bureau of the Census provisional estimate as of July 1, 1974.
[2] Violent crime is offenses of murder, forcible rape, robbery, and aggravated assault; property crime is offenses of burglary, larceny-theft and motor vehicle theft.

the discrepancy between crimes known to have occurred and arrests made in connection with the known crimes varies considerably from one offense category to another. As shown in Figure 1, a drawing from the *Uniform Crime Reports* of 1974, police departments cleared by arrest 80 percent of the murders, 78 percent of the negligent manslaughters, 51 percent of the forcible rapes, 63 percent of the aggravated assaults, 27 percent of the robberies, 18 percent of the burglaries, 20 percent of the larcenies, and 15 percent of the auto thefts. It should be pointed out that the police count a clearance when they have identified someone they believe to be an offender of a known offense, have sufficient evidence to charge the person, and actually take him into custody. Also, the arrest of one person can conceivably clear several crimes, or, on the other hand, *several* persons may be arrested in the process of clearing one known offense.

The extent to which criminal statistics may be reduced between

Murder and non-negligent man-slaughter	Forc-ible rape	Robbery	Aggra-vated assault	Burglary	Larceny-theft	Motor vehicle theft
20,600	55,209	441,290	452,724	3,020,742	5,227,696	973,773
9.7	26.1	208.8	214.2	1,429.0	2,473.0	460.6
16,398	47,332	418,722	368,267	2,498,217	4,288,854	877,347
16,690	48,125	421,753	373,902	2,546,649	4,362,298	893,186
10.8	31.2	273.7	242.6	1,652.6	2,830.9	579.6
1,176	2,838	11,503	37,140	217,984	543,859	44,513
1,313	3,111	12,567	40,781	237,608	589,654	48,501
5.7	13.4	54.2	175.9	1,024.9	2,543.5	209.6
1,996	3,272	5,696	30,425	202,655	239,153	26,568
2,597	3,973	6,970	38,041	236,485	275,744	31,996
7.6	11.6	20.4	111.5	693.2	808.3	93.8

[3] The percentage representing area actually reporting will not coincide with the ratio between reported and estimated crime totals since these data represent the sum of the calculations for individual states which have varying populations, portions reporting, and crime rates.

known crimes and convicted persons received in prisons was noted by C. C. Van Vechten in an analysis of "criminal case mortality" in several jurisdictions.[39] Distinguishing between seven levels of criminal procedure, Van Vechten found that for all of the crimes known in the District of Columbia 35.7 percent resulted in offenses cleared, 10.0 percent in persons charged, 7.5 percent in judicial prosecutions, 5.9 percent in convictions, 3.7 percent in sentences in prison, and 3.6 percent in prisoners received from courts. The marked decrease from the first procedural level to the last demonstrates the difficulty of using criminal statistics far removed from the offense itself as measures of the "actual" amount of criminality.

Perhaps the most critical problem in the use of official criminal statistics as indicators of the incidence of criminality, even when "offenses known to the police" are employed, is that there exists an unknown amount of criminality that never becomes a part of the public record. For various

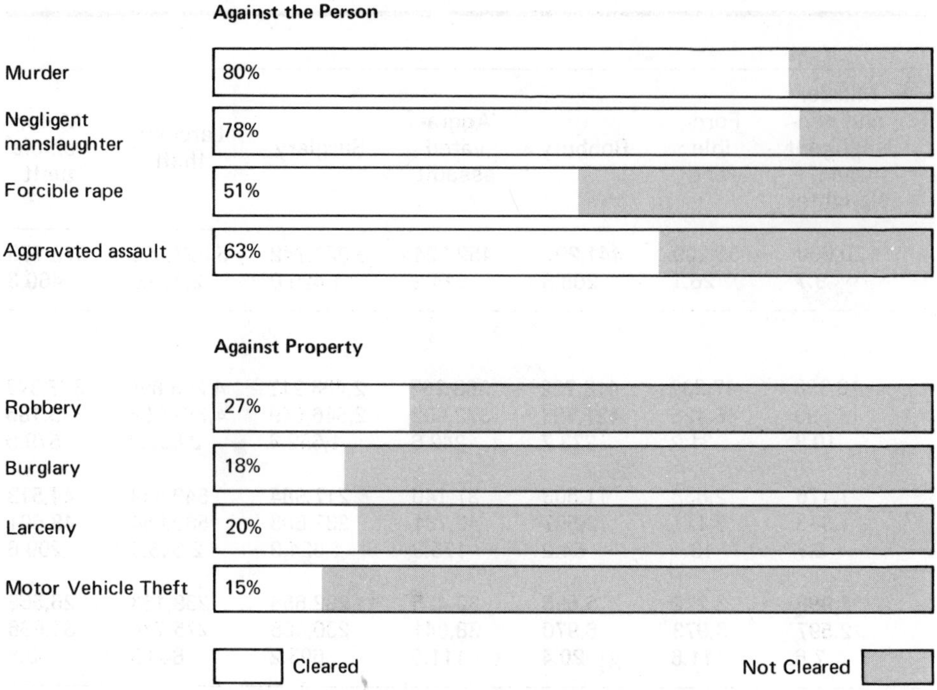

Against the Person

Murder	80%
Negligent manslaughter	78%
Forcible rape	51%
Aggravated assault	63%

Against Property

Robbery	27%
Burglary	18%
Larceny	20%
Motor Vehicle Theft	15%

Cleared   Not Cleared

Figure 1. Crimes Cleared by Arrest, 1974
  SOURCE: Federal Bureau of Investigation, *Uniform Crime Reports, 1974* (Washington, D.C.: U.S. Government Printing Office, 1975), p. 43.

reasons many criminal offenses are never reported to the police, or when reported are not recorded by the police. Any given violation of the criminal law is likely to carry with it a certain probability that it will come to the attention of the law-enforcement agencies. The probability that an offense will not be reported or recorded is related to a number of factors: (1) Some offenses are known only to the offender, and, thus, are not likely to be reported by the offender. (2) Because of a lack of knowledge of the criminal law, victims and witnesses will not report criminal violation. (3) Witnesses to an offense may not want to report the offense because of inconvenience, embarrassment, fear, or lack of interest in law enforcement. (4) The victim or witness may fear the possibility of being implicated in the violation or in other violations if investigated. (5) The victim or witness may fear reprisal if the criminal offense is reported. (6) Friends and relatives may try to protect the offender and, therefore, not report the offense. (7) The victim may fear unfavorable publicity and embarrassment. (8) Social values

TABLE 2. REASONS GIVEN FOR NOT REPORTING VICTIMIZATIONS

	Personal	Household	Commercial
Nothing could be done; lack of proof	34	38	37
Not important enough	28	32	33
Police would not want to be bothered	5	7	4
Too inconvenient or time-consuming	3	2	5
Private or personal matter	6	5	—
Did not want to become involved	—	—	1
Fear of reprisal	2	1	0
Reported to someone else	10	3	8
Other and not available	12	12	12
	100%	100%	100%

SOURCE: National Crime Panel, *Crime in Eight American Cities, Advance Report,* (Washington, D.C.: Dept. of Justice, 1974), p. 6.

and public opinion do not favor the full enforcement of certain criminal laws. (9) Some criminal offenses because of their nature are not readily visible to the general public or law-enforcement agencies. (10) Law-enforcement agencies may wish to conceal some criminal offenses.[40]

The National Crime Panel's survey of victimization in eight American cities yielded the percentage distribution in Table 2 of reasons advanced by victims for not reporting personal, household, and commercial victimizations.

The existence of considerable amounts of "hidden criminality" has been indicated in a number of studies in criminology. In an examination of the extent to which official statistics measure juvenile delinquency, Robison found that about a third of the behavior problems known to New York City agencies did not become court cases.[41] Murphy, Shirley, and Witmer found in a study of boys who were in a special counseling program that many were "unofficial delinquents." The juvenile offenses were known by certain authorities but were handled informally.[42] In a study of the delinquent behavior reported by Texas college students committed in their high school days and college years, Porterfield found that the college students had engaged in similar amounts and forms of delinquent behavior as had the juveniles who were officially processed in court.[43] The college students, because of their advantageous backgrounds, had not been referred to court for their illegal acts while the other juveniles had been officially handled.

In a more recent investigation, Short and Nye compared the self-reported juvenile behavior of samples of students in three midwestern high schools and three western high schools to the reported delinquency of a sample of juveniles in a western training school.[44] They found, among other things, that delinquent conduct among the noninstitutional students was extensive and that there were similarities between the institutional and noninstitutional students in self-reported delinquent conduct. A number of other recent studies using the self-reporting techniques of measuring delinquency have investigated differences according to social class, sex, race, religion, family relations, and rural-urban residence.[45]

Adult criminality also is much more widespread than is reflected in official criminal statistics. James S. Wallerstein and Clement J. Wyle published in 1947 the responses of a sample of New York residents to a questionnaire containing 49 offense categories.[46] When the respondents, 1,020 men and 678 women, were asked to check the offenses they had committed, 91 percent of the sample admitted that they had committed one or more of the offenses. The men had on the average committed 18 of the offenses and the women averaged 11 offenses each. For some of the particular offense categories, 89 percent of the men admitted to larceny, 85 percent to disorderly conduct, 49 percent to assault, and 35 percent to concealed weapons. Among the women in the sample, 83 percent admitted to larceny, 81 percent to malicious mischief, 76 to disorderly conduct, 74 percent to indecency, and 39 percent to auto misdemeanors.

More recently, the preliminary report of the National Crime Panel's victimization studies has demonstrated conclusively the fact that adult criminality is more widespread than official criminal statistics would have us believe. Table 3 shows the average rate of victimization by type per one thousand population in eight sampled cities. The rates are considerably above the official crime statistics for these offense categories in these locations over comparable time periods.

Biasing influences on arrest records for all categories of criminally defined behavior further distort our perception of the real world and what is actually happening out there. For example, it was recently reported with regard to drug-related arrests that "these patterns (of drug arrests) reflect systematic biases in the operations of police assigned to the Narcotics Division. These and other such biases argue that we ought not to rely on indices of drug activity derived from arrest records."[47]

There are, furthermore, many special forms of reported offenses that are not collected in the traditional sources of criminal statistics.[48] Among these offenses are those that occur in commerce and industry, management–labor relations, union management, income-tax reporting, and social security and public administration. These offenses are for the most part dealt with by state and federal regulatory agencies. The statistics in regard to these offenses, therefore, are in the files and reports of the

TABLE 3. AVERAGE VICTIMIZATION RATES FOR PERSONS AGE 12 AND OVER, BY TYPE OF VICTIMIZATION IN EIGHT SELECTED AMERICAN CITIES

(Average rate per 1000 population age 12 and over, based on surveys during the months July through November 1972 of victimizations during the previous 12 months.)

Type of victimization	Average rate per 1000
Crimes of violence	51
Rape and attempted rape	2
Robbery	19
Robbery and attempted robbery with injury	6
Serious assault	3
Minor assault	2
Robbery without injury	8
Attempted robbery without injury	6
Assault	30
Aggravated assault	14
With injury	5
Attempted assault with weapon	9
Simple assault	16
With injury	4
Attempted assault without weapon	12
Crimes of theft	91
Personal larceny with contact	9
Purse snatching	3
Attempted purse snatching	1
Pocket picking	5
Personal larceny without contact	82

SOURCE: Adapted from National Crime Panel, *Crime in Eight American Cities, Advance Report*, (Washington, D.C.: U.S. Department of Justice, 1974), p. 11. The eight cities are: Atlanta, Baltimore, Cleveland, Dallas, Denver, Newark, Portland, and St. Louis.

Note: Detail may not add to total shown because of rounding. In general, small differences between any two figures in this table are not statistically significant because of sampling.

respective agencies. Such criminal records do not usually become a part of official criminal statistics. Reliance on the traditionally collected criminal statistics obscures the prevalence of these and other crimes. Official statistics thus serve better as indicators of the reaction of society to certain kinds of offenses than as measures of the amount of criminality in society, and if we are looking for the rates of crime in American society, we are not likely to find them in the statistics gathered thus far by government agencies.

Crime = Crime Index Offenses
Crime Rate = Number of offenses per 100,000 inhabitants

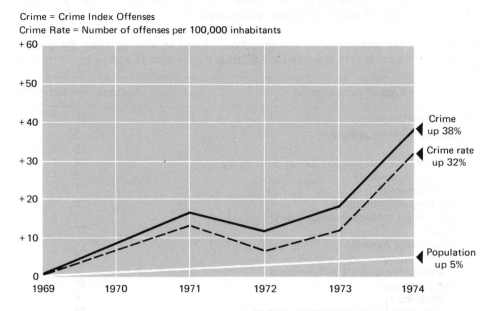

Figure 2.   Crime and Population, 1969–1974 (Percent change over 1969)
  SOURCE: Federal Bureau of Investigation, *Uniform Crime Reports, 1974* (Washington, D.C.: U.S. Government Printing Office, 1975), p. 12.

THE MEANING OF CRIME RATES

The use of official criminal statistics as measures of the incidence of criminality is thus a questionable practice. Furthermore, to criticize the existing criminal statistics and to advocate better crime-reporting procedures is to accept the assumption that official statistics can in themselves serve as indexes of the actual amount of crime. Nevertheless, official criminal statistics continue to be used as indicators of criminality in society. Numerous studies have drawn upon official statistics in the attempt to draw conclusions about the *extent* of crime and delinquency and the *characteristics* of offenders.[49]

The conclusions often reached in the use of official criminal statistics is that the crime rate is higher than it "should be" and that, in addition, the crime rate has continued to increase steadily since World War II. The student of crime, and the entire public, will continue to be periodically reminded that the crime rate for the current year is higher than that of previous years. Newspapers report as news the releases of the annual *Uniform Crime Reports.* We are reminded by the FBI that our crime rate continues to in-

Limited to murder, forcible rape, robbery and aggravated assault

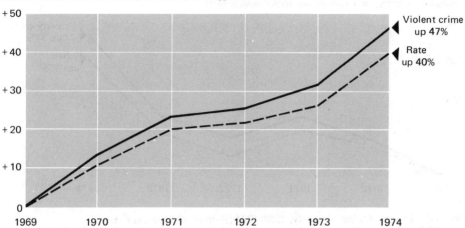

Figure 3.   *Crimes of Violence, 1969–1974 (Percent change over 1969)*
   SOURCE: Federal Bureau of Investigation, *Uniform Crime Reports, 1974* (Washington, D.C.: U.S. Government Printing Office, 1975), p. 13.

crease sharply. Figures 2, 3, and 4 from the *Uniform Crime Reports* are typical of the kind of graphic description that is periodically presented to the public. Once knowing that the crime rate is increasing, we are expected to experience collective alarm. The reader is not usually, however, provided with the additional information that it is not certain what the criminal statistics mean. They may mean only that law-enforcement procedures change from year to year. The crime rate may not reflect the actual amount of crime so much as it reflects the way police departments operate and change in their operations.

   There are other processes that could also be taking place as concomitant events, events that—if known and integrated into a total understanding of the crime picture—may well alter the public's frame of reference about the meaning of criminal statistics. Two common examples of such concomitant events can be cited, examples falling under the heading "I have some bad news and some good news." First, the crime rate may drop in traditional dangerous or perilous areas of an urban center, but at the same time rise sharply in the rest of the city. Such a development could reflect a spatial shift in law-enforcement personnel and nothing more. Second, one particular legal category of crime, for example, auto theft, could decline sharply during one time period while other legal categories of

Limited to burglary, larceny-theft and motor vehicle theft

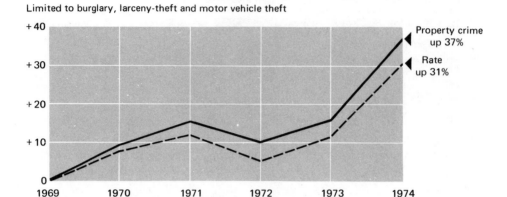

Figure 4. Crimes Against Property, 1969–1974 (Percent change over 1969)
SOURCE: Federal Bureau of Investigation, *Uniform Crime Reports, 1974* (Washington, D.C.: U.S. Government Printing Office, 1975), p. 14.

crime, for example, rape and burglary, were on the ascendancy during that same time period. This could reflect merely the results of reorganization of bureaus in the police department. Both of these sets of concomitant events actually did occur in the city of New York in late 1974 and early 1975.[50]

It may well be that the wrong question is being asked of our criminal statistics. Official criminal statistics, in the first place, represent only a fraction of some unknown amount of offensive behavior in any given geographical area. In this use of criminal statistics, there is much "hidden criminality," and the statistics are "dark figures." Second, since most of human behavior can at some time be labeled as criminal by those with the authority to so label, the statistics reflect the policies and behaviors of the agencies engaged in the administration of criminal law. The fact is that *all* human behavior has a probability of becoming defined as criminal in one of the stages of criminal procedure.

Thus, the conception of official criminal statistics must be broadened to include the fact that criminal statistics also represent the process of labeling behavior as criminal. Rather than assuming that criminal statistics indicate only the *incidence of criminal behavior* in a population, it must be assumed as well that criminal statistics reflect differentials in the *administration of criminal law.*[51] These two conceptions of criminal statistics may not necessarily be regarded as mutually exclusive. A third meaning of criminal statistics is that they reflect a combination of the first two conceptions, that is, that they reflect a mixture of the *incidence of criminality and the administration of criminal law.*

A fourth meaning of criminal statistics, on a distinct conceptual level, is that they are indicators of the *socially recognized volume of crime.* In this conception, official statistics are viewed as production figures from the standpoint of the society. Whether there is more or less "actual" criminality, strict or lenient administration of criminal law, or some combination of criminality and administration is not the issue. The crucial question is why societies and their agencies report, manufacture, or produce the volume of crime that they do.

With a similar notion in mind, Cressey has suggested that the kind of reporting system that is devised in a society serves useful purposes for the varying personnel that are engaged in the control, treatment, and prevention of crime. A vagueness in criminal statistics is useful because it decreases the wide range of ideological and theoretical commitments of the many persons dealing with criminals. Thus, Cressey suggests a "sociology of crime reporting":

> The kind and amount of statistics compiled on crime and delinquency are, in a very real sense, an index of social concern about crime and delinquency. Why do we report and compile what we can do? What pressures are there on workers in the field to report some deviations and not others? What pressures are there for and against establishment of uniform categories for reporting and compilation? Why do we ask the personnel who are in direct contact with criminals to look at what they look at?[52]

For us, then, the meaning of criminal statistics is clear: They represent the nature and extent of crime recognized in any given society or jurisdiction at any particular time.

POLITICS OF AMERICAN CRIME RATES

In the final analysis crime rates have to be understood as *political* devices. It is for political purposes that criminal statistics are gathered. And likewise it is according to political needs that criminal statistics are recorded and interpreted. American crime rates are thus subject to a great manipulation, from their inception to their use. It is impossible to know from any statistic the "true" rate of crime. Whether crime is increasing or decreasing in American society is a question that can never be answered in any objective way beyond the politics of the times.

Crime rates, therefore, are used to justify or instigate a multitude of political (including social and economic) interests. High crime rates, for example, are used by the police to rationalize the need for more personnel and equipment. At the same time crime rates cannot be drastically reduced by the police without jeopardizing the allocation of further appropriations. The contradiction is that the police have an interest in maintaining both a high and low rate of crime concurrently.

In recent years politicians have made crime rates an issue in their political campaigns. Many candidates for various offices have promised to reduce the crime rate. Barry Goldwater, the Republican presidential candidate, introduced "law and order" into the campaign of 1964. The rhetoric was escalated by the candidates in the 1968 presidential campaign. Each candidate developed his own version of law and order as a battle cry in the campaign. Richard Nixon, then the Republican candidate, touched it off in his acceptance speech at Miami, charging that "some of our courts in their decisions have gone too far in weakening the peace forces as against the criminal."[53] In even greater detail, Nixon presented his position on law and order in a paper, "Toward Freedom from Fear." His position was made clear: "Just as justice dictates that innocent men go free, it also means that guilty men must pay the penalty of their crimes. It is the second part of justice to which the nation must begin to address itself in earnest. . . . By now Americans, I believe, have learned the hard way that a society that is lenient and permissive for criminals is a society that is neither safe nor secure for innocent men and women."[54]

The Democratic candidate, Hubert Humphrey, responded by promising to halt "rioting, burning, sniping, mugging, traffic in narcotics, and disregard for law." But he added that "the answer lies in reasoned effective action by our authorities, not in attacks on our courts, our laws or our Attorney General."

The former governor of Alabama, George Wallace, running as an independent candidate, took the extreme position on the law and order issue. His solution was simple: Free the police of all restraint. Wallace repeated his position every place he went, usually bringing the house down with the message: "If you walk out of this hotel tonight and someone knocks you on the head, *he'll* be out of jail before *you're* out of the hospital, and on Monday morning they'll try the policeman instead of the criminal. That's right, we're going to have a *police* state for folks who burn the cities down. They aren't going to burn any more cities." The law and order issue was becoming a racist euphemism for suppressing the demands of blacks in the urban ghettoes.

The law and order issue, with its own variations, was repeated in the presidential election of 1972. This time, Richard Nixon, the incumbent, explicitly used criminal statistics to bolster his position. This time, however, he argued that the crime rates were actually *decreasing* during his administration. George McGovern, the Democratic candidate, refuted Nixon's use of criminal statistics. A "numbers game" was being played with the American crime rates. McGovern nevertheless found it necessary to offer similar law and order programs for the control of crime. Crime control now was clearly a means for preventing the destruction of the established order.

Ironically, those very people in national political life, the nation's "leaders"—Richard Nixon, Spiro Agnew, John Mitchell, H. R. Haldeman, John Ehrlichman, to name but the most notorious—who posed as the most patriotic Americans during the late 1960s and early 1970s, controlling crime in order to prevent the destruction of the established order, were the very ones who almost succeeded in subverting and bringing down that established order *in their own way.* Unfortunately, these people saw their own way of subverting the liberties, rights, and freedoms of citizens as healthy protective bastions against the surge of crime that threatened existing arrangements. The end result of this dialectic of crime and crime control was a United States Department of Justice, bereft of respect, the object of public ridicule and cynicism. Out of this debacle also emerged the final realization that from 1968 onward, the massive infusion of federal resources into crime control had utterly failed to reduce crime rates.

> *In one of his last statements as Attorney General, William B. Saxbe*
> *described as "a dismal failure" the Federal effort to reduce*
> *crime despite "the billions in anti-crime funds awarded since 1968,"*
> *and analysts in the Office of Management and Budget are*
> *now highly dissatisfied with the way LEAA [Law Enforcement*
> *Assistance Administration] has spent its money.*[55]

The ultimate use of criminal statistics for political ends is currently being planned and implemented. By improving the techniques of national surveys, as first used in research for the President's Crime Commission, the government is developing a system for the continuous monitoring of crime. The objective, however, is not merely to get a more complete record of otherwise unreported crime, but to gather information that can be used to devise more effective means of law enforcement. As an administrative official of the Information and Statistics Service (of LEAA) observed recently regarding these new statistical methods: "Actually, under-reporting is only of marginal interest to our study. We are attempting to design a statistical methodology that will allow us to continuously monitor the character-

istics of crime in the country; who are the victims; what is the genesis of a certain type of crime; where, how and when does it occur. These are the questions we want answers to to provide tolls for planning responses by police and other social agencies."[56]

We are well on the road to a national crime-data reporting system. A national data bank, with instant retrieval possibilities, will provide the most rational and political device for the authoritarian control of the population. The use of criminal statistics has progressed to its ultimate control purpose. Crime rates are now explicitly used to protect the class and governmental interests of the social and economic system.

THE METHODOLOGY OF EXPLANATION

Traditionally all scientific enterprises were based on the faith that there is a knowable order. Science was thus a tautology: Order was assumed and that assumption led to the discovery of order. Furthermore, science has assumed a special kind of order; a *causal order*. The principle of causality has served as a foundation for all the sciences. Causality has been both a methodological device and a substantive theory of reality. Until fairly recent times the concept went unquestioned.

The object of most of the explanation in criminology has been to find the "causes of crime." The search for the causes of crime continues to be a principal concern of criminologists.[57] All such efforts assume that phenomena can be divided into units, or variables, and that the variables can then be causally linked. The study of criminal behavior, for the most part, is devoted to establishing that an "A is the cause of B," B being crime and A being a social phenomenon, preferably some kind of pathology.

Modern thought in the philosophy of science, however, tends to either dispense with the concept of causation or use it with qualified meaning. Even in the physical sciences the concept of causation has lost much of its utility. What is occurring is a revision in the conception of the natural world and the relation of the observer to it. The basic challenge of modern physics to the principle of causality is in the idea that the very act of observing has an influence on that which is being observed.[58] Since causal statements depend upon a knowledge of the present state of a phenomenon in order to calculate the future state of another phenomenon, skepticism regarding the scientist's ability to objectively observe the present state of affairs casts doubt on the application of the laws of causality.

The implication of modern philosophy is the rejection of the idea that science is a "copy of reality." Even that which many of us regard as real, such as atoms, are the *constructs* of the scientist. The same may be true of causality: Causality is a construct that has been used by the scientist in an attempt to understand the world he or she experiences.

A danger that the social scientist must guard against in a reading of modern science is the temptation to imitate completely the scientific model of the physical sciences. There has been the tendency in the social sciences to copy the philosophical assumptions of the physical sciences as well as their particular methods and techniques. But how, then, is the concept of causation to be used in the social sciences, particularly in criminology? In addition to recognizing that causation is initially a construct, we must make a distinction between the physical world and the social world. The basic differences and the corresponding methods of investigation have been described by Alfred Schutz in the following way:

> *The world of nature, as explored by the natural scientist, does not "mean" anything to molecules, atoms, and electrons. But the observational field of the social scientist—social reality—has a*

> *specific meaning and relevance structure for the human beings living, acting, and thinking within it.*[59]

Following this reasoning, it is important to make a distinction in the social sciences between *methodological causation* and *social causation*. This is essentially the approach Robert M. MacIver took in his argument that the phenomena with which the social sciences deal exhibit a special kind of substantive causal process, different in significant respects from the causation of phenomena in the physical world.[60] Since social causation is a distinctive kind of causation, he continued, the methodology of the social sciences should be developed accordingly. MacIver maintained that there are a number of distinct levels of causal analysis. The social scientist, he insists, is concerned with the sociopsychological nexus of phenomena. The phenomena of interest to the sociologist are those arising out of the individual and collective "dynamic assessments." Since human beings are immersed in their strivings, purposes, and goals, the assessment of behavior by man must be a basic part of causal analysis. Man himself, as a conscious social being, is the agent of causation and, according to MacIver, must be so considered in the study of social behavior.

A similar argument has been advanced by Pitirim A. Sorokin in an attempt to liberate sociology from the concepts and methods of the physical sciences.[61] After distinguishing between several forms of interconnections between sociocultural phenomena, Sorokin concludes that most empirically grounded sociocultural systems are bound together as causal-meaningful unities. Hence, for Sorokin and MacIver, as well as for some other social scientists, social causation may be conceived of as a special form of causation, one that combines methodological causation with substantive causation because of the nature of the social world that human beings construct.

Once realizing that the concept of causation must have a special meaning in the social sciences, *alternatives* to causal explanation can be considered. Causal explanation is only one form of explanation and cannot be equated with explanation in general.[62] Certainly when causal analysis is not appropriate for either methodological or substantive purposes, other forms of explanation should be used. Many of the important contributions in sociology have been presented in other than causal form, as empirical generalizations, classifications, statistical descriptions, probabilities, and developmental stages. Generally social scientists have been interested in social structure, the functioning of systems and their parts, regularities of behavior, patterns, and processes. All of these concerns have been pur-

sued for the most part without the aid of cause-and-effect reasoning. It is obvious that there would be a science of human social behavior without the notion of causality.[63]

Another explanatory approach available to criminology as an alternative to causative reasoning involves the use of phenomenological assumptions. This approach takes human consciousness and its intended meanings as the proper locus for an understanding of social behavior. Drawing from the works of several scholars, Edward Tiryakian observes that "existential phenomenology applied to sociology seeks the *roots* of social existence."[64] Such an approach, a "sociology in depth" as George Gurvitch has phrased it, attempts to get at the dynamic complexity of social reality not arrived at by the traditional scientific concepts and methods. Gurvitch has suggested that the surface of the readily observable may be penetrated through the analysis of various depth levels, ranging from the ecological surface to the collective mentality.[65] Existential phenomenology has the promise of providing a method and a body of concepts for the substantive analysis of the wholeness of social phenomena and the processes by which social phenomena become, change, and possibly disintegrate, all in respect to man's subjective awareness of his own and others' actions.

There is one other form of explanation that is qualitatively different from all the rest. Rather than attempting merely to *describe* the existing order, the purpose is to understand what *is* in terms of what *could be.* This involves a *dialectical* form of thought that allows us to examine all the contradictions in social existence. The dialectical method, drawing from Marx, involves "research into the manifold ways in which entities are internally related. It is a voyage of exploration that has the whole world for its object, but a world which is conceived of as relationally contained in each of its parts."[66] Moreover, in being able to *critically* understand existing conditions, we can suggest ways of thinking and acting that will allow for a new existence.

THEORIZING IN CRIMINOLOGY

There are a number of approaches to theorizing in criminology, with each separate approach, or "mode of thought" containing its own assumptions about the methodology of explanation and the nature of social and human reality. Consequently, each mode of thought carries with it both a specific relation to the dominant order and a unique set of social consequences.

The four thought modes in criminology will be briefly reviewed in the following order: (1) the positivistic, (2) the social constructionist, (3) the phenomenological, and (4) the dialectical materialist.[67]

POSITIVISM

The positivistic mode of thought begins with realist assumptions about existence. That is, the primary objective is to "discover" the laws of the real world. It follows the simple epistemology that absolutely separates the knower from the known. Objectivity is assumed possible because of the belief that an order exists that is independent of the observer; and given enough knowledge, accumulated systematically, the scientist could predict future events and control their occurrence. Following such a mechanistic conception of the relation of social facts, the positivist usually couches explanations in causal terms. Finally, positivists regard their scientific activity as being "value free."

The intellectual failure of positivism is that of not being reflexive, and its political failure, as related to this intellectual failure and largely as a result of it, is its acceptance of the status quo. There is no questioning of the established order, just as there is no examination of scientific assumptions. The official reality is the one within which the positivist operates, the one that he or she accepts and supports.[68] Consequently, the efforts of criminologists operating in the positivist thought mode are devoted almost solely to established interests. Attention traditionally has been on the violator of criminal law, rather than on the legal system itself.[69] Solutions of the crime problem are usually framed in terms of changing the law-breaker rather than altering the legal system.

SOCIAL CONSTRUCTIONISM

Social constructionist thought begins with a recognition of philosophical idealism. Social constructionists work with an ontology that questions the existence of an objective reality apart from the individual's imagination. It is assumed that objects cannot exist *independently* of our minds, that any reality is important only as long as it can be perceived. The epistemological assumption is that observations are based on mental constructions formed in the mind of the observer, rather than on the raw apprehension of the physical world.

Hence, following these assumptions, the social scientist's constructs have to be founded upon the world created by social actors. The world that is important to the social constructionist is the one created by the social actions of human beings, through interaction and intercommunication with others.[70] This *social reality* involves the social meanings and the products of the subjective world of everyday life.

The failure of social constructionist thought is its inability to provide a stance that would allow us to transcend the official reality. While social constructionists furnish us with the beginnings for an examination of multiple realities, they fail to provide a yardstick for judging the superiority of one reality over another. Social relativism prevails at the expense of a critical understanding of the social world. The social constructionist perspective, however, has given new vitality to the study of crime and the law. Crime and other forms of stigmatized behavior are viewed first as categories that are created and imposed upon some persons by others.[71] Crime thus exists because of the social construction and application of the label of crime; and criminal law, similarly, is not autonomous to society, but is itself a social construction, created by those who are in positions of power.[72]

PHENOMENOLOGY

Phenomenological thought begins by examining the process by which we understand the world. Explanation as a form of thought is itself examined.

Phenomenologists, while differing considerably among themselves, generally agree that our knowledge of the physical world comes from our experiences of objects in that world.[73] But, they continue, when we talk about the physical world we are not limited by these experiences. That is, we are not limited by our actual experiences; we are able to speak of and share visions of *possible* experiences, thus altering our perception of things in the world. As long as a physical object exists in the world, it is possible to experience it. What is important is that an object is perceivable. We are capable of perceiving the essence of things.

Consciousness itself thus remains the source of our understanding of the world. Knowledge about the world cannot stand apart from our sense of things. Any understanding of an objective thing can come about only through our consciousness of the thing; reality is to be found in our consciousness of it. The essential is thus what the human mind understands through its consciousness, in the course of its experience of the world. Any objectivity is to be achieved by means of our own subjectivity, that is, through our consciousness.

The urge to think forces us to transcend our conventional knowledge about the world and our place in it. It is in the transcendental thinking of the phenomenologist that we find the inspiration for moving beyond the conventional wisdom of the age, including our contemporary knowledge of crime and the legal order. Instead of reifying the social order, or giving an account of ordered existence, the movement is toward a transcendence of our experience. Phenomenological thought, however, lacks the critical edge of dialectical materialist theory.

DIALECTICAL MATERIALISM

Here we finally arrive at critical theory. Through the demystifying exercise of self-reflection, the dialectical materialist approach to theory seeks to expunge or obliterate as much as is humanly possible all prior suppositions and assumptions in order to be open to every possible alternative to the existing reality. By taking this point of departure it seeks to minimize the possibility of a false consciousness that is rooted in an uncritical acceptance of a reified social order, a reified social order that is at the same time alienating and oppressive. Dialectical materialism thus is best conceived of as a liberating force, a struggle toward the birth of a new consciousness.

This new consciousness that dialectical materialism seeks to constitute is truly a liberating force in the life of a people, for the possession of it frees us to choose a better life, to build an alternative society, one free

from alienation, dominance, repression, and hierarchy. For without critical thought we are inexorably chained to the only form of society we know, the existing one. Thus we are not free. To know the richness and variety of possible alternative social lives is to be free to choose them, and conversely, not to know of any other possibilities is to be indentured to that which is. Social structures have that power over us who have created them, a power to be resisted constantly: They blot out, obliterate, the possibility of alternative social structures. For in aspiring to the rewards that an existing system offers, we are blinded to consideration of alternative social existences. This is the message of Herbert Marcuse in his discussion of the "one dimensional" character of our present reality.[74]

The dialectical materialist mode involves critical thought.[75] It is a mode that exposes false beliefs, practices, and social structures by submitting them to juxtaposition and comparison with contradictory beliefs, practices, and social structures. It is only by way of dialectical thought that our minds can break the hold that the forces of current reality have on us and "determine the direction and control the consequences of these forces."[76] Our odyssey involves a search, not for objective reality, but for a negation of the established order so that we may begin anew.

This mode of thought, further, is *materialistic* in that it has developed out of historical materialism as formulated by Marx. It tells us that the study of our existing legal reality and world of crime is the study of a process rooted ultimately in material reality, that of production, a process, moreover, operating within a system that has certain set limits to its potential growth and development. As materialist, it turns our critical focus onto the nature of our current legal reality in terms of its precise role in relation to a unique mode of production, advanced capitalism. Thus, critical materialism guides criminological theory toward constructing an understanding of how legal structures and processes affect the productive enterprise of our society, and thus ultimately the culture that infuses and gives life and meaning to that society.[77]

Guided by dialectical materialism, then, criminological theory of the future will "explain the structural and the class differences existing within and between capitalist societies in contributing further to our understanding of the antagonisms that result, as Marx understood, from the lack of correspondence between the development of material production and the development of social and legal relations."[78] It will involve itself in analyzing the real processes by which laws are formulated, supported and enforced, or abandoned depending upon the class interests they protect and extend and depending upon their usefulness to specific material arrangements of production. Finally, such a criminological theory at the same time maintains a firm realization that "the legal norms in question are inextricably connected with the developing contradictions in (capitalist) societies."[79]

NOTES

1. Denis Carrol and Jean Pinatel, "Report on the Teaching of Criminology," in *The University Teaching of Social Sciences: Criminology* (UNESCO, 1957), p. 15.
2. Stanton Wheeler, "The Social Sources of Criminology," *Sociological Inquiry*, 32 (Spring 1962), p. 141.
3. Walter Reckless, *The Crime Problem*, 4th ed., (Englewood Cliffs, N.J.: Prentice-Hall, 1967), pp. 1–10.
4. John Wildeman, *The Crime Fighters*, unpublished PhD dissertation, New York University, 1971, p. 13.
5. Marvin E. Wolfgang, "Criminology and the Criminologist," *Journal of Criminal Law, Criminology and Police Science*, 54 (June 1963), p. 162.
6. Nico Stehr and Lyle E. Larson, "The Rise and Decline of Areas of Specialization," *The American Sociologist*, 7 (August 1972), pp. 3–6.
7. Discussions of the substance of criminology in the United States can be found in Marshall B. Clinard, "Criminological Research," in Robert K. Merton, Leonard Broom, and Leonard S. Cottrell, Jr., eds., *Sociology Today* (New York: Basic Books, 1959), pp. 509–536; Donald R. Cressey, "Crime," in Robert K. Merton and Robert A. Nisbet, eds., *Contemporary Social Problems*, 2d ed. (New York: Harcourt Brace

Jovanovich, 1966), pp. 136–192; Gilbert Geis, "Sociology and Crime," in Joseph S. Roucek, ed., *Sociology of Crime* (New York: Philosophical Library, 1961), pp. 7–33; Daniel Glaser, "The Sociological Approach to Crime and Correction," *Law and Contemporary Problems,* 23 (Autumn 1958), pp. 683–702; Frank E. Hartung, "A Critique of the Sociological Approach to Crime and Correction," *Law and Contemporary Problems,* 23 (Autumn 1958), pp. 703–734; Ned Polsky, *Hustlers, Beats, and Others* (Chicago: Aldine, 1967), pp. 117–149; Stanton Wheeler, "Delinquency and Crime," in Howard S. Becker, ed., *Social Problems: A Modern Approach* (New York: Wiley, 1966), pp. 201–276; Elmer H. Johnson, *Crime, Correction, and Society,* 3d ed. (Homewood, Illinois: Dorsey Press, 1974), pp. 3–19; Martin Haskell and Lewis Yablonski, *Crime and Delinquency,* 2d ed., (Chicago: Rand McNally, 1974), chap. 1, passim.

8. George B. Vold, *Theoretical Criminology* (New York: Oxford University Press, 1958), pp. v–vi.

9. For an extended discussion of this theme, see Richard Quinney, *The Social Reality of Crime* (Boston: Little, Brown, 1970), chap. 1.

10. C. Ray Jeffery, "The Historical Development of Criminology," *Journal of Criminal Law, Criminology and Police Science,* 50 (June 1959), p. 9.

11. Austin T. Turk, "Prospects for Theories of Criminal Behavior," *Journal of Criminal Law, Criminology and Police Science,* 55 (December 1964), p. 460.

12. George Cole, *Criminal Justice: Law and Politics* (Belmont, Calif.: Duxbury Press, 1972); Patrick Murphy, *Our Kindly Parent—The State: The Juvenile Justice System* (New York: Viking Press, 1974); Ronald Akers and Richard Hawkins, eds., *Law and Control in Society* (Englewood Cliffs, N.J.: Prentice-Hall, 1975); William J. Chambliss, ed., *Criminal Law in Action* (Santa Barbara, Calif.: Hamilton Publishing Company, 1975).

13. Michael Banton, *The Policeman in the Community* (London: Tavistock, 1964); Egon Bittner, "The Police on Skid-Row: A Study of Peace Keeping," *American Sociological Review,* 32 (October 1967), pp. 699–715; Abraham S. Blumberg, *Criminal Justice* (New York: Quadrangle, 1967); Howard S. Becker, *Outsiders* (New York: Free Press, 1963); William J. Chambliss, "A Sociological Analysis of the Law of Vagrancy," *Social Problems,* 12 (Summer 1964), pp. 67–77; Aaron V. Cicourel, *The Social Organization of Juvenile Justice* (New York: Wiley, 1968); John P. Clark, "Isolation of the Police: A Comparison of the British and American Situations," *Journal of Criminal Law, Criminology and Police Science,* 56 (September 1965), pp. 307–319; C. Ray Jeffery, "The Development of Crime in Early English Society," *Journal of Criminal Law, Criminology and Police Science,* 47 (March–April 1957), pp. 647–666; Wayne R. La Fave, *Arrest* (Boston: Little, Brown, 1965); Alfred R. Lindesmith, *The Addict and the Law* (Indiana University Press, 1965); Donald J. Newman, *Conviction* (Boston: Little, Brown, 1966); Arthur Niederhoffer, *Behind the Shield* (Garden City, N.Y.: Doubleday, 1967); Irving Piliavin and Scott Briar, "Police Encounters with Juveniles," *American Journal of Sociology,* 70 (September 1964), pp. 206–214; Jerome H. Skolnick, *Justice Without Trial* (New York: Wiley, 1966); David Sudnow, "Normal Crimes: Sociological Features of the Penal Code in a Public Defender Office," *Social Problems,* 12 (Winter 1965), pp. 255–276.

14. See, for example, Earl Rubington and Martin Weinberg, *Deviance: The Interactionist Perspective,* 2d ed., (New York: Macmillan, 1973).

15. See the discussion and references in Marshall B. Clinard and Richard Quinney, *Criminal Behavior Systems: A Typology,* 2d ed. (New York: Holt, Rinehart and Winston, 1973).

16. See, for example, Elmer H. Johnson, *Crime, Correction and Society,* 3d ed. (Homewood, Ill.: Dorsey Press, 1974); Richard R. Korn and Lloyd W. McCorkle, *Criminology and Penology* (New York: Holt, Rinehart and Winston, 1959); Sutherland and Cressey, *Principles of Criminology,* 9th ed. (Philadelphia: Lippincott, 1974); Paul W. Tappan, *Crime, Justice and Correction* (New York: McGraw-Hill, 1960).

17. Donald R. Cressey, ed., *The Prison* (New York: Holt, Rinehart and Winston, 1961); Don C. Gibbons, *Changing the Lawbreaker* (Englewood Cliffs, N.J.: Prentice-Hall, 1965);

Daniel Glaser, *The Effectiveness of a Prison and Parole System* (Indianapolis: Bobbs-Merrill, 1964); Malcolm W. Klein, *Street Gangs and Street Workers* (Englewood Cliffs, N.J.: Prentice-Hall, 1971); Solomon Kobrin, "The Chicago Area Project—A 25-Year Assessment," *Annals of the American Academy of Political and Social Science,* 322 (March 1959), pp. 19–29; Walter B. Miller, "The Impact of a 'Total Community' Delinquency Control Project," *Social Problems,* 10 (Fall 1962), pp. 168–191; Lloyd W. McCorkle, Albert Alias, and F. Lovell Bixby, *The Highfields Story* (New York: Holt, Rinehart, and Winston, 1957); James F. Short, Jr., and Fred L. Strodtbeck, *Group Process and Gang Delinquency* (University of Chicago Press, 1965); Gersham M. Sykes, *The Society of Captives* (Princeton University Press, 1958); Clyde B. Vedder and Barbara A. Kay, eds., *Penology: A Realistic Approach* (Springfield, Ill.: Thomas, 1969).

18. See Sarah Boggs, "Formal and Informal Crime Control: An Exploratory Study of Urban, Suburban, and Rural Orientations," *Sociological Quarterly,* 12 (Summer 1971), pp. 319–327; Alexander L. Clark and Jack P. Gibbs, "Social Control: A Reformulation," *Social Problems,* 12 (Spring 1965), pp. 402–406; James E. Conklin, "Dimensions of Community Response to the Crime Problem," *Social Forces,* 18 (Winter 1971), pp. 373–385; John A. Gardiner, "Public Attitudes Toward Gambling and Corruption," *Annals of the American Academy of Political and Social Science,* 374 (November 1967), pp. 123–134; Jennie McIntyre, "Public Attitudes Toward Crime and Law Enforcement," *Annals of the American Academy of Political and Social Science,* 374 (November 1967), pp. 34–46; Donald J. Newman, "Public Attitudes Toward a Form of White Collar Crime," *Social Problems,* 4 (January 1957), pp. 228–232; Elizabeth A. Rooney and Don C. Gibbons, "Social Reactions to 'Crime Without Victims,'" *Social Problems,* 13 (Spring 1966), pp. 400–410; Erwin O. Smigel, "Public Attitudes Toward Stealing as Related to Size of the Victim Organization," *American Sociological Review,* 21 (June 1956), pp. 320–327.

19. Peter Manning, "Review Essay," in *Contemporary Sociology,* 2:2 (March 1973), pp. 123–128. Manning was reviewing Stanley Cohen, ed., *Images of Deviance;* Daniel Glaser, *Social Deviance;* Edwin Lemert, *Human Deviance, Social Problems and Social Control;* David Matza, *Becoming Deviant;* and Edwin Schur, *Labeling Deviant Behavior.*

20. James A. Inciardi, *Careers in Crime* (Skokie, Ill.: Rand McNally, 1975). See also Peter Letkemann, *Crime As Work* (Englewood Cliffs, N.J.: Prentice-Hall, 1975).

21. Anthony Platt, "The Triumph of Benevolence: The Origins of The Juvenile Justice System in the United States," in Richard Quinney, ed., *Criminal Justice in America: A Critical Understanding* (Boston: Little, Brown, 1974), pp. 356–389. A clear exposition of the liberal ideology, especially in regard to the issue of value neutrality is found in Donald Black, "The Boundaries of Legal Sociology," in Donald Black and Maureen Mileski, eds., *The Social Organization of Law* (New York: Seminar Press, 1973), pp. 41–56.

22. Ian Taylor, Paul Walton, and Jock Young, "Advances Toward a Critical Criminology," *Theory and Society,* 1 (Winter, 1974), p. 443.

23. Union of Radical Criminologists, *Newsletter,* 3 (May 1973), p. 1.

24. Ibid.

25. Taylor, Walton, and Young, "Advances Toward a Critical Criminology," pp. 455–460 passim. On criminal statistics, see also Roger Hood and Richard Sparks, *Key Issues in Criminology* (New York: McGraw-Hill, 1970), esp. chap. 1.

26. Ibid., p. 454.

27. Ibid., p. 460.

28. Sources of criminal statistics are discussed, among other places, in Ronald H. Beattie, "Sources of Statistics on Crime and Correction," *Journal of the American Statistical Association,* 54 (September 1959), pp. 582–592; Walter A. Lunden, *Facts on Crimes and Criminals* (Ames, Iowa: The Art Press, 1961); James A. McCafferty, "Prisoner Statistics—National and State," *Proceedings of the American Statistical Association* (1960), pp. 25–33; Edward B. McConnell, "Judicial Criminal Statistics," *National*

Probation and Parole Association Journal, 3 (July 1957), pp. 250–262; Edward E. Schwartz, "Statistics of Juvenile Delinquency in the United States," *Annals of the American Academy of Political and Social Science,* 261 (January 1949), pp. 9–20.

29. Thorsten Sellin, "The Measurement of Criminality in Geographic Areas," *Proceedings of the American Philosophical Society,* 97 (April 1953), p. 163.

30. Louis N. Robinson, "History of Criminal Statistics, 1908–1933," *Journal of Criminal Law, Criminology and Police Science,* 24 (May–June 1933), p. 126. Also see C. E. Gehlke, "Development of Criminal Statistics in the Past Century," *Proceedings of the American Prison Association* (1931), pp. 176–190.

31. These and other surveys are discussed in Virgil Peterson, *Crime Commissions in the United States* (Chicago Crime Commission, 1945).

32. National Crime Panel, *Crime in Eight American Cities, Advance Report* (Washington, D.C.: Dept. of Justice, 1974), p. III.

33. Austin Turk, *Criminality and the Legal Order* (Skokie, Ill.: McNally, 1972), p. 8.

34. Ronald H. Beattie, "Problems of Criminal Statistics in the United States," *Journal of Criminal Law, Criminology and Police Science,* 46 (July–August 1955), p. 178.

35. Edwin H. Sutherland and Donald R. Cressey, *Criminology,* 9th ed. (Philadelphia: Lippincott, 1974), p. 25.

36. See, for example, Peter P. Lejins, "Uniform Crime Reports," *Michigan Law Review,* 64 (April 1966), pp. 1011–1033; David J. Pittman and W. F. Handy, "Uniform Crime Reporting: Suggested Improvements," *Sociology and Social Research,* 46 (January 1962), pp. 135–143; Sophia M. Robinson, "A Critical View of the Uniform Crime Reports," *Michigan Law Review,* 64 (April 1966), pp. 1031–1054; Thorsten Sellin, "The Uniform Criminal Statistics Act," *Journal of Criminal Law, Criminology and Police Science,* 40 (March–April 1950), pp. 679–700; Leslie T. Wilkins, "New Thinking in Criminal Statistics," *Journal of Criminal Law, Criminology and Police Science,* 56 (September 1965), pp. 277–284; Marvin E. Wolfgang, "Uniform Crime Reports: A Critical Appraisal," *University of Pennsylvania Law Review,* 111 (April 1963), pp. 708–738.

37. Ronald H. Beattie, "Criminal Statistics in the United States—1960," *Journal of Criminal Law, Criminology and Police Science,* 51 (May–June 1960), pp. 49–65.

38. Thorsten Sellin, "The Basis of a Crime Index," *Journal of Criminal Law, Criminology and Police Science,* 22 (September–October 1931), p. 346.

39. C. C. Van Vechten, "Differential Criminal Case Mortality in Selected Jurisdictions," *American Sociological Review,* 7 (December 1942), pp. 833–839.

40. Based on Marshall B. Clinard, *Sociology of Deviant Behavior,* rev. ed. (New York: Holt, Rinehart and Winston, 1963), pp. 20–21; and Thorsten Sellin, *Research Memorandum on Crime and the Depression* (New York: Social Science Research Council, 1936), pp. 69–70.

41. Sophia M. Robison, *Can Delinquency be Measured?* (New York: Columbia University Press, 1936).

42. Fred J. Murphy, Mary M. Shirley, and Helen L. Witmer, "The Incidence of Hidden Delinquency," *American Journal of Orthopsychiatry,* 16 (October 1946), pp. 686–696.

43. Austin L. Porterfield, *Youth in Trouble* (Fort Worth: The Leo Potishman Foundation, 1946).

44. James F. Short, Jr., and F. Ivan Nye, "Extent of Unrecorded Juvenile Delinquency: Tentative Conclusions," *Journal of Criminal Law, Criminology and Police Science,* 49 (November–December 1958), pp. 296–302.

45. Among the studies are Ronald L. Akers, "Socio-Economic Status and Delinquent Behavior: A Retest," *Journal of Research in Crime and Delinquency,* 1 (January 1964), pp. 38–46; John P. Clark and Eugene P. Wenninger, "Socio-Economic Class and Areas as Correlates of Illegal Behavior among Juveniles, *American Sociological Review,* 27 (December 1962), pp. 826–834; Robert A. Dentler and Lawrence J. Monroe, "Social Correlates of Early Adolescent Theft," *American Sociological Review,* 26 (October 1961), pp. 733–743; Maynard L. Erickson and Lamar T. Empey, "Court Records, Undetected Delinquency and Decision-Making," *Journal of Criminal*

Law, Criminology and Police Science, 54 (December 1963), pp. 456–469; F. Ivan Nye and James F. Short, Jr., "Socioeconomic Status and Delinquent Behavior," *American Journal of Sociology,* 63 (January 1958), pp. 381–389; Albert J. Reiss and Albert Lewis Rhodes, "The Distribution of Juvenile Delinquency in the Social Class Structure," *American Sociological Review,* 26 (October 1961), pp. 720–732; Harwin L. Voss, "Socio-Economic Status and Reported Delinquent Behavior," *Social Problems,* 13 (Winter 1966), pp. 314–324. Studies of self-reported delinquency are summarized in Robert H. Hardt and George E. Bodine, *Development of Self-Report Instruments in Delinquency Research: A Conference Report* (Syracuse, N.Y.: Syracuse University Youth Development Center, 1965).

46. James S. Wallerstein and Clement J. Wyle, "Our Law-Abiding Law-Breakers," *Probation,* 25 (April 1947), pp. 107–112.

47. Lois B. DeFleur, "Biasing Influences on Drug Arrest Records: Implications for Deviance Research," *American Sociological Review,* 40 (February 1975), pp. 83–103, quoted from abstract.

48. Harry Manuel Schulman, "The Measurement of Crime in the United States," *Journal of Criminal Law, Criminology and Police Science,* 57 (December 1966), pp. 485–486.

49. See, for example, John C. Ball, Alan Ross, and Alice Simpson, "Incidence and Estimated Prevalence of Recorded Delinquency in a Metropolitan Area," *American Sociological Review,* 29 (February 1964), pp. 90–93; E. Jackson Baur, "The Trend of Juvenile Offenses in the Netherlands and the United States," *Journal of Criminal Law, Criminology and Police Science,* 55 (September 1964), pp. 359–369; Joseph W. Eaton and Kenneth Polk, *Measuring Delinquency* (Pittsburgh: University of Pittsburgh Press, 1961); Thomas P. Monahan, "On the Incidence of Delinquency," *Social Forces,* 39 (October 1960), pp. 66–72; Austin L. Porterfield, "A Decade of Serious Crimes in the United States: Some Trends and Hypotheses," *American Sociological Review,* 13 (February 1948), pp. 44–54; Thorsten Sellin, "Crime," *American Journal of Sociology,* 47 (May 1942), pp. 898–906; Thorsten Sellin, "Crime and Delinquency in the United States: An Overview," *Annals of the American Academy of Political and Social Science,* 339 (January 1962), pp. 11–23; Harry Willbach, "The Trend of Crime in New York City," *Journal of Criminal Law, Criminology and Police Science,* 29 (May–June 1938), pp. 62–75.

50. *The New York Times,* 2 December 1974, p. 1, and 8 February 1975, p. 1.

51. Such an approach to criminal statistics is suggested in John I. Kitsuse and Aaron V. Cicourel, "A Note on the Uses of Official Statistics," *Social Problems,* 11 (Fall 1963), pp. 131–139; Donald J. Newman, "The Effect of Accommodations in Justice Administration on Criminal Statistics," *Sociology and Social Research,* 46 (January 1962), pp. 144–155; Stanton Wheeler, "Criminal Statistics: A Reformulation of the Problem," *Journal of Criminal Law, Criminology and Police Science,* 58 (September 1967), pp. 317–324.

52. Donald R. Cressey, "The State of Criminal Statistics," *National Probation and Parole Association Journal,* 3 (July 1957), pp. 240–241. A similar view is presented in Albert D. Biderman and Albert Reiss, Jr., "On Exploring the 'Dark Figure' of Crime," *Annals of the American Academy of Political and Social Science,* 374 (November 1967), pp. 1–15.

53. Quoted in Fred J. Cook, "There's Always a Crime Wave—How Bad's This One?" *The New York Times Magazine,* October 6, 1968, p. 38. The quotations from the other presidential candidates are also in Cook's article.

54. Quoted in Albert J. Reiss, "Crime, Law and Order as Election Issues," *Transaction,* 5 (October 1968), p. 3.

55. *The New York Times,* 24 March 1975, p. 30, editorial.

56. *The New York Times,* 27 April 1973, p. 1.

57. Critical discussions of causal explanation, however, are found in Hermanus Bianchi, *Position and Subject Matter of Criminology* (Amsterdam: North-Holland, 1956); David Matza, *Delinquency and Drift* (New York: Wiley, 1964); Walter C. Reckless, *The Crime Problem* (Englewood Cliffs, N.J.: Prentice-Hall, 1967).

58. Mario Bunge, *Causality: The Place of the Causal Principle in Modern Science* (New York: Harcourt Brace Jovanovich, 1963); Percy W. Bridgman, *Reflections of a Physicist* (New York: Philosophical Library, 1950); see especially Werner Heisenburg, *Physics and Philosophy: The Revolution in Modern Science* (New York: Harper & Row, 1958); and Stephen Toulmin, *The Philosophy of Science* (New York: Harper & Row, 1960).

59. Alfred Schutz, "Concept and Theory Formation in the Social Sciences," in Maurice Natanson, ed., *Philosophy of the Social Sciences* (New York: Random House, 1963), p. 242.

60. Robert M. MacIver, *Social Causation* (New York: Harper & Row, 1964, originally published in 1942).

61. Pitirim A. Sorokin, *Sociocultural Causality, Time and Space* (Durham: Duke University Press, 1943). See also Sorokin, *Sociological Theories of Today* (New York: Harper & Row, 1966), pp. 17–31.

62. See Robert Brown, *Explanation in Social Science* (Chicago: Aldine, 1963); Abraham Kaplan, *The Conduct of Inquiry* (New York: Intext, 1964); and Ernest Nagel, *The Structure of Science* (New York: Harcourt Brace Jovanovich, 1961).

63. For a full discussion of the notion of causality, see Ernest Gellner, *Cause and Meaning in the Social Sciences* (London: Routledge & Kegan Paul, 1973).

64. Edward A. Tiryakian, "Existential Phenomenology and the Sociological Tradition," *American Sociological Review*, 39 (October 1965), pp. 674–688. Also see James L. Heap and Philip A. Roth, "On Phenomenological Sociology," *American Sociological Review*, 38 (June 1973), pp. 354–367.

65. George Gurvitch, *The Spectrum of Social Time* (Dorchecht, Holland: D. Reidel, 1964).

66. Bertell Ollman, *Alienation: Marx's Conception of Man in Capitalist Society* (Cambridge University Press, 1971), p. 62.

67. The following discussion is adapted and greatly condensed from Richard Quinney, *Critique of Legal Order: Crime Control in Capitalist Society* (Boston: Little, Brown, 1974), pp. 8–14.

68. See John H. Schaar, "Legitimacy in the Modern State," in Philip Green and Sanford Levinson, eds., *Power and the Community: Dissenting Essays in Political Science* (New York: Random House [Vintage Books], 1970), esp. pp. 303–308.

69. See C. Ray Jeffery, "The Structure of American Criminological Thinking," *Journal of Criminal Law, Criminology and Police Science*, 46 (January 1956), pp. 658–672.

70. See Alfred Schutz, *The Problem of Social Reality: Collected Papers I* (The Hague: Martinus Nijhoff, 1962); and Peter L. Berger and Thomas Luckmann, *The Social Construction of Reality* (Garden City, N.Y.: Doubleday, 1966).

71. Howard S. Becker, *Outsiders: Studies in the Sociology of Deviance* (New York: Free Press, 1963).

72. Richard Quinney, *The Social Reality of Crime* (Boston: Little, Brown, 1970).

73. See Quentin Lauer, *Phenomenology: Its Genesis and Prospect* (New York: Harper & Row, 1965); Pierre Thevanaz, *What Is Phenomenology?*, James M. Edie, ed. (New York: Quadrangle, 1962).

74. Herbert Marcuse, *One-Dimensional Man* (Boston: Beacon Press, 1964), p. 9.

75. Herbert Marcuse, *Reason and Revolution* (Boston: Beacon Press, 1960), especially pp. vii–xiv and 3–29. On the development of the Frankfurt School of critical theory, see Martin Jay, *The Dialectical Imagination: A History of the Frankfurt School and the Institute of Social Research, 1923–1950* (Boston: Little, Brown, 1973).

76. Irving Zeitlin, speaking of the negative-critical thought of the philosophers of the Enlightenment, in his *Ideology and the Development of Sociological Theory* (Englewood Cliffs, N.J.: Prentice-Hall, 1968), p. 5.

77. Taylor, Walton, and Young, "Advances Toward a Critical Criminology," p. 468.

78. Ibid., p. 470.

79. Ibid., p. 472.

CRIME AND PUNISHMENT IN THE UNITED STATES

A critical understanding of crime requires an investigation of the relation of crime to the control of crime. Emerging patterns of criminally defined behavior and the control of crime develop together, both in relation to the underlying political economy. That which threatens the existing social and economic order becomes the object of crime control. In this chapter we will discuss some of the crucial aspects of crime and punishment in the United States.

CRIME IN AN EMERGING SOCIETY

In order to understand the character of crime and crime control in the contemporary United States, it is necessary to cover a number of topics that relate to the development of the crime problem. The first consideration is the concept of crime in reference to English common law, for crime as a legal concept was an English import that was tempered by the American experience. The criminal laws of the colonies were similar to English laws because of the stipulation in the colonial charters that the laws created in the colonies should not contradict the laws of England.[1] In addition, continuity with English law was assured because the early settlers from England brought with them the only legal heritage they knew, that of English common law. Furthermore, English common law was perpetuated later through the popularity of such codifications as Sir Edward Coke's *Institutes* and Sir William Blackstone's *Commentaries on the Laws of*

England. Finally, American lawyers trained in England were successful in adapting English common law to colonial conditions.[2]

English common law, however, took a particular direction in the colonies because of the nature of the colonists who came to America. Many of the settlers were religious dissidents who left England to establish a social order that would correspond to their radical religious beliefs. The Massachusetts Bay Colony, in particular, was founded as a Puritan community that would be an example of godliness to the world. This "City upon a Hill," as Governor John Winthrop metaphorically referred to the settlement, incorporated Puritan religious principles into its legal order.

The Puritan settlers adhered to a conception of the covenant that viewed government as originating in a compact among the people. Moreover, the power of the state was regarded as legitimate because it was a government inspired by the decrees of God. An implication of the idea of the covenant was that law had divine origins and that such law was to be authoritatively administered by the leaders of the community. Governor Winthrop forcefully expressed these ideas to the settlers when he declared that "the determination of law belongs properly to God; He is the only lawgiver, but He hath given power and gifts to man to interpret His laws; and this belongs principally to the highest authority in a commonwealth, and subordinately to other magistrates and judges according to their several places."[3]

In order to follow God's Word in the formulation of criminal laws, the settlers in Massachusetts Bay Colony turned to the Scriptures. Consequently, most of the provisions of the criminal (or capital) laws of the legal code of the colony were annotated by chapter and verse from the Old Testament. Some provisions corresponded almost exactly to certain biblical passages. In substance the provisions included the crimes of idolatry, witchcraft, blasphemy, bestiality, sodomy, adultery, rape, man stealing, treason, false witness with intent to take life, cursing or smiting a parent, stubbornness or rebelliousness on the part of a son against his parents, and homicide committed with malice.[4] All of the crimes were punishable by death.

The legal authority of the state was thus religiously supported both literally and figuratively. The implications for the further development of law in the United States were that law (and government in general) existed to regulate imperfect humans, that political leaders must be obeyed, and that the welfare of the whole is more important than that of the individual. For the Puritans, crime was an act against God and the orderliness of nature itself. The criminal, according to the Puritan theological doctrine, belonged to a category of permanent misfits who were predestined to oppose society.

This form of reaction, as a "deployment pattern," has been described by Kai T. Erikson in the following way:

> To characterize the New England deployment pattern in a word, we may say (1) that the Puritans saw deviant behavior as the special property of a particular class of people who were more or less frozen into deviant attitudes; and (2) that they generally thought it best to handle the problem by locking these people into fairly permanent deviant roles. Puritan theories of human development began with the assumption that men do not change a

great deal as they mature or are exposed to different life experiences, and in this sense the settlers of the Bay had little faith in the promise that men might "reform" or overcome any pronounced deviant leanings. A person's character, like his social estate, is fixed by the preordained pattern of human history, and if he should somehow indicate by his surly manners and delinquent ways that he is not a very promising candidate for conversion, the community was not apt to waste many of its energies trying to change him or mend his character. In a very real sense, he belonged to a deviant "class" and was not expected to improve upon that condition.[5]

Our contemporary reaction to crime has been shaped by the Puritan concept of crime.

Although the early, pre-Revolutionary criminal codes were primarily religious, the focus of the criminal law began to change after the American Revolution. There was a dramatic shift from the pre-Revolutionary notion that the function of the criminal law was to enforce the morals and religion of the community. The post-Revolutionary view was that the purpose of the criminal law was to protect property and physical security. The state became actively involved, through its use of the criminal law, in promoting stability of the social order.[6] Moreover, political acts against the state and its economy were, under the new constitution, controlled by the criminal law. The new state elite, instead of being worried about sinners, "feared organized groups of malcontents bent upon reconstruction of society. . . . In short, their fear was that the economically underprivileged would seek material gain by banding together to deprive more privileged persons of their wealth and standing."[7] Criminal law and crime control served the major objective: to promote order in an emerging capitalist society. The crime control programs of today continue to serve the same purpose. That which threatens the hegemony of the capitalist class and the state becomes the object of the law and law enforcement, and we are told by the state that this is the morally correct way to do things.

CRIME AND PUNISHMENT
THE AMERICAN WAY

The possibility of a criminal sanction exists for every citizen in the state. Indeed, the primary purpose of the criminal sanction is to warn the citizenry that a violation of the law will lead to deprivation and punishment of some kind. In addition, the imposition of a sentence for an adjudicated offense is the state's retaliation against those who fail to abide by its dictates. A criminal sentence is the state's last attempt to preserve the established order and to punish those who have transgressed the rules of order.

The state has devised various schemes to punish the offender. Not only are there the concrete forms of capital and corporal punishment, but the state has created punishments that supposedly "rehabilitate" ("treat" or "correct") the offender as well. The objective of such schemes is to bring the deviant back into the established order. The complete program requires both a punishment for threatening the established system and a form of treatment that will readapt the offender to the existing social and economic order. Like all the other aspects of the legal system, custody and corrections function in America to preserve the existing political economy.

Confinement of offenders to an institution, as a means of dealing with crime, developed within a particular historical context in the United States. Following the American Revolution, the government became greatly concerned about the protection of the new social order, including the eradication of any conduct that threatened that order. The development of the penitentiary was an attempt by leaders in the Jacksonian period to promote stability in the new nation. "Legislators, philanthropists, and local officials, as well as students of poverty, crime and insanity were convinced that the nation faced unprecedented dangers and unprecedented opportunities. The asylum, they believed, could restore a necessary social balance to the new republic, and at the same time eliminate long-standing problems. At once nervous and enthusiastic, distressed and optimistic, they set about constructing and arranging institutions."[8] The penitentiary would attempt to rehabilitate offenders and at the same time stand as a guide to right action for the rest of society.

The prison movement spread in the early 1820s from New York and Pennsylvania throughout the rest of the country. Two systems of prison organization, the "congregate" system at Auburn, New York, and the "separate" system in Philadelphia, provided competing models. The controversy between the two models represented differing concepts of crime and punishment. In the Philadelphia model, as practiced at Eastern State Penitentiary in Philadelphia, prisoners were placed in solitary confinement. Inmates could then supposedly reflect upon their crimes and gain spiritual insight and strength for their own reformation. The Auburn system of New York, in comparison, emphasized congregate activities rather than separate confinement. Although the inmates spent the night in individual cells, they

worked together during the day. Hence the emphasis in the Philadelphia prison was on the possibilities of personal conversion, whereas the Auburn prison stressed external discipline and forced rehabilitation.

The outcome of the controversy between the two prison systems was that the Auburn system eventually became the model for nearly all maximum-security prisons in the United States. Regimentation, reflecting adoption of the Auburn system, became the standard mode of prison life in the United States. The convict's daily life was strictly controlled. The military style of command pervaded all aspects of prison life. In organization as well as in architecture, the prison symbolized obedience, order, and rigidity. The prison provided a model for the whole society: "The functioning of the penitentiary—convicts passing their sentences in physically imposing and highly regimented settings, moving in lockstep from bare and solitary cells to workshops, clothed in common dress, and forced into standard routines—was designed to carry a message to the community. . . . By demonstrating how regularity and discipline transformed the most corrupt persons, it would reawaken the public to these virtues. The penitentiary would promote a new respect for order and authority."[9] Custody in the prison today is essentially the same as it was at an earlier time. Though there are now more sophisticated programs in rehabilitation or treatment, the daily life of the inmate remains one of routine and regimentation.[10] The modern trend toward corrections is a continuation of the objectives of custody. The goals of custody and corrections are tied to the single purpose of the state itself: to control and manipulate those whose behavior threatens existing arrangements. That custody and corrections both serve the same objective, and are often administered within the same setting, becomes evident in a critical understanding of crime control in the United States.[11]

In the movement from custody and prison reform (in which prisons are to be made more livable) to treatment (within the prison as well as outside of it), the aim is that of "transforming man."[12] We are now in an age in which "people-changing" is a skill and a profession, as well as a moral injunction. In the new applications of corrections, dangerous techniques are being practiced and undemocratic procedures are being instituted.[13] What is emerging is a new authoritarianism, concealed under the terminology of treatment and professionalism. The consequence may be a "correctional therapeutic community" where any deviant will be treated and readjusted to the prevailing order. Through indoctrination and coercion the new professional worker (the "expert") aids the state in preserving the established arrangements.

Thus, correctional reform, following the liberal ideology, has become the control of crime and criminals by means of scientific knowledge and professional management. Prisons are to be made into therapeutic centers, where offenders will be scientifically managed and manipulated, and finally reintegrated into society. This is all to be done, of course, as humanely as possible, according to precepts of liberalism.[14]

The true nature of liberal reforms is illustrated whenever the functions of corrections are threatened by those subject to its operations. For example, in Attica prison, over forty persons were killed by the state when the prisoners threatened the state's conception of the prison. At the time of the uprising, in September of 1971, the New York State Corrections Department was instituting a liberal reform program. Corrections Commissioner Russel G. Oswald could then write that "the main impact of the new direction for the department is the recognition of the individual as a human being and the need for basic fairness throughout our day-to-day relationships with each other."[15] Under the covering veil of such liberal-reform notions, Governor Rockefeller could order the state troopers to fire upon and murder the prisoners and their guards. If what the state is doing for these people is indeed for their own good, then the state is *right* in killing them if they resist.

Further, despite the fact that in 1972 the McKay Commission, New York State's special commission on Attica, was highly critical in its final report of indiscriminate police use of weapons and ammunition that "virtually assured the death or serious injury of innocent persons" during the

retaking of the prison, to date not one law-enforcement person has been indicted. On the other hand, 62 inmates have been named in 42 indictments for alleged crimes related to the uprising. The state's chief prosecutor in the Attica affair was charged by his chief assistant, who resigned his post in protest in December of 1974, with "deliberately blocking the full investigation of material evidence to the grand jury insofar as it relates to possible crimes by law officers."[16] Early in 1975 a prosecution witness, a man who had been an Attica inmate during the uprising, testified that he had lied in naming five fellow-inmates to a grand jury investigating the killing of two Attica prison inmates. He had lied, he said, because: "They [at least seven correction officers] beat me for at least half an hour . . . I was made to crawl around on the floor and shout 'White power!' and kiss their feet . . . I gave an interview under an atmosphere of the most intense terror I have ever known. I gave an interview to save my life."[17] Such things happen when the functions of corrections are threatened by those subject to its operations.

Corrections and custody, then, accompanied by legal murder, that is, execution, provide the state with the ultimate means of controlling that which threatens the social and economic system.[18] Once the category of "criminal" is attached, control is established possibly for a lifetime, with the legal restrictions never being completely removed. Upon conviction for a crime an offender automatically loses a variety of rights and privileges held out to the citizenry. A number of civil rights—rights such as the right to vote, the right to enter into a legally binding contract, the right to obtain a license to practice a profession, rights possessed by others by fact of citizenship—are typically lost by those persons convicted of felonies and certain misdemeanors. Most state statutes and constitutions provide for deprivation of some rights upon criminal conviction.

In addition to the loss of numerous civil rights, convicted persons are usually prohibited from participating in other activities regulated by the state. They may be barred from obtaining professional, occupational, and business licenses, or from other kinds of employment. The procedures for restoring such privileges are not always clear.

It is in the lawlessness of the prison that the politics of custody and punishment are most dramatically displayed. Screened from public visibility and control, the prison develops its own rules and fosters its own order of lawlessness.

> *There is almost nothing the prison cannot do, and does not do to inmates, including keeping them beyond the expiration dates of their sentences (via procedures declaring them dangerous or mentally ill). It can and does transfer them far from their families; limit and restrict their visitors; censor what they read, what they may write; decide whom they may associate with inside, what medicine or other medical care they will or will not receive, what education they may or may not have, whether they will be totally locked up, for weeks, months, occasionally even years, or enjoy limited physical freedom. Inmates' personal property may be misplaced and destroyed, incoming and outgoing letters sometimes not delivered, and, in the extreme, prisoners may be starved, brutalized and killed.*[19]

Not only is the prison a lawless agency, in practical everyday reality immune from the law, but the very existence of the prison is political in nature. Furthermore, "the prison system helps to sustain the myth that certain groups of people (for example, blacks, the Spanish-speaking, Indians, poor whites) are inferior, defective, dangerous, not to be trusted: it discourages challenges to the existing political and economic order by reminding members of those groups that the violence of the state can and will be unleashed against them if they get out of line."[20]

The social organization of the prison serves to maintain the political goals of imprisonment. The purpose of prison organization is to keep prisoners powerless. Through its own lawlessness, through "classification" and segregation, through the administration of the various dehumanizing schemes of confinement, prison officials are able to maximize security. In fact, it is the aim of prison administrators to keep inmates as unorganized among themselves as possible, to prevent them from joining forces.

> *To this end, psychological solitary confinement is substituted, to the fullest extent possible, for physical isolation. This permits inmates to work and participate in prescribed activities, but it minimizes the danger of violence, revolt or riot. To facilitate the state of unorganization or anomie, administrators always admonish inmates to "do your own time," and consistently, officially distribute rewards such as parole and good-time allowances to inmates who remain isolated from other prisoners.*[21]

That the psychological solitary confinement of the prison is not dissimilar to that of an insane asylum was pointed up by Max Horkheimer and Theodore Adorno, writing about the Nazis' political use of prisons back in 1944: "Since de Tocqueville, the bourgeois republics have attacked man's soul, whereas the monarchies attacked his body; similarly the penalties inflicted in these republics also attack man's soul. The new martyrs do not die a slow death in the torture chamber but instead waste away spiritually as invisible victims in the great prison buildings, which differ in little but name from madhouses."[22]

The political intentions of the state, however, are not always successfully achieved. Contained within the politics of custody and punishment are the contradictions that threaten the existence of the prison. Totalitarian control, even under the guise of "rehabilitation," contains the seeds of its own destruction. Occurring within the prison today is a revolt against both the prison and the society that makes the prison necessary. George Jackson, writing to his lawyer from Soledad Prison in California, indicated the extent of revolutionary consciousness among blacks in that prison.

> *Nothing has improved, nothing has changed in the weeks since your team was here. We're on the same course, the blacks are fast losing the last of their restraints. Growing numbers of blacks are openly passed over when paroles are considered. They have become aware that their only hope lies in resistance. They have learned that resistance is actually possible. The holds are beginning to slip away. Very few men imprisoned for economic crimes or even crimes of passion against the oppressor feel*

that they are really guilty. Most of today's black convicts have come to understand that they are the most abused victims of an unrighteous order. Up until now, the prospect of parole has kept us from confronting our captors with any real determination. But now with the living conditions deteriorating, and with the sure knowledge that we are slated for destruction, we have been transformed into an implacable army of liberation. The shift to the revolutionary anti-establishment position that Huey Newton, Eldridge Cleaver, and Bobby Seale projected as a solution to the problems of America's black colonies has taken firm hold of these brothers' minds. They are now showing great interest in the thoughts of Mao Tse-tung, Nkrumah, Lenin, Marx, and the achievements of men like Che Guevara, Giap, and Uncle Ho.[23]

And before being assassinated in prison, Jackson wrote about the transformation resulting from the prison experience:

This camp brings out the very best in brothers or destroys them entirely. But none are unaffected. None who leave here are normal. If I leave here alive, I'll leave nothing behind. They'll never count me among the broken men, but I can't say that I am normal either. I've been hungry too long. I've gotten angry too often. I've been lied to and insulted too many times. They've pushed me over the line from which there can be no retreat. I know that they will not be satisfied until they've pushed me out of this existence altogether. I've been the victim of so many racist attacks that I could never relax again. My reflexes will never be normal again.[24]

Prisoners are moving from riot to revolution, and the state is responding with an intensification of repression. As observed in prison revolts, most notably at Attica and San Quention, prison officials and state authorities resort to a range of repressive measures, including political transfers, torture, assassination, and authorized violence. Moreover, new techniques are being developed and applied to deal with the revolutionary movement within prisons. Tranquilizing drugs, lobotomies, an electronic technology, surveillance, and the like are being used on rebellious prisoners. At the same time, however, the growth of a political consciousness among prisoners is making it more difficult for the state to maintain its control.

The state has enlisted the aid and assistance of both the social and physical sciences in its struggle to maintain and increase its control

over the minds and bodies of its captive population. In this regard it is interesting to note that the *Social Science and Humanities Index* (the *Social Science Index* is a separate index as of 1974) added to its listings two new subheadings in 1972, one on "Prison Psychology" and another on "Prisoner Treatment." The new wave in the social sciences is people control.[25] In line with this is the newly constructed United States Bureau of Prisons behavior modification center at Butner, North Carolina, at a cost of some $13 million.[26]

The extensive use of the technology of electronic brain control on parolees and other social "incorrigibles" is not only on the horizon, it is in fact here, according to some observers. Electronic stimulation of the brain (ESB) research is rapidly advancing as a result of federal funding diverted to domestic control concerns in the vacuum following the withdrawal of U.S. military commitments from Southeast Asia and the consequent drying up of monies available for research on control of foreign populations. "Electronic control (ESB) of prisoners is the cheapest and most effective way to remedy the chronic problems of this country's penal system."[27]

Other developments are moving forward under the predominant liberal ideology. Indications are that behavior modification programs in the prisons of this country are quietly growing amidst public apathy and ignorance. These programs amount to "the 'Final Solution' without the ovens" according to some.[28] It seems to be that such programs are being tested out and implemented principally on the federal level, for this is where most of our tax money surfaces. It also appears that this type of research is proceeding without public knowledge.

Some of the victims of our prisons manage to have their voices heard before a wider audience, and what they have to say is deeply disturbing to Americans who care to listen. These voices from the depths testify to experiences of sheer horror, a horror imposed by the ultimate sanity of the state. A prisoner writes on the use of drugs to control inmates:

> *Prolixin is worse. A usual dose of it lasts a month. Comments of a person while on a second dose of Prolixin: "I feel like I'm not within myself," "This drug is just terrible," "It creates a very painful reality," "It comes on in waves," "It feels like there is a machine in my mind and that is all there is." . . . One case I'm thinking of, when coming off the drug experienced an initial great awakening from the recognized year's spaced-out quality, but soon he regressed back a bit from the initial euphoria— "climbing out of a hole," he called it. He is bitter at having been forced to take the drug (four or five hacks came into his cell and injected him).[29]*

Instead of changing the oppressions of our existing order, the response of the American state is to control and manipulate those disruptive elements within the society. The prison and the larger society are inextricably linked.

> *The society in which prisoners are brutalized and killed at Soledad and San Quentin and Attica and Tucker Farm in Arkansas is the same society which slaughtered Indians and then Vietnamese, in which Panther leaders are shot to death while they sleep, in which voter registration workers are killed in Mississippi. It is a society in which both unemployment and corporate benefits are high and the possibility of satisfying work is denied to the many while urgent social needs go unmet.[30]*

The cover of secrecy and lawlessness is being stripped away from the prison as prisoners fight for their rights and revolt against the repression of the prison.

> *The prison itself has produced the prisoner movement. This movement is still in its infancy; prisoners are only just now coming*

to an informed sense of identity and a consciousness of
the possibilities of collective action. Prisoners' unions, strikes, revolts
—these are the first visible signs of these stirrings. It is from the
prisoner movement, the ex-convcit movement, that leadership will
come in struggles relating to the prison—and no doubt in other
struggles as well. But support from all of us is needed, and must be
forthcoming, not only for prisoners' sakes, but for our own.
For the prison indeed oppresses not just those who are locked behind
its bars. It reaches out to every one of us.[31]

As American society is further threatened by its own contradictions, new forms of crime control are being and will continue to be instituted. According to some authorities, we are already entering an era in which the most subtle and totalitarian methods are being devised and practiced.[32] Only with the development of an alternative kind of society, based on socialist principles rather than on principles of hierarchy, competition, and domination—principles inherent to capitalism—can these forms of manipulation and control be challenged and removed.

CRIME CONTROL IN URBAN AMERICA

As the United States increased in population, the place of residence shifted from the country to the city. Following the American Revolution, only about 5 percent of the population lived in cities. The figure rose steadily to about 40 percent in 1900, 64 percent in 1960, and to nearly 80 percent today. With this trend to urban residence, there has been a shift in the locus of crime. Today crime is regarded as principally an urban problem. The character of the urban criminal environment is indicated in the official criminal statistics. Each year the Total Crime Index is the highest in the large urban aggregates (the Standard Metropolitan Statistical Areas). Comparatively, the smaller cities have medium rates, while the rural areas have the lowest rates of crime. Today we tend to equate crime with urban living.

In the rural America of the seventeenth and eighteenth centuries, crime was dealt with by means of fairly crude enforcement and administrative procedures. The law offices of England served American needs. Rural areas and villages handled their crime problem through night watchmen, constables, sheriffs, and justices of the peace. With the development of cities, however, more elaborate law-enforcement facilities were established. City governments in the United States organized their own police forces.

London's police system (based on the Metropolitan Police Act of 1829) was adopted by New York City in 1844. During the next ten years similar law-enforcement systems were organized in Chicago, Boston, and Philadelphia. By the turn of the century most of our cities had their own systems for the enforcement and administration of criminal law.

The development of a professional police force in cities was an attempt by the dominant class in the city to control the behavior of those classes that rebelled against the oppressive urban conditions. In Boston, for example, the problem of mob violence "soon compelled the municipality to take a more significant step, to create a new class of permanent professional officers with new standards of performance."[33] The newly emerging police force in the cities thus served to maintain the order desired by the ruling class by quelling civil unrest, and it was not created merely to control crime.

The role of the police was now to prevent disorder. That is, in a preventive conception of law enforcement, "the police take the initiative and seek out those engaged in violating the law—those engaged in specific behaviors that are designated as illegal."[34] Preventing crime became a rational way of maintaining public order. Thus, the rise of the police in cities is related to the class structure of the city:

> *During the first half of the 19th century, the professional police*
> *increasingly took over and expanded the duties of the constableship.*
> *This led to the police themselves becoming specialists in the*
> *maintenance of public order, which involved a transition to*
> *emphasizing the prevention of crime, and the role of law as ideal*
> *became an attempt to enforce laws as real prescriptions governing*
> *conduct. In this way the police, as an agency of the state, took*
> *over the function of social control from the members of the local*
> *community. The historical sources of the change were economic*
> *inequality and increasing riots. Thus the police became an agency*
> *of those with wealth and power, for suppressing the attempts*
> *by the have-nots to re-distribute the wealth and power.*[35]

By the middle of the 1800s the forces of urbanization and industrialization were well under way in the cities of this country. With increasing class conflict, the consequences for the development of crime were considerable. Whereas the major problems of crime had involved such activities as street fighting, public drunkenness, brawls, and minor theft, the criminal activities of the large city now related to the problems of the rapidly growing city. The influx of immigrants and the formation of slum areas had their effects upon the character of urban crime. Furthermore, an underworld with a fair degree of sophistication developed in a number of cities. Prostitution, theft, robbery, gambling, and numerous rackets emerged as urban forms of criminal activity.[36] In New Orleans, by the 1880s, there were well-organized gangs of burglars, pickpockets, and sneak thieves. The San Francisco waterfront was crowded with brothels, saloons for gambling, and boarding houses from which many a sailor was shanghaied to the Orient. The New York criminal scene flourished in the rapidly growing slum areas of lower Manhattan. One observer in 1873 estimated that New York had up to three hundred professional thieves, five thousand prostitutes, and at least $4–5 million dollars worth of stolen goods was handled yearly by fences.[37]

In 1887 the Society for the Prevention of Crime was formed in New York City by a distinguished group of private citizens, among whom were such figures as Peter Cooper, David Whitney, and William Prentice. The society took as its motto, *Urbis Salus Vigilantia* ("The City is Safe through Vigilance"). The following year they published their constitution in their Second Annual Report, which, along with their occasional Bulletins, was to become a yearly publication through to 1922. According to the constitution the society's object was the ". . . prevention of crime . . . and the eradication of the sources and causes of crime and vice . . . especially by the suppression of tippling houses."[38] The attack was on. The weapons in the battle then were much the same as they are today as wielded by the society's latter-day, nationwide counterpart, the National Council on Crime and Delinquency: "The methods of operation shall be to arouse a correct public opinion, to assist in the prosecution of law breakers, to disseminate information by means of the press . . . and by all other feasible means to influence correct legislation in favor of the measures recommended by the Society."[39]

The flavor and texture of urban crime in the latter decades of the nineteenth century comes through in these Annual Reports. The society fought drug use (principally opium); gambling of every imaginable kind; "smutty" and lewd weekly magazines; pimps, procurers, and prostitutes ("Assignation Houses"); corruption among the police and high city officials; "the evils of the liquor traffic"; and so forth. Rarely in the pages of the society's Annual Reports and Bulletins, however, does one encounter our more modern urban crimes of rape, robbery, burglary, mugging, murder, or kidnapping.

We are all aware of the high rates of crime today in American cities. Yet, because of the lack of historically comparative figures it is difficult to know whether crime is greater today than in the past. There is some evidence to indicate, nevertheless, that an increase in crime may not be as apparent as some would believe. For example, a study of New York Police Department statistics for the period 1916 to 1936 shows, first, that the crime rate for offenses against the person was higher than the rate for some of the same offenses today; and, second, that the crime rate for offenses against the person steadily decreased between 1916 and 1936.[40] In another study, the arrest reports of the Boston police were investigated for the years 1849 to 1951.[41] The conclusion reached was that the rate for the combined major crimes declined over the one-hundred-year period. Murder, larceny, and assault clearly declined, while burglary and robbery showed a downward trend except for periodic upswings. Manslaughter increased around the turn of the century but has declined recently from this higher level. Only forcible rape has shown a clear tendency to increase during the last one hundred years. The overall crime rate in Boston for the seven major offenses has declined steadily to a level of about one-third that in 1875.

In the study of the changing crime problem in Boston, the author notes that his conclusion of the downward drift of the crime rate stands in marked contrast to the popular belief that crime is growing more rampant and more serious every year. In an explanation of this contradiction, he writes:

> *This belief has been largely fostered by the annual reports issued by the FBI, where appalling increases in crime and delinquency are monotonously recorded. The FBI has been issuing these reports only since 1930, and [as shown in this study] the crime rate in Boston has, indeed, risen slightly since then. But even if we assume that the* long-term trend *in Boston and other major metropolitan centers has been downward, we need not conclude that there is a basic contradiction between these data and the trends traced by the annual reports of the FBI. The migration pattern of this nation over the last one hundred years has been from areas of low crime rates, that is, rural areas and small towns, to areas of high crime rates, that is, large urban centers; and a chronic increase in the crime rate in the entire society is not inconsistent with a steady decrease in the crime rates of its large cities.*[42]

Thus, the apparent rise in crime is in part a result of the movement of the population to urban centers. Although crime rates may have actually declined in some cities, the national crime rate may be higher because a larger proportion of the nation's population now resides in cities, in cities that nevertheless have relatively higher crime rates than rural areas.[43] Also, the forces that produce crime, including both the agencies of crime control that define behavior as criminal and the social and economic conditions that make criminal behavior appropriate, are largely found in urban-industrial United States. Therefore, as a greater proportion of the population resides in cities, the greater the chances of an increasing crime problem, and as the ratio of police to population fluctuates, the crime rate fluctuates.

But what supports and gives character to the crime problem as it now exists in the United States? Numerous studies have explored the relation of urban crime rates to structural characteristics of cities.[44] Generally, it has been found that the population characteristics (such as economic, family, racial, and ethnic characteristics) of an area are associated with offense rates. Yet, underlying these associations are processes that produce both the crime problem and the population composition of social areas, as well as the relation between the two. These processes can be briefly suggested.

A basic feature of modern cities is the manifestation of class divisions, reflected in the residents' work, cultural values, and ideology. All the forces of the advanced capitalist world are being worked out in American cities. A consequence of this condition is that a common community is impossible to achieve in the existing city. Not only is there a lack of common objectives, but the urban environment is devoid of the means for living our lives together. All the inhumane aspects of the city —the materialistic exploitation, the brutalization of the person, and the abuses suffered from the physical arrangements—are thus free to take their toll on the human spirit.

> *Just as the bourgeois marketplace makes each individual a stranger to another, so the bourgeois city estranges . . . central and fringe areas (of the city) from each other. The paradox of the bourgeois city is that it unites these areas internally not in the felicitous heterogeneity of unity in diversity that marked the medieval commune—a heterogeneity unified by mutual aid and a common municipal tradition—but rather in the suspicions, anxieties and hatreds of the stranger from the "other" ghetto. . . . No longer are the elements of the city cemented by mutual aid, a shared culture, and a sense of community; rather, they are cemented by a social dynamite that threatens to explode the urban tradition into its very antithesis.[45]*

Without economic well-being and some sense of community, each person is subject to victimization by another. Moreover, such victimization is made personally legitimate by the realization that we are victims of the conditions of modern urban living. When we finally come to recognize that we are victims of an unjust system, we will also finally recognize that this same system that is victimizing us is forcing us to victimize our fellows.

Those who are oppressed in the modern city, that is, persons of the working-class, may turn to criminal activities as an appropriate way to survive in capitalist America. Many contemporary actions are either natural responses to exploitation or conscious efforts to achieve unfulfilled hopes. Actions against others—in the form of such personal offenses as assault, murder, and robbery—may be expressions not of personal pathology but of conscience and condition.

Simultaneously, as citizens as well, we fear the physical attacks that may befall us while we are in our homes or on the street. Urban dwellers today have a new consciousness of crime. They no longer *feel* safe. The subjective awareness of crime is greater today than ever before. A good portion of this increased awareness is a result of a sense of losing control over our lives, resulting from the oppressions of the world we have made for ourselves. In addition, the customary relation between the assailant and the victim seems to be breaking down; we have reason to fear for our safety. In some other age, in some other place, we had the opportunity of knowing our assailants: a friend, a spouse, or some other acquaintance. In the large city today, however, there is less certainty as to who is going to be the assailant. We have less control over the certainty of our spatial movements and our personal encounters. In the process we are losing the possibility of lives that could be lived together. A new urban community seems necessary. The one we have is much too frightening and brutal to sustain. Urban America as we know it has become outmoded, and like the dinosaur is threatened with extinction unless we radically restructure our urban institutions along truly humanitarian and socialist lines, free from alienation, competition, hierarchy, and exploitation. Such restructuring, for example, would accord priority to decentralized power structures of community control over massive, dehumanized, and centralized power structures.

The official response of the state to the product of these processes, urban crime, has been to create and strengthen as much as possible urban police forces. Urban crime then cannot be understood outside the context of urban law enforcement. The vast body of scholarly literature on law enforcement is growing at a considerable rate, and the question of why this is so has been left relatively unattended by sociological criminologists to date. There are several fruitful hypotheses that could be suggested and tested, the most promising being that the professional and popular fixation on the police in our society is best likened to a nation's fixation on its military forces when that nation is at war and threatened with imminent invasion. That is, it reflects a siege mentality. The next task would then obviously be to inquire why the country is at war, over what issues, and what must be done to effect a cessation of hostilities.

The most extensive publishing effort along these lines has been made by one publishing company that has recently reprinted 35 volumes on the police in the United States in order to "provide a much needed service to scholars in law and the social sciences, to police and other public administrators."[46] There is indeed a wealth of material on law enforcement here, published documents and volumes spanning the more than one-hundred-year period between 1860 and 1967. Other contemporary books on the police being published range in content from analysis of police administrative behavior through how the behavioral sciences can serve police effectiveness.[47]

One immediately evident reason for this increased interest in the police in the scholarly literature over the past several years is that it is the result of the infusion of billions of federal dollars into state and local law-enforcement agencies. President Johnson's Safe Streets and Crime Control Act of 1967 resulted in the creation of the Law Enforcement Assistance Administration (LEAA) in 1968. Since then $4.2 billion has been pumped into this country's criminal justice system, with 40 percent of that staggering total, or $1.68 billion, going directly to law enforcement bodies across the country. Professional and academic research interests have always followed where the money led, and criminologists are no different.

One outstanding and controversial public issue that has emerged out of urban law enforcement is that of killing by the police and the killing of police. It is in the cities that police work is the most dangerous and that the probability of citizens being killed by police bullets is the highest. The more fatalities there are among the police in our cities, the more tense, defensive, and "jumpy" the police become, increasing proportionately their readiness to "shoot first and ask questions later" out of motives of sheer self-defense. Innocent citizens of the cities get shot when this state of affairs is reached. Illustrative of this is the death of the 24-year-old woman who was slain in the East New York section of Brooklyn in December of 1974 when she was caught in police crossfire. It turned out that a Housing Authority officer and a Correction Department officer were exchanging fire, shooting to kill one another in a dual case of mistaken identity.

This type of police-citizen encounter has been on the increase in urban America. The probability, furthermore, of police killing police is escalating. Again, illustrative of this was the mutual killing of two peace officers, one a New York City police officer and the other a City Housing policeman, in Man-

hattan early in February of 1975. It was another case of mistaken identity and highly nervous officers.[48] In violation of regulations and law, a great many black urban police do not carry weapons in the cities when off duty. The reason is simple: They know better than anyone else that a black man in civilian clothes who carries a weapon in our cities is courting death from his fellow, uniformed officers.

Elsewhere studies have indicated decisively that there is a movement among law-enforcement personnel in the cities toward the use of types of weaponry and ammunition that have a tendency to wound more seriously and to kill more frequently. For example, an American Civil Liberties study report claims that some police departments in Massachusetts, California, Connecticut, Hawaii, Pennsylvania, Texas, Virginia, and Washington are beginning surreptitiously to adopt the use of soft-headed, hollow-nosed bullets (the dreaded "dumdum"). Use of these bullets has been frequently banned in international treaties in an attempt to limit the conduct of war.[49]

We the people are told, with ample documentation and coverage of police funerals from the mass media, that urban law-enforcement personnel give their lives to protect us from criminals. A death toll is kept in every city. And sadly it is true: police do die in the line of duty. But recall the last time that television news covered the funeral of a construction worker who died while on duty. The fact is that the men and women who build our buildings, run our railroads, mine our coal, extinguish our fires, and farm our lands suffer a greater statistical probability of losing their lives in the course of their work than do police personnel.[50] The occupational risks in law enforcement are less dangerous than those in the several major industries and occupations cited above, occupations that keep our society going.

Another issue that reaches deeply to touch a raw and sensitive nerve of urban police forces is that of police corruption. Corruption is simultaneously recognized and not recognized, admitted and denied, exposed and concealed by the police themselves, city police administrators, police unions, and the general public. The recent and comprehensive report of the National Advisory Commission on Criminal Justice Standards and Goals, entitled simply *Police,* claims to represent, "the most up-to-date and proven experience in the police field available today."[51] This massive document is 668 pages in length, and yet a scant three pages deal with "Positive Prevention of Police Misconduct" and only *one-half* of a page touches on police corruption.

City police especially are perhaps the most exposed occupational group—with the exception of professional politicians—to the temptations of corruption. At virtually every turn and in virtually every manner they may be corrupted. A recent article suggests a classificatory scheme of police corruption. Eight types or classes of police corruption are outlined: (1) corruption of authority, (2) kickbacks, (3) opportunistic theft, (4) shakedowns, (5) protection of illegal activities, (6) the fix, (7) direct criminal activities, and (8) internal payoffs.[52] Lawrence Sherman, in *Police Corruption: A Sociological Perspective,* constructs a theory of police corruption out of 14 separate propositions divided into four subheadings: the nature of community structure, organizational characteristics of the department, legal opportunities, and corruption controls.[53] He recognizes that "the problem of police corruption is merely a slice of the larger problem of official corruption in American society."[54] Indeed, the larger framework within which to really come to an adequate understanding of police corruption and the larger problem of official corruption is ultimately that of the relationship between the liberal state as a control institution and the structure of capitalist corporate economy.

Finally, one recent and pervasive reaction of urban law enforcement departments in this country to many of the ills cited above, and indeed to the growing chasms between the police and the people, has been the establishment and financing of "community relations bureaus." This development was made historically necessary by the insistence of law enforcement in the United States in viewing the public as an "adversary with dangerous outlines."[55] Consequently, an organizational means of drawing the police closer to the urban communities they serve is being attempted. The development of police-community relations bureaus is for the most part a failing effort to "cool out" minority neighborhoods.

CONTROL OF MORAL ORDER

Much of crime control in America involves the enforcement of morality. The control of morality is at the same time the control of the more material aspects of society. That is, laws on private and public morality reflect the desire to preserve all aspects of life. If the moral base of social and economic life should be threatened, then the social and economic order itself might give way. Thus, laws regulating various sexual activities, drinking, vagrancy, drug use, and the like are enacted to control the total environment, even the most intimate aspects of one's life, so that the existing order can be secured and perpetuated according to the interests of the established order.[56]

The range of sexual conduct that is covered by law is so extensive that the law makes potential criminals of most of the adolescent and adult population.[57] One of the principal reasons for such complete control over sexual behavior is to protect a particular kind of family system, a family system that preserves the existing institutions in American society. A great number of state laws seek to control acts that might otherwise endanger the chastity of women before marriage. There are the numerous laws in regard to rape (statutory and forcible), fornication, incest, and sexual deviance of juveniles. The criminal laws on adultery also exist to protect the family by preventing sexual relations outside the marriage bond. Through these laws the cherished monogamous family pattern is preserved.

Some of our criminal laws on sexual behavior were formulated to protect specific aspects of marriage and family life in relation to the larger social order. Several southern states, for instance, enacted laws to prevent marriages between blacks and whites. In 1967, however, the Supreme Court ruled that an antimiscengenation statute of Virginia was unconstitutional. Such "slavery laws," held over from a bygone era, had been originally formulated to ensure the slavery status of blacks and in more recent times have been used to maintain segregation of the races.

Criminal law has also been formulated to prevent the exposure of members of the society to that which is regarded by some as lewd or obscene. The Comstock Act of 1873 stands in American criminal law as a landmark in the control of obscenity. Before that time the common law was not clear on the issue. In fact, obscenity was not considered to be a problem before the nineteenth century. By the middle of the nineteenth century a new concept of obscenity had emerged, given an identity by the Victorian Age.[58] The protection of women and the young became a concern of several segments of the population. Finally, in 1873, with considerable pressure for a statutory law, the Comstock law was enacted, providing for the censorship of literature and other printed matter that might come in the hands of the innocent.

Today well-organized groups, such as the National Organization for Decent Literature, continue to pressure courts and legislatures for statutes and decisions on the regulation of obscenity. The interest in controlling "obscene" materials has recently been supported in the 1973 Supreme Court decision, *Miller* v. *California*, which establishes new standards for judging the contents of books, magazines, plays, and movies. This new decision abandons the 1957 ruling, *Roth* v. *United States*, which had allowed sexual materials that were of "redeeming social value." The new decision gives local committees and states the power to determine what is obscene, without reference to a national standard. State and local courts may now punish the printing or sale of works that appeal to the "prurient interest in sex." Such judgment is to be based on "contemporary community standards." In giving new direction to obscenity law, the Supreme Court is allowing the power structure within the community to establish standards that will protect its own order. What is at stake in obscenity law is no less than the preservation of the existing order.

The laws in regard to prostitution vary greatly throughout the country. In most states the act of solicitation is a misdemeanor punished by a fine or a jail sentence of one year. Repeated apprehensions may result in a strong charge of felony. In some states laws have been enacted to control not only solicitation by prostitutes but also the activities of the exploiters and customers of prostitutes. While prostitution may be defined as a crime, the conduct is frequent in all societies. The laws remain, however, as a representation of what some in society expect in the ideal moral order.

There are moves in the United States to revise the prostitution laws. Supposedly to make the statutes less discriminatory toward women, suggestions are being made to reduce the penalties and include the male patrons in the law. But countering these moves is the desire by some groups, especially community leaders and law-enforcement agents, to "clean up" certain areas of the city. In the revision of the New York State law on

prostitution, for example, the final law was written by those groups that have the most power and resources to shape public policy.[59] In the end it is not the class interests of the prostitutes that are being considered in the law, but the class interests of those who make the law. Their order prevails through the criminal law.

Criminal penalties for homosexual acts in the United States have tended to be severe. Some states provide penalties of ten or more years imprisonment. In actuality, however, a relatively small proportion of persons are arrested for homosexual acts and when penalties are administered they tend to be lenient. While a moral connotation is still attached to homosexuality by many people, the trend may be toward the removal of certain homosexual acts from the list of crimes. In 1955 the American Law Institute concluded that homosexual behavior between consenting adults in private should be removed from the criminal law.[60] The state of Illinois, in revising its penal code in 1961, adopted the institute's recommendation. Similar legal reforms are currently under consideration, although other states have been reluctant to revise their homosexual statutes. The Supreme Court of the United States continues to rule in favor of statutes that criminalize homosexual behavior.

Although drinking itself is not a crime, being drunk in public may result in a criminal arrest. The person who drinks excessively may be apprehended simply because he is disturbing the community's sense of propriety or because being intoxicated may lead to other acts of public nuisance or disturbance. To become intoxicated and exuberant in one's own home is proper middle-class behavior, but to be drunk in public is to violate the Puritanical standards of moral strength and personal discipline.

The likelihood exists that public drunkenness will not be treated as crime in the future. A legal change has occurred already in the United States. In 1966 the United States Court of Appeals for the District of Columbia ruled that a chronic alcoholic cannot be convicted of the crime of public drunkenness. Since the defendant to a drunkenness charge "has lost the power of self-control in the use of intoxicating beverages," the court held, the defendant thus lacks the necessary criminal intent to be guilty of a crime and cannot therefore be punished under the criminal law. Similar rulings and legislative measures may eventually eliminate a vast portion of criminal offenses.

The current trend in the law associated with drinking and drunkenness is in part an extension of the forces that operated in the repeal of the Eighteenth Amendment. The repeal of the constitutional amendment in 1933 marked the end of the "great experiment" known as Prohibition, which had been established through the Volstead Act and ratified through the Eighteenth Amendment in 1920. The movement to place a ban on drinking and the liquor trade was an assertion of the rural Protestant mind against the urban culture that had emerged at the end of the nineteenth century and the beginning of the twentieth. Prohibition meant for a significant portion of the population the stamping out of sin in an evil society. The rural element was temporarily successful, in the enactment of Prohibition legislation, but succumbed within 13 years to the inevitable.

But Prohibition was to fail as law as it was to fail as a noble experiment. An outdated morality could not be enforced through criminal law. Rural interests were replaced by the interests of a new social order.

> *The old order of the country gave way to the new order of the cities. Rural morality was replaced by urban morality, rural voices by urban voices, rural votes by urban votes. A novel culture of skyscrapers and suburbs grew up to oust the civilization of the general store and Main Street. A technological revolution broadcast a common culture over the various folkways of the land. It is only in context of this immense social change, the metamorphosis of Abraham Lincoln's America into the America of Franklin Roosevelt, that the phenomenon of national prohibition can be seen and understood. It was part of the whole process, the last hope of the declining village. It was less of a farce than a tragedy, less of a mistake than a proof of changing times.*[61]

Vagrancy has been a crime in virtually every state in the United States. Since the state statutes have had their heritage in English law, the common law meaning of the term "vagrancy" is either stated or implied in the statutes. Accordingly, a vagrant is an idle person, beggar, or person wandering without being able to give a good account of himself. Most important to the vagrancy concept, then, is the nature of the person. "Vagrancy is the principal crime in which the offense consists of being a certain kind of person rather than in having done or failed to do certain acts."[62]

Vagrancy laws are widely used on the community level to detain various kinds of questionable and suspicious persons. The vagrancy laws and their enforcement thus are aimed at potential criminals, are used sometimes in lieu of other charges, and often are the means to rid the community of those who do not meet the standards of the respectable members.

However, the vagrancy laws are currently being evaluated and questioned. One writer has stated, "The time is surely at hand to modernize the vagrancy concept or, better yet, to abandon it altogether for statutes which will harmonize with notions of a decent, fair, and just administration of criminal justice, and which will at the same time make it possible for police departments to discharge their responsibilities in a reasonable manner."[63] Along these lines, a significant change in vagrancy law has been made in the state of New York. In 1967 the New York Court of Appeals ruled unconstitutional a statute of 1788 that provided for the arrest of persons with no visible means of support. The court ruled that the law "constitutes an overreaching of the proper limitations of the police power."[64] Furthermore, the court said that the statute has little use "other than, perhaps, as a means of harassing, punishing or apprehending suspected criminals in an unconstitutional fashion." The old statute was declared unconstitutional on the ground that it interfered with the liberty of a citizen to conduct himself as he sees fit as long as he does not interfere with the rights of others. Such repeal, which is occurring in other states as well, will end the use of laws of the vagrancy type to enforce community order. However, *other* means of maintaining public order, legal or extra-legal, are certain to be substituted for vagrancy law.

Before the turn of this century there was no significant legislation concerning the manufacture or distribution of narcotic drugs. In a short time, however, states and the federal government enacted laws for the control of drugs. The legislation of morality in these cases involved a shift in the conception of drug use, requiring a different manner of handling the problem. The shift consisted of moving drug users from one category to another, from a problem shared by the general population to one predominantly of the lower classes, the "unrespectable" parts of society.[65]

The Harrison Act passed by Congress in 1914 had the effect of defining users of certain drugs as criminals. In technical language the Harrison Act required that all drug handlers be registered and that the fact of securing drugs be made a matter of record.[66] But through the interpretation of the act, the court rulings in specific cases, and the enactment of supplementary laws, criminal sanctions were provided for the unathorized possession, sale, or transfer of drugs. In addition to the federal statutes and rulings, the states have enacted their own antinarcotic laws. In the United States, penalties for violation of drug laws have become more severe in recent years. The possession of narcotics, for example, is now a felony instead of a misdemeanor.

Furthermore, other policies are being instituted to control the "drug problem." For example, there is a trend to handle drug addiction as a disease, with the addict being a "sick" person. Substitute drugs, such as methadone, are being administered to addicts. The federal government is establishing new laws, such as the Comprehensive Drug Control Act of 1970. In the process, the state is creating the possibility of controlling the population through the administration of drugs. The question is not so much the use of drugs per se, but who is going to control their use.

Moreover, the state, in defining drug use and addiction as a problem, is conditioning the public to respond by condemning the drug user, rather than questioning the kind of social order that makes drug use a viable alternative to the everyday reality. In teaching us to believe that the problem is in the morality or physical condition of the drug user, rather than in the pathology of the existing social order, those who rule maintain their order without instituting any fundamental changes. To control the moral order is to secure the social, economic, and political order of the society.

NOTES

1. See Roscoe Pound, "The Development of American Law and Its Deviation from English Law," *Law Quarterly Review,* 67 (January 1951), pp. 49–66; Julius Goebel, Jr., "King's Law and Local Custom in Seventeenth Century New England," *Columbia Law Review,* 31 (March 1931), pp. 416–448; Edwin C. Surrency, "Revision of Colonial Laws," *American Journal of Legal History,* 9 (July 1965), pp. 189–202; Elizabeth Caspar Brown, *British Statutes in American Law, 1776–1836* (Ann Arbor: University of Michigan Law School, 1964).
2. Perry Miller, *The Life of the Mind* (New York: Harcourt Brace Jovanovich, 1965), pp. 99–265.
3. Quoted in Richard B. Morris, *Studies in the History of American Law,* 2d ed. (New York: Joseph M. Mitchell, 1959), p. 35.
4. See George Lee Haskins, *Law and Authority in Early Massachusetts* (New York: Macmillan, 1960), pp. 141–162.
5. Kai T. Erikson, *Wayward Puritans: A Study of the Sociology of Deviance* (New York: Wiley, 1966), pp. 196–197.
6. David J. Rothman, *The Discovery of the Asylum* (Boston: Little, Brown, 1971), especially pp. 57–78.
7. William E. Nelson, "Emerging Notions of Modern Criminal Law in the Revolutionary Era: An Historical Perspective," *New York University Law Review,* 42 (May 1967), p. 463.
8. Rothman, *The Discovery of the Asylum,* p. xviii. See also Harry E. Barnes, *The Repression of Crime: Studies in Historical Penology* (Montclair, N.J.: Patterson Smith, 1969).
9. Rothman, *The Discovery of the Asylum,* p. 107.
10. See Lawrence E. Hazelrigg, ed., *Prison Within Society* (Garden City, N.Y.: Doubleday, 1968). Also Harry E. Barnes, *The Evolution of Penology in Pennsylvania* (Montclair, N.J.: Patterson Smith, 1968).
11. For a striking contrast in two different approaches to what is happening behind the walls of United States prisons today, see Robert Carter, Daniel Glaser, and Leslie Wilkins, eds., *Correctional Institutions* (New York: Lippincott, 1972); and the editors of *Ramparts* magazine and Frank Browning, eds., *Prison Life* (New York: Harper & Row, 1972). Also see Leonard Orland, *Justice, Punishment, Treatment—the Correctional Process* (New York: Free Press, 1973). For the prison as a coercive state apparatus, see Vladimir I. Lenin, *State and Revolution* (New York: International Publishers, 1935).
12. Robert Martinson, "The Age of Treatment: Some Implications of the Custody-Treatment Dimension," *Issues in Criminology,* 2 (Fall 1966), pp. 275–293.
13. Also see American Friends Service Committee, *Struggle for Justice: A Report on Crime and Punishment in America* (New York: Hill and Wang, 1971); Francis A. Allen, "Criminal Justice, Legal Values and the Rehabilitative Ideal," *Journal of Criminal Law, Criminology and Police Science,* 50 (September–October 1959), pp. 226–232. For a devastating critique of the therapeutic mystique in corrections, see Jock Young, "The Zookeepers of Deviance," *Catalyst,* (Summer 1970), pp. 38–46.
14. See Jessica Mitford, *Kind and Usual Punishment* (New York: Knopf, 1973).

15. *The New York Times,* 16 September 1971, p. 43.
16. Quoted in *The New York Times,* 8 April 1975, p. 24. The McKay Commission's investigation of the Attica revolt is presented in *Attica, the Official Report of the New York State Special Commission on Attica* (New York: Bantam Books, 1972).
17. *The New York Times,* 23 January 1975, p. 21.
18. On legal murder, see William Bowers, *Executions in America* (Lexington, Mass.: Lexington Books, 1974).
19. David F. Greenberg and Fay Stender, "The Prison as a Lawless Agency," *Buffalo Law Review,* 21 (Spring 1972), p. 806.
20. Ibid., p. 820.
21. Donald R. Cressey, in the foreword to Donald Clemmer, *The Prison Community* (New York: Holt, Rinehart and Winston, 1958), p. ix.
22. Max Horkheimer and Theodore Adorno, *Dialectic of Enlightenment* (New York: Herder and Herder, 1972), p. 228. *Originally Dialektik der Aufklarung,* 1944.
23. George Jackson, *Soledad Brother: The Prison Letters of George Jackson* (New York: Bantam Books, 1970), p. 30. See also Min Sun Yee, *The Melancholy History of Soledad Prison* (New York: Harper's Magazine Press, 1973).
24. Ibid., p. 32.
25. See, for example, L. A. Bennett, "Application of Self-Esteem Measures in a Correctional Setting: Changes in Self-Esteem During Incarceration," *Journal of Research in Crime and Delinquency,* 11 (January 1974), pp. 9–15; M. J. Irvine and P. Gendreau, "Detection of the False Good and Bad Response on the Sixteen Personality Factors Inventory in Prisoners and College Students," *Journal of Consulting and Clinical Psychology,* 42 (June 1974), pp. 456–466; N. L. Bert, "Self-Concept of Neurotic and Sociopathic Criminal Offenders," *Psychological Reports,* 34 (April 1974); p. 622; C. E. Cobb, "Behavior Modification in the Prison System," *Black Scholar,* 5 (May 1974), pp. 41–44; F. B. Raymond, "To Punish or to Treat?", *Social Work,* 19 (May 1974), pp. 305–312; B. J. Morrison et al., "Effect of Electrical Shock and Warning or Cooperation in a Non-Zero-Sum Game," *Journal of Conflict Resolution,* 15 (March 1971), pp. 605–608; T. E. Deiker, "Crossvalidation of MMPI Scales of Aggression on Male Criminal Criterion Groups," *Journal of Consulting and Clinical Psychology,* 42 (April 1974), pp. 196–202; W. T. Austin and F. L. Bates, "Ethnological Indicators of Dominance and Territory in a Human Captive Population," *Social Forces,* 52 (June 1974), pp. 447–455.
26. Aryeh Neier and Alberto Mares, "A Program to Cripple Federal Prisoners," *New York Review of Books,* 21 (7 March 1974), p. 23.
27. Dr. Gerald Smith, quoted in the University of Massachusetts newspaper, *The Massachusetts Daily Collegian,* 14 February 1973, p. 14.
28. "Positive Reinforcement of Prison," *Anarchist Black Cross Bulletin,* 7 (January 1974), p. 15.
29. Quotation from a letter to the editor, signed "An Anarchist Captive," *The Match,* December 1972, p. 7.
30. Greenberg and Stender, "The Prison as a Lawless Agency," p. 837. On the fascist nature of control in the United States, see George Jackson, *Blood in My Eye* (New York: Bantam Books, 1972), pp. 111–163.
31. Greenberg and Stender, "The Prison as a Lawless Agency," p. 838.
32. Nicholas N. Kittrie, *The Right to be Different: Deviance and Enforced Therapy* (Baltimore: Johns Hopkins Press, 1971).
33. See Roger Lane, *Policing the City: Boston, 1882–1885* (Cambridge: Harvard University Press, 1967), p. 26.
34. Evelyn L. Parks, "From Constabulary to Police Society: Implications for Social Control," *Catalyst* (Summer 1970), p. 80.
35. Ibid., pp. 81–82.
36. Herbert Asbury, *The French Quarter* (New York: Knopf, 1936); Herbert Asbury, *The Barbary Coast* (Garden City, N.Y.: Garden City Publishing Co., 1933); Herbert

Asbury, *The Gangs of New York* (New York: Knopf, 1928); Richard O'Connor, *Hell's Kitchen* (Philadelphia: Lippincott, 1958).

37. Gustav Lening, *The Dark Side of New York Life and Its Criminal Classes* (New York: Frederick Gerhard, 1873), pp. 71 and 158. Other contemporary accounts of crime in New York are found in Charles Loring Brace, *The Dangerous Classes of New York* (New York: Wynkoop and Hallenback, 1872); Edward Crapsey, *The Nether Side of New York* (New York: Sheldon and Co., 1872); Richard K. Fox, *The Man Traps of New York* (New York: Richard Fox Proprietor Police Gazette, 1881); Matthew Hale Smith, *Sunshine and Shadow in New York* (Hartford: J. B. Burr and Co., 1869).

38. *Constitution, By-Laws and Charter of the Society For the Prevention of Crime and Second Annual Report,* 1878, p. 5.

39. Ibid.

40. Harry Willbach, "The Trend of Crime in New York City," *Journal of Criminal Law, Criminology and Police Science,* 29 (May–June 1938), pp. 62–75.

41. Theodore N. Ferdinand, "The Criminal Patterns of Boston Since 1849," *American Journal of Sociology,* 73 (July 1967), pp. 84–99.

42. Ibid., pp. 98–99.

43. In further explanation, Ferdinand writes the following in a footnote (p. 99): "To illustrate the validity of this conclusion, consider the following hypothetical example. Suppose we have a society of 1,000,000 in which 80 percent of the population lives in villages where the crime rate is 40 percent per 1,000. The remaining 20 percent lives in urban areas where the crime rate is 100 per 1,000. The crime rate for such a society would be 52 per 1,000. Now suppose the village crime remains at 40 per 1,000, the urban crime rate *drops* to 60 per 1,000, and the percentage in urban areas rise to 90 percent of the total, which is still 1,000,000. The crime rate for the society has risen to 58 per 1,000 even though the rate has fallen sharply in the cities." In addition, the apparent rise in crime can be attributed to the change in age structure in the United States, which is also a concomitant of a shift to urban residence. That is, the younger age groups (which are ordinarily arrested for offenses) are increasing faster than the other categories. See Philip C. Sagi and Charles F. Wellford, "Age Composition and Patterns of Change in Criminal Statistics," *Journal of Criminal Law, Criminology and Police Science,* 59 (March 1968), pp. 29–36.

44. Among these studies are Sarah L. Boggs, "Urban Crime Patterns," *American Sociological Review,* 30 (December 1965), pp. 899–908; Ronald J. Chilton, "Continuity in Delinquency Area Research: A Comparison of Studies for Baltimore, Detroit, and Indianapolis," *American Sociological Review,* 29 (February 1964), pp. 71–83; Marshall B. Clinard, "The Process of Urbanization and Criminal Behavior," *American Journal of Sociology,* 48 (September 1942), pp. 202–213; Bernard Lander, *Toward an Understanding of Juvenile Delinquency* (New York: Columbia University Press, 1954); Richard Quinney, "Structural Characteristics, Population Areas, and Crime Rates in the United States," *Journal of Criminal Law, Criminology and Police Science,* 57 (March 1966), pp. 45–52; Calvin F. Schmid, "Urban Crime Areas: Part II," *American Sociological Review,* 25 (October 1960), pp. 655–678; Karl Schuessler, "Components of Variation in City Crime Rates," *Social Problems,* 9 (Spring 1962), pp. 314–323; David Sears and John McConohay, "Participation in the Los Angeles Riot," *Social Problems,* 17:1 (Summer 1969), pp. 3–20. For a critique of this approach, see Judith A. Wilks, "Ecological Correlates of Crime and Delinquency," in President's Commission on Law Enforcement and Administration of Justice, *Crime and Its Impact—An Assessment* (Washington, D.C.: U.S. Government Printing Office, 1967), pp. 138–156.

45. Murry Bookchin, *The Limits of the City* (New York: Harper & Row, 1974), p. 76.

46. Quoted from the publisher's blurb for Robert M. Fogleson, ed., *Police in America* (New York: Arno Press, 1971), p. 2. The entire series costs $532.

47. Alan Bent, *Politics of Law Enforcement* (Lexington, Mass.: Lexington Books, 1974); Alan Coffey, *Police Intervention into Family Crisis* (Santa Cruz, California: Davis Publishing Company, 1974); John Gardiner and D. Olson, *Theft of the City* (Indiana University Press, 1974); Sharon and Jack Goldsmith, *The Police Community— Dimensions of an Occupational Subculture* (Palisades, California: Palisades Publishers, 1974); V. A. Leonard and H. W. More, *Police Organization and Management*, 4th ed. (Mineola, N.Y.: Foundation Press, 1975); James Munro, *Administrative Behavior and Police Organization* (Cincinnati: W. H. Anderson, 1974); Jerome Skolnick and Thomas Gray, eds., *Police in America* (Boston: Little, Brown, 1975); Leonard Steinberg and D. McEvoy, *Police and the Behavioral Sciences* (Springfield, Ill.: Thomas, 1974); and Jerry Wilson and P. Fugua, *Police and the Media* (Boston: Little, Brown, 1975).

48. *The New York Times*, 3 February 1975, p. 1.

49. See *The New York Times* editorial on this issue, "To Stop or Kill?," 11 November 1974.

50. Paul Takagi, "A Garrison State in 'Democratic' Society," *Crime and Social Justice*, 1 (Spring–Summer 1974), p. 28.

51. From the Preface, E. M. Davis, Chairman of the Task Force on Police, National Advisory Commission on Criminal Justice Standards and Goals, *Police* (Washington, D.C.: U.S. Government Printing Office, 1973), p. viii.

52. Julian Roebuck and Thomas Parker, "A Typology of Police Corruption," *Social Problems*, 21 (1974), pp. 423–437.

53. Lawrence Sherman, ed., *Police Corruption: A Sociological Perspective* (Garden City, N.Y.: Doubleday [Anchor Books], 1974), pp. 1–39.

54. Ibid., p. vii.

55. Peter Manning, "Survey Review: Recent Books on the Police," *Contemporary Sociology*, 4 (September 1975), p. 484. This is a fine review of the recent literature in this area.

56. These laws are discussed in greater detail in Richard Quinney, *Criminology: Analysis and Critique of Crime in the United States* (Boston: Little, Brown, 1975), chap. 7.

57. See Morris Ploscowe, "Sex Offenses: The American Legal Context," *Law and Contemporary Problems*, 25 (Spring 1960), pp. 217–225; also Gerhard O. W. Mueller, *Legal Regulation of Sexual Conduct* (Dobbs Ferry, N.Y.: Oceana, 1961).

58. Henry H. Foster, Jr., "The 'Comstock Load'—Obscenity and the Law," *Journal of Criminal Law, Criminology and Police Science*, 48 (September–October 1957), pp. 245–258.

59. Pamela A. Roby, "Politics and Criminal Law: Revision of the New York State Penal Law on Prostitution," *Social Problems*, 17 (Summer 1969), pp. 83–109.

60. See Martin Hoffman, *The Gay World* (New York: Basic Books, 1968), pp. 77–97.

61. Andrew Sinclair, *Era of Excess: A Social History of the Prohibition Movement* (New York: Harper & Row, 1964), pp. 5–6.

62. Forrest W. Lacey, "Vagrancy and Other Crimes of Personal Condition," *Harvard Law Review*, 66 (May 1953), p. 1203. Also see Caleb Foote, "Vagrancy-Type Law and Its Administration," *University of Pennsylvania Law Review*, 104 (March 1956), pp. 603–650.

63. Arthur H. Sherry, "Vagrants, Rogues, and Vagabonds—Old Concepts in Need of Revision," *California Law Review*, 48 (October 1960), p. 567.

64. See *The New York Times*, 8 July 1967, pp. 1 and 9.

65. Troy Duster, *The Legislation of Morality: Laws, Drugs, and Moral Judgment* (New York: Free Press, 1970), pp. 3–28.

66. Alfred R. Lindesmith, *The Addict and the Law* (Indiana University Press, 1965), chap. 1.

5

THE FUTURE OF CRIME AND SOCIAL JUSTICE

Given an understanding of some important aspects of crime in the United States, we can venture into a concluding discussion of the future of crime and social justice in this country. Two things are certain; First, crime is undergoing great change in the United States; and second, the problem of crime will be an integral part of the United States as long as the society is based on a capitalist political economy. The real problem today is not the problem of crime but the problem of advanced capitalist society.

THE CHANGING CHARACTER OF CRIME

Crime is becoming more political in the United States. That is, the behaviors of the criminally defined are political, and the actions of the state in labeling the behaviors as criminal are inherently political. This is also to say that crime is one of the most characteristic qualities of contemporary society. At stake is the fundamental issue of social justice and the possibility of creating an authentic existence.

In relation to the politics of crime, two seemingly opposing trends are underway in the United States. On the one hand, there is the liberal trend toward the "decriminalization" of a number of crimes. Along with the increasingly political use of the criminal law, in other words, there is the legal reform movement resulting in the decreased use of the criminal law for the regulation of certain everyday behaviors. The laws that are involved are primarily those that pertain to the control of public morality, the laws that sanction prostitution, abortion, homosexuality, drunkenness, and vagrancy. The argument being presented in these legal reforms is that the criminal law should not interfere with the liberty of a person to conduct himself or herself as long as another person is not being harmed. The proper function of the law, instead, is the protection of the lives and property of citizens, but also "the preservation of public order and decency."[1] This actually leaves us where we began: Anything and everyone can be restricted by criminal law. Even in the legal reform movement, the attempt is to protect the established order.

Alongside the legal reform movement, but closely tied to it in objective, is the increasing use of criminal law in other areas of control. If law-enforcement efforts are diverted from some forms of conduct, more time, personnel, and technology can be directed to the control of other kinds of behavior. The criminal law is increasingly being focused upon the protection of the existing order. As the capitalist system is further threatened by its own contradictions, crime control is one of the major instruments for the prevention of changes that would otherwise destroy the capitalist order.[2]

Thus, the new ideology of crime control, while being couched in reformist terminology, is actually for the control of anything that threatens the political economy of capitalism. New forms of control and manipulation are being devised and instituted. The older punitive philosophy is being modernized by more subtle techniques of control. Scientific knowledge and professional management are used to "rehabilitate" anyone who threatens domestic order. Prisons are being made into "therapeutic centers" where offenders are expertly managed and manipulated, and "reintegrated" into society. Methods of "behavior modification" are being practiced in "correctional facilities."

That we are entering a new kind of society, or rather the development of an advanced capitalism, seems evident from our critical study of the crime problem. The capitalist state, in its support of an advanced capitalism that cannot respond to human needs and still exist, must remake itself. The modern state, with its capitalist ruling class, maintains its control over internal challenges by developing and institutionalizing the instruments of science and technology. This "new-style" fascism, as it is being called, is a complex of modernized control mechanisms. It is a pervasive form of control; indeed, a managed society. As Bertram Gross has described this new order: "A managed society rules by a faceless and widely dispersed complex of warfare-welfare-industrial-communications-police bureaucracies caught up in developing a new-style empire based on a technocratic ideology,

a culture of alienation, multiple scapegoats, and competing control net-works."[3] Not only will the economy be managed, but the total society will be managed by the modern state. This is a state removed from the will and needs of the people.

It is our conviction that only a vision of the future that goes beyond the reform of capitalism can provide us with a humane existence. Crime control in the United States is a crucial indication of the kind of world that can increasingly develop under present images and theories of society and human nature. A way out of this possible future is found in the struggle for a socialist society.

PUBLIC CONSCIOUSNESS ABOUT CRIME

The crime and social justice of the future will ultimately be anchored in our current social reality of crime and our current reactions to this social reality. Crime as a "social disease" has always been a focal concern of the American public, and this concern over crime has in our day reached an unparalleled degree. The important question is, Why is this so?

One response to this question is that the public's concern over crime is the direct result of the government's desire to persuade us all that crime is our common enemy and that an all-out crusade against crime is to our common benefit. The American people are thus depicted as standing united against that growing band of evil outsiders called criminals. What is really happening here, though? Why does the state invest so much in making the public think and react in this manner? Could it be that it is only by having the people react to crime in this manner that the state can legitimate its increasingly totalitarian crime-control policies? If this suggestion is accurate, then we are left with the inescapable conclusion that the state as we now know it in this country, the handmaiden of our capitalist economy,[4] finds it useful to manipulate public opinion in order to gain legitimacy for severe control policies, policies that protect the peculiar political economy that is currently inflicting increasing suffering upon us all.

Thus, the objective of the state is to prevent the people of this country from forming a different social reality of crime, one that is alien to the interests of those who occupy and control elite power positions. Such a social reality would see criminally defined behavior in another light: Crime rates are the result of an over-controlling state coupled with a failing capitalist economy, an economy doomed by its internal contradictions to ultimate collapse.

Crime became a major concern in the 1960s, a concern that continues unabated in the 1970s, officially and publicly. The explanations for the sharp rise in public concern about crime are generally of two kinds.[5] According to the first explanation, the concern about crime is an irrational response of the public to the rapid social changes that have supposedly taken place in the past decade. According to the second, the public's reaction to crime is largely justified by the increase in the crime rate. The establishment of the President's Crime Commission in 1965 was justified by these kinds of explanations. And the Crime Commission even subjected the public reaction to study: "A chief reason that this Commission was organized was that there is widespread public anxiety about crime. In one sense, this entire report is an effort to focus that anxiety on the central problem of crime and criminal justice. A necessary part of that effort has been to study as carefully as possible the anxiety itself."[6] The President's Crime Commission and the resulting Omnibus Crime Bill were also justified —officially—by the public's concern about crime.

An understanding of the public's current formulation of the social reality of crime, an understanding that is rooted in critical theory, would be this: Public opinion cannot be separated from the powerful and influential forces of opinion-molding that come from official sources. Thus, the state apparatus, responding to the interests of capitalism, is responsible for defining the official reality of crime that many of us uncritically accept without examination or question. Public opinion is influenced by official policies, policies that in turn are formed by the needs of a capitalist economy.

We are authoritatively informed by the press and other mass media that the actual crime statistics support our increasing fear of crime, a fear documented by the scientifically reliable public opinion polls. We are told by these same authoritative sources that there are homicidal people at large amongst us because, "Plea Bargains Resolve 8 of 10 Homicide Cases: Reduced Charges Found to Bring Probation or 10 Years at Most."[7] Imagine the reaction of the citizen reading this over morning coffee. Again, a "scientifically reliable" poll finds added public worry over crime and crime control issues.[8] How else are we expected to think? Where else do we find information that formulates our perception of this reality? It is no great cause for wonder that the public's fear of crime is a real fear in the minds of the people. But it is being carefully manipulated.

That the public would deal severely with offenders is indicated in a national survey that asked a sample of the public the best way of dealing with an adult convicted of a specific crime.[9] The alternative sentences, from a list of seven crimes ranging from embezzlement to murder, were probation, a short prison sentence with parole, or a long prison sentence. The use of probation found little favor with the public. We are nowhere told that the cost of probation amounts to only a fraction of the cost of incarceration, thus easing our tax burden. Considering each of the crimes, only about a quarter of the respondents felt that probation was an appropriate sentence. Only for prostitution, judged more harshly by women than men, did as much as 26 percent of the public consider probation appropriate.

All of these findings have to be placed in the context of the official ideology of crime and crime control. What is striking is the correspondence between public opinion and official ideology and policy. But rather than follow the traditional assumption that official policy reflects public opinion, we are suggesting that officials use public opinion for their own advantage; and that at the same time government officials manipulate public opinion to suit the policies they are establishing. It is to be expected that public opinion and official ideology will be the same. Given the nature of political and economic power distributions in American society, the official ideology and reality shape public consciousness about crime.[10] Americans, despite Watergate and Vietnam, still tend to accept uncritically the official definitions of reality conveyed to them from the media and government officials.

We must, however, become considerably more critical in our evaluations. Until we create a critical imagination, one capable of unmasking the contradictions spawned by existing political and economic structures, one shared by all, the social reality of crime will be a reflection of the needs of the capitalist order. A true and genuine public consciousness must be created, not only with regard to crime, but with regard to all of social reality.

A STRUGGLE FOR SOCIAL JUSTICE

Any social problem, crime included, is understandable only if it is seen within the framework of the social, economic, and political structure of the society. We are convinced that the problem of crime in the United States is really the problem of capitalist society. Consequently, the crime problem in the United States cannot be solved within the context of the political economy of capitalism.

Earlier we projected one possible future for American society: oppressive and totalitarian, a frozen and permanent alienation. But we do not close on this note; for these things, as all things social, are dialectical in nature. An emergence of freedom from bondage, of optimism from pessimism, is always on the edge of the possible.

The alternative tomorrow that we have also been suggesting, then, is indeed possible. This is a world freed from the dehumanizing conditions and contradictions of capitalism, freed from the brutality of class oppression, hierarchy, and domination. Only then can be begin to adequately consider solutions to the problem of crime.

Such a world comes to pass only through socialist, revolutionary struggle. That the struggle has already begun is indicated by a widespread discontent among the American people; by emergent liberation movements in all oppressed groups; by the gradual withdrawal of legitimacy from the institutions of the society; by the growing critical imagination; and by everyday struggles in the community and in places of work. All of these are part of the struggle for a new world, one in which class divisions are no longer present and one in which a captialist system will be replaced by a more efficient and humane economic organization.

We are engaged in a common struggle, a struggle of truly historical significance, against the oppressions and contradictions of the capitalist state and economy. What the new socialist society to be born from that struggle will look like can be known only in the struggle for social justice. But it will be a society dedicated to our common existence. It will be a world relieved of the burden of crime as we know it today in the United States.

NOTES

1. See Norval Morris and Gordon Hawkins, *The Honest Politician's Guide to Crime Control* (University of Chicago Press, 1970), p. 26.
2. See Richard Quinney, *Critique of Legal Order: Crime Control in Capitalist Society* (Boston: Little, Brown, 1974).
3. Bertram Gross, "Friendly Fascism, A Model for America," *Social Policy,* 1 (November–December 1970), p. 46. Gross goes on to suggest that this "new-style" fascism, will differ strikingly from traditional fascism: "Under techno-urban fascism, certain elements previously regarded as inescapable earmarks of fascism would no longer be essential. Pluralistic in nature, techno-urban fascism would need no charismatic dictator, no one-party rule, no mass fascist party, no glorification of the state, no dissolution of legislatures, no discontinuation of elections, no distrust of reason. It would probably be a cancerous growth *within* and *around* the White House, the Pentagon, the broader political establishment" (p. 46).
4. For a demonstration of this argument, see David Gordon, "Recession Is Capitalism as Usual," *The New York Times Magazine,* 27 April 1975, p. 18.
5. Frank F. Furstenberg, Jr., "Public Reaction to Crime in the Streets," *The American Scholar,* 41 (Autumn 1971), pp. 601–610. For a detailed discussion of public opinion about crime, see Quinney, *Critique of Legal Order,* pp. 149–162.

6. President's Commission on Law Enforcement and Administration of Justice, *The Challenge of Crime in a Free Society* (Washington, D.C.: U.S. Government Printing Office, 1967), p. 49.

7. *The New York Times,* 27 January 1975, p. 1.

8. *The New York Times,* 29 October 1974, p. 1.

9. Louis Harris and Associates, *The Public Looks at Crime and Corrections* (Washington, D.C.: Joint Commission on Correctional Manpower and Training, 1968), pp. 11–12.

10. On this theme see Richard Quinney, *Criminology: Analysis and Critique of Crime in America* (Boston: Little, Brown, 1975), pp. 259–277.

SELECTED BIBLIOGRAPHY

Ronald L. Akers, "Toward a Comparative Definition of Law," *Journal of Criminal Law, Criminology and Police Science,* 56 (September 1965), pp. 301–306.

Francis A. Allen, *The Borderland of Criminal Justice:* University of Chicago Press, 1964.

American Friends Service Committee, *Struggle for Justice: A Report on Crime and Punishment in America,* New York: Hill and Wang, 1971.

Hannah Arendt, "Thinking and Moral Considerations," *Social Research,* 38 (Autumn 1971), pp. 417–446.

Gustave Aschaffenburg, *Crime and Its Repression,* trans. Adalbert Albrecht, Boston: Little, Brown, 1913.

Michael Banton, *The Policeman in the Community,* London: Tavistock, 1964.

Ronald H. Beattie, "Sources of Statistics on Crime and Correction," *Journal of American Statistical Association,* 54 (September 1959), pp. 582–592.

Howard S. Becker, *Outsiders: Studies in the Sociology of Deviance,* New York: Free Press, 1963.

Jeremy Bentham, *An Introduction to the Principles of Morals and Legislation,* corrected ed., Oxford: Clarendon Press, 1823.

Hermanus Bianchi, *Position and Subject Matter of Criminology: Inquiry Concerning Theoretical Criminology,* Amsterdam: North-Holland, 1956.

Albert D. Biderman and **Albert J. Reiss, Jr.,** "On Exploring the 'Dark Figure' of Crime," *Annals of the American Academy of Political and Social Science,* 374 (November 1967), pp. 1–15.

Egon Bittner, *The Functions of the Police in Modern Society,* National Institute of Mental Health, Washington, D.C.: U.S. Government Printing Office, 1970.

Alan F. Blum, "Theorizing," in Jack D. Douglas, ed., *Understanding Everyday Life: Toward the Reconstruction of Sociological Knowledge,* Chicago: Aldine, 1970.

Abraham S. Blumberg, *Criminal Justice,* New York: Quadrangle, 1967.

Abraham S. Blumberg, ed., *Current Perspectives on Criminal Behavior,* New York: Knopf, 1974.

Sarah L. Boggs, "Formal and Informal Crime Control: An Exploratory Study of Urban, Suburban, and Rural Orientations," *Sociological Quarterly,* 12 (Summer 1971), pp. 319–327.

Sarah L. Boggs, "Urban Crime Patterns," *American Sociological Review,* 30 (December 1965), pp. 899–908.

Willem A. Bonger, *Criminality and Economic Conditions,* trans. Henry P. Horton, Boston: Little, Brown, 1916.

Willem A. Bonger, *Introduction to Criminology,* trans. Emil Van Loo, London: Methuen, 1936.

Charles Booth, *Life and Labour of the People of London,* 2d ed., 9 vols., Toronto: Macmillan, 1892–1897.

William Bowers, *Executions in America,* Lexington, Mass.: Lexington Books, 1974.

Charles Loring Brace, *The Dangerous Classes of New York,* 3d ed., Montclair, N.J.: Smith Patterson, 1880.

Paul Breines, ed., *Critical Interruptions,* New York: Herder & Herder, 1972.

Percy W. Bridgman, "Determinism in Modern Science," in Sidney Hook, ed., *Determinism and Freedom in the Age of Modern Science,* New York: Macmillan, 1961, pp. 57–75.

Mario Bunge, *Causality: The Place of the Causal Principle in Modern Science,* New York: Harcourt Brace Jovanovich, 1963.

Ernest W. Burgess, "The Study of the Delinquent as a Person," *American Journal of Sociology,* 28 (May 1923), pp. 657–680.

Robert W. Burgess and **Ronald L. Akers,** "A Differential Association-Reinforcement Theory of Criminal Behavior," *Social Problems,* 14 (Fall 1966), pp. 128–147.

Cyril Burt, *The Young Delinquent,* Englewood Cliffs, N.J.: Prentice-Hall, 1925.

Daniel Callahan, *Abortion: Law, Choice and Morality,* New York: Macmillan, 1970.

Nathaniel Cantor, *Crime and Society,* New York: Holt, Rinehart and Winston, 1939.

Robert Carter, Daniel Glaser, Leslie Wilkins eds., *Correctional Institutions,* Philadelphia: Lippincott, 1972.

Ruth Shonle Cavan, *Criminology,* 3d ed., New York: Crowell, 1962.

Center for Research on Criminal Justice, *The Iron Fist and the Velvet Glove,* Berkeley, Calif.: Center for Research on Criminal Justice, 1975.

William J. Chambliss, ed., *Criminal Law in Action,* Santa Barbara, Calif.: Hamilton Publ. Co., 1975.

William J. Chambliss, "A Sociological Analysis of the Law of Vagrancy," *Social Problems,* 12 (Summer 1964), pp. 66–77.

William J. Chambliss and **Robert B. Seidman,** *Law, Order, and Power,* Reading, Mass.: Addison-Wesley, 1971.

Bradley Chapin, *The American Law of Treason: Revolutionary and National Origins:* University of Washington Press, 1964.

Paul Chevigny, *Police Power: Police Abuse in New York City,* New York: Pantheon Books, 1969.

Ronald J. Chilton, "Continuity in Delinquent Area Research: A Comparison of Studies for Baltimore, Detroit, and Indianapolis," *American Sociological Review,* 29 (February 1964), pp. 71–83.

Aaron V. Cicourel, *The Social Organization of Juvenile Justice,* New York: Wiley, 1968.

Alexander L. Clark and **Jack P. Gibbs,** "Social Control: A Reformulation," *Social Problems,* 12 (Spring 1965), pp. 402–406.

Marshall B. Clinard ed., *Anomie and Deviant Behavior,* New York: Free Press, 1964.

Marshall B. Clinard, "Criminological Research," in Robert K. Merton, Leonard Broom, and Leonard S. Cottrell, Jr., eds., *Sociology Today,* New York: Basic Books, 1959, pp. 509–536.

Marshall B. Clinard, "Sociologists and American Criminology," *Journal of Criminal Law, Criminology, and Police Science,* 41 (January–February 1951), pp. 549–577.

Marshall B. Clinard and **Richard Quinney,** *Criminal Behavior Systems: A Typology,* 2d ed., New York: Holt, Rinehart and Winston, 1973.

Richard A. Cloward and **Lloyd E. Ohlin,** *Delinquency and Opportunity,* New York: Free Press, 1960.

Albert K. Cohen, *Delinquent Boys,* New York: Free Press, 1955.

Albert K. Cohen, Alfred Lindesmith, and **Karl F. Schuessler,** eds., *The Sutherland Papers:* Indiana University Press, 1956.

Patrick Colquhoun, *Treatise on the Police of the Metropolis,* 7th ed., London: J. Mawman, 1806.

James E. Conklin, "Dimensions of Community Response to the Crime Problem," *Social Forces,* 18 (Winter 1971), pp. 373–385.

Edward Crapsey, *The Nether Side of New York,* New York: Shelden & Co., 1872.

Ed Cray, *The Enemy in the Streets: Police Malpractice in America,* Garden City, N.Y.: Doubleday, 1972.

Donald R. Cressey, ed., *The Prison,* New York: Holt, Rinehart and Winston, 1961.

Donald R. Cressey, "The State of Criminal Statistics," *National Probation and Parole Association Journal,* 3 (July 1957), pp. 240–241.

Donald R. Cressey, *Theft of the Nation: The Structure and Operations of Organized Crime in America,* New York: Harper & Row, 1969.

F. James Davis, "Law as a Type of Social Control," in F. James Davis, Henry H. Foster, Jr., C. Ray Jeffery, and E. Eugene Davis, *Society and the Law,* New York: Free Press, 1962, pp. 39–63.

Melvin L. De Fleur and **Richard Quinney,** "A Reformulation of Sutherland's Differential Association Theory and a Strategy for Empirical Verification," *Journal of Research in Crime and Delinquency,* 3 (January 1966), pp. 1–22.

Stanley Diamond, "The Rule of Law Versus the Order of Custom," *Social Research,* 38 (Spring 1971), pp. 42–72.

Troy Duster, *The Legislation of Morality: Drugs, and Moral Judgment,* New York: Free Press, 1970.

Lamar Empey, "Delinquency Theory and Recent Research," *Journal of Research in Crime and Delinquency,* 4 (January 1967), pp. 28–42.

Frederick Engels, *The Origin of the Family, Private Property, and the State,* New York: International Publishers, 1942.

Kai T. Erikson, *Wayward Puritans: A Study in the Sociology of Deviance,* New York: Wiley, 1966.

Richard A. Falk, Gabriel Kolko, and **Robert Jay Lifton,** eds., *Crimes of War,* New York: Random House, 1971.

Enrico Ferri, *Criminal Sociology,* trans. J. I. Kelly and John Lisle, Boston: Little, Brown, 1917.

Arthur E. Fink, *Causes of Crime: Biological Theories in the United States, 1800–1915:* University of Pennsylvania Press, 1938.

Richard Flacks, "Towards a Socialist Sociology: Some Proposals for Work in the Coming Period," *The Insurgent Sociologist,* 2 (Spring 1972), pp. 18–27.

Lawrence M. Friedman, *A History of American Law,* New York: Simon & Schuster, 1973.

Wolfgang Friedmann, *Law in a Changing Society,* 2d ed., New York: Columbia University Press, 1972.

Lon L. Fuller, *The Morality of Law,* New Haven: Yale University Press, 1964.

Richard C. Fuller, "Morals and the Criminal Law," *Journal of Criminal Law, Criminology, and Police Science,* 32 (March–April 1942), pp. 624–630.

Frank F. Furstenberg, Jr., "Public Reaction to Crime in the Streets," *The American Scholar,* 40 (Autumn 1971), pp. 601–610.

John F. Galliher, "Explanations of Police Behavior: A Critical Review and Analysis," *Sociological Quarterly,* 12 (Summer 1971), pp. 308–318.

Raffaele Garofalo, *Criminology,* trans. Robert Wyness, Boston: Little, Brown, 1914.

Gilbert Geis, *Not the Law's Business? An Examination of Homosexuality, Abortion, Prostitution, Narcotics and Gambling in the United States,* National Institute of Mental Health, Washington, D.C.: U.S. Government Printing Office, 1972.

Gilbert Geis, "Sociology and Crime," in Joseph S. Roucek, ed., *Sociology of Crime,* New York: Philosophical Library, 1961, pp. 7–33.

Gilbert Geis, ed., *White-Collar Criminal: The Offender in Business and the Professions,* New York: Atherton Press, 1968.

Jeff Gerth, "The Americanization of 1984," *SunDance,* 1 (April–May 1972), pp. 58–65.

Don C. Gibbons, *Changing the Lawbreaker,* Englewood Cliffs, N.J.: Prentice-Hall, 1965.

Don C. Gibbons, "Crime and Punishment: A Study in Social Attitudes," *Social Forces,* 47 (June 1969), pp. 391–397.

John L. Gillin, *Criminology and Penology,* Englewood Cliffs, N.J.: Prentice-Hall, 1926.

Morris Ginsberg, *On Justice in Society,* Baltimore: Penguin Books, 1965.

Daniel Glaser, *Adult Crime and Social Policy,* Englewood Cliffs, N.J.: Prentice-Hall, 1972.

Daniel Glaser, "Criminality Theories and Behavior Images," *American Journal of Sociology,* 61 (March 1956), pp. 433–444.

Daniel Glaser, *The Effectiveness of a Prison and Parole System,* Indianapolis: Bobbs-Merrill, 1964.

Daniel Glaser, "The Sociological Approach to Crime and Correction," *Law and Contemporary Problems,* 23 (Autumn 1958), pp. 683–702.

Sheldon and **Eleanor Glueck,** *Physique and Delinquency,* New York: Harper & Row, 1956.

Sheldon and **Eleanor Glueck,** *Unraveling Juvenile Delinquency,* New York: Commonwealth Fund, 1956.

Abraham Goldstein, *The Insanity Defense,* New Haven: Yale University Press, 1967.

David M. Gordon, "Capitalism, Class, and Crime in America," *Crime and Delinquency,* 19 (April 1973), pp. 163–185.

Charles Goring, *The English Convict: A Statistical Study,* London: His Majesty's Stationery Office, 1913.

Gene Grabiner, "The Limits of Three Perspectives on Crime: 'Value-Free Science,' 'Objective Law' and State 'Morality,' " *Issues in Criminology,* 8 (Spring 1973), pp. 35–48.

Bertram Gross, "Friendly Fascism: A Model for America," *Social Policy,* 1 (November–December 1970), pp. 44–52.

Ellen Elizabeth Guillot, *Social Factors in Crime: As Explained by American Writers of the Civil War and Post Civil War Period,* published PhD dissertation: University of Pennsylvania, 1943.

Jürgen Habermas, *Knowledge and Human Interests,* trans. Jeremy J. Shapiro, Boston: Beacon Press, 1971.

Jürgen Habermas, *Theory and Practice,* Boston: Beacon Press, 1973.

Jürgen Habermas, *Toward a Rational Society,* Boston: Beacon Press, 1970.

Jürgen Habermas, *Legitimation Crisis,* Boston: Beacon Press, 1975.

Michael Hakeem, "A Critique of the Psychiatric Approach to Crime and Correction," *Law and Contemporary Problems,* 23 (Autumn 1958), pp. 650–682.

Jerome Hall, *General Principles of Criminal Law,* 2d ed., Indianapolis: Bobbs-Merrill, 1960.

Jerome Hall, *Theft, Law, and Society,* 2d ed., Indianapolis: Bobbs-Merrill, 1952.

Norwood Russell Hanson, *Patterns of Discovery:* Cambridge University Press, 1965.

Robert H. Hardt and **George E. Bodine,** *Development of Self-Report Instruments in Delinquency Research: A Conference Report:* Syracuse University Youth Development Center, 1965.

Henry M. Hart, Jr., "The Aims of the Criminal Law," *Law and Contemporary Problems,* 23 (Summer 1958), pp. 401–441.

H. L. A. Hart, *The Concept of Law,* London: Oxford University Press, 1961.

H. L. A. Hart, *Law, Liberty, and Morality:* Stanford University Press, 1963.

Clayton A. Hartjen, *Crime and Criminalization,* New York: Praeger, 1974.

Frank E. Hartung, *Crime, Law, and Society,* Detroit: Wayne State University Press, 1965.

Frank E. Hartung, "A Critique of the Sociological Approach to Crime and Correction," *Law and Contemporary Problems,* 23 (Autumn 1958), pp. 703–734.

George Lee Haskins, *Law and Authority in Early Massachusetts,* New York: Macmillan, 1960.

S. R. Hathaway and **Elio D. Monachesi,** *Analyzing and Predicting Delinquency with the MMPI:* University of Minnesota Press, 1953.

Lawrence E. Hazelrigg, ed., *Prison Within Society,* Garden City, N.Y.: Doubleday, 1968.

William Healy, *The Individual Delinquent,* Boston: Little, Brown, 1915.

William Healy and **Augusta F. Bronner,** *New Light on Delinquency and Its Treatment,* New Haven: Yale University Press, 1936.

Ester Heffernan, *Making It in Prison: The Square, the Cool, and the Life,* New York: Wiley, 1972.

Martin Heidegger, *What Is a Thing?,* trans. W. B. Barton, Jr., and Vera Deutsch, Chicago: Henry Regnery Company, 1967.

Werner Heisenberg, *Physics and Philosophy: The Revolution in Modern Science,* New York: Harper & Row, 1958.

Travis Hirschi and **Hanan C. Selvin,** *Delinquency Research: An Appraisal of Analytic Methods,* New York: Free Press, 1967.

E. Adamson Hoebel, *The Law of Primitive Man,* Cambridge: Harvard University Press, 1954.

Roger Hood and **Richard Sparks,** *Key Issues in Criminology,* New York: McGraw-Hill, 1970.

E. A. Hooton, *The American Criminal: An Anthropological Study,* Cambridge, Mass.: Harvard University Press, 1939.

Max Horkimer, *Critical Theory: Selected Essays,* New York: Seabury Press, 1975.

Max Horkimer and **Theodore Adorno,** *Dialectic of Enlightenment,* New York: Herder & Herder, 1972.

David Horowitz, *Empire and Revolution: A Radical Interpretation of Contemporary History,* New York: Random House, 1969.

Irving Louis Horowitz and **Martin Liebowitz,** "Social Deviance and Political Marginality: Toward a Redefinition of the Relation Between Sociology and Politics," *Social Problems,* 15 (Winter 1968), pp. 145–296.

Dick Howard and **Karl E. Klare,** eds., *The Unknown Dimension: European Marxism Since Lenin,* New York: Basic Books, 1972.

James A. Inciardi, *Careers in Crime,* Skokie, Ill.: Rand McNally, 1975.

John Irwin, *The Felon,* Englewood Cliffs, N.J.: Prentice-Hall, 1970.

George Jackson, *Blood in My Eye,* New York: Random House, 1972.

Martin Jay, *The Dialectical Imagination: A History of the Frankfort School and the Institute of Social Research, 1923–1950,* Boston: Little, Brown, 1973.

C. H. S. Jayewardene, "The English Precursors of Lombroso," *British Journal of Criminology,* 4 (October 1963), pp. 164–170.

C. Ray Jeffery, *Crime Prevention Through Environmental Design,* Beverly Hills, Calif.: Sage, 1971.

C. Ray Jeffery, "The Development of Crime in Early English Society," *Journal of Criminal Law, Criminology and Police Science,* 47 (March–April 1957), pp. 647–666.

C. Ray Jeffery, "The Structure of American Criminological Thinking," *Journal of Criminal Law, Criminology and Police Science,* 46 (January–February 1956), pp. 658–672.

Olof Kinberg, *Basic Problems of Criminology,* Copenhagen: Levin & Munkgaard, 1935.

Otto Kirchheimer, *Political Justice: The Use of Legal Procedure for Political Ends:* Princeton University Press, 1961.

John I. Kitsue and **Aaron V. Cicourel,** "A Note on the Uses of Official Statistics," *Social Problems,* 11 (Fall 1963), pp. 131–139.

Malcolm W. Klein, *Street Gangs and Street Workers,* Englewood Cliffs, N.J.: Prentice-Hall, 1971.

Gabriel Kolko, *The Triumph of Conservatism: A Reinterpretation of American History, 1900–1916,* New York: Free Pres, 1963.

Barry Krisberg, *Crime and Privilege,* Englewood Cliffs, N.J.: Prentice-Hall, 1975.

Thomas S. Kuhn, *The Structure of Scientific Revolutions:* University of Chicago Press, 1962.

Wayne R. LaFave, *Arrest: The Decision to Take a Suspect into Custody,* Boston: Little, Brown, 1965.

Bernard Lander, *Toward an Understanding of Juvenile Delinquency,* New York: Columbia University Press, 1954.

Johannes Lange, *Crime and Destiny,* trans. Charlotte Haldane, New York: Liveright, 1930.

Quentin Lauer, *Phenomenology: Its Genesis and Prospect,* New York: Harper & Row, 1965.

Robert Lefcourt, *Law Against the People: Essays to Demystify Law, Order and the Courts,* New York: Random House, 1971.

Peter P. Lejins, "Uniform Crime Reports," *Michigan Law Review,* 64 (April 1966), pp. 1011–1030.

Edwin M. Lemert, *Human Deviance, Social Problems, and Social Control,* Englewood Cliffs, N.J.: Prentice-Hall, 1967.

Yale Levin and **Alfred R. Lindesmith,** "English Ecology and Criminology of the Past Century," *Journal of Criminal Law and Criminology,* 27 (March–April 1937), pp. 810–816.

Alfred R. Lindesmith, *The Addict and the Law:* Indiana University Press, 1965.

Alfred R. Lindesmith and **H. Warren Dunham,** "Some Principles of Criminal Typology," *Social Forces,* 19 (March 1941), pp. 307–314.

Alfred R. Lindesmith and **Yale Levin,** "The Lombrosian Myth in Criminology," *American Journal of Sociology,* 42 (March 1937), pp. 653–671.

Cesare Lombroso, *Crime, Its Causes and Remedies,* trans. H. P. Horton, Boston: Little, Brown, 1911.

A. R. Louch, *Explanation and Human Action:* University of California Press, 1969.

Staughton Lynd, *Intellectual Origins of American Radicalism,* New York: Pantheon Books, 1968.

Robert M. MacIver, *Social Causation,* New York: Harper & Row, 1964 (originally published in 1942).

Bronislav Malinowski, *Crime and Custom in Savage Society,* Boston: Routledge & Kegan Paul, 1926.

Hermann Mannheim, *Comparative Criminology,* Boston: Houghton Mifflin, 1965.

Peter K. Manning, "The Police: Mandate, Strategies, and Appearances," in Jack D. Douglas, ed., *Crime and Justice in American Society,* Indianapolis: Bobbs-Merrill, 1971, pp. 149–193.

Herbert Marcuse, *Counterrevolution and Revolt,* Boston, Beacon Press, 1972.

Herbert Marcuse, *Reason and Revolution,* Boston: Beacon Press, 1960.

John M. Martin, Joseph P. Fitzpatrick, and **Robert E. Gould,** *The Analysis of Delinquent Behavior: A Structural Approach,* New York: Random House, 1968.

Robert Martinson, "The Age of Treatment: Some Implications of the Custody-Treatment Dimension," *Issues in Criminology,* 2 (Fall 1966), pp. 275–293.

Karl Marx, *The Grundrisse,* trans. David McLellan, New York: Harper & Row, 1971.

Karl Marx, *Selected Writings in Sociology and Social Philosophy,* trans. T. B. Bottomore, New York: McGraw-Hill, 1964.

David Matza, *Becoming Deviant,* Englewood Cliffs, N.J.: Prentice-Hall, 1969.

David Matza, *Delinquency and Drift,* New York: Wiley, 1964.

Karl Menninger, *The Crime of Punishment,* New York: Viking Press, 1969.

Robert K. Merton, "Social Structure and Anomie," *American Sociological Review,* 3 (October 1938), pp. 672–682.

Hank Messick, *Lansky,* New York: Putnam Sons, 1971.

Jerome Michael and **Mortimer J. Adler,** *Crime, Law, and Social Science,* New York: Harcourt Brace Jovanovich, 1933.

Ralph Miliband, *The State in Capitalist Society,* New York: Basic Books, 1969.

Martin B. Miller, "The Indeterminate Sentence Paradigm: Resocialization or Social Control," *Issues in Criminology,* 7 (Fall 1972), pp. 101–124.

Jessica Mitford, *Kind and Usual Punishment,* New York: Knopf, 1973.

Albert Morris, *Criminals and the Community:* Melbourne University Press, 1953.

Norval Morris and **Gordon Hawkins,** *The Honest Politician's Guide to Crime Control:* University of Chicago Press, 1969.

Terence Morris, *The Criminal Area: A Study in Social Ecology,* Boston: Routledge & Kegal Paul, 1958.

Gerhard O. W. Mueller, "Tort, Crime, and the Primitive," *Journal of Criminal Law, Criminology, and Police Science,* 46 (September–October 1955), pp. 303–332.

William E. Nelson, "Emerging Notions of Modern Criminal Law in the Revolutionary Era: An Historical Perspective," *New York University Law Review,* 42 (May 1967), pp. 450–482.

Donald J. Newman, *Conviction,* Boston: Little, Brown, 1966.

Donald J. Newman, "The Effect of Accommodations in Justice Administration on Criminal Statistics," *Sociology and Social Research,* 46 (January 1962), pp. 144–155.

Donald J. Newman, "White Collar Crime," *Law and Contemporary Problems,* 23 (Autumn 1958), pp. 735–753.

Arthur Niederhoffer, *Behind the Shield,* Garden City, N.Y.: Doubleday, 1967.

Lloyd E. Ohlin, ed., *Prisoners in America,* Englewood Cliffs, N.J.: Prentice-Hall, 1973.

Bertell Ollman, *Alienation: Marx's Conception of Man in Capitalist Society,* London: Cambridge University Press, 1971.

Enzo Paci, *The Function of the Social Sciences and the Meaning of Man,* trans. Paul Piccone and James E. Hansen, Evanston, Ill.: Northwestern University Press, 1972.

Herbert L. Packer, *The Limits of the Criminal Sanction:* Stanford University Press, 1968.

John Pallas and **Bob Barber,** "From Riot to Revolution," *Issues in Criminology,* 7 (Fall 1972), pp. 1–19.

Evelyn L. Parks, "From Constabulary to Police Society: Implications for Social Control," *Catalyst* (Summer 1970), pp. 76–97.

Maurice Parmelee, *Criminology,* New York: Macmillan, 1918.

Coleman Phillipson, *Three Criminal Law Reformers: Beccaria, Bentham, Romilly,* London: Dent, 1923.

Luke O. Pike, *A History of Crime in England,* 2 vols., London: Smith, Elder, 1873–1876.

Irving Piliavin and **Scott Briar,** "Police Encounters with Juveniles," *American Journal of Sociology,* 70 (September 1964), pp. 206–214.

David J. Pittman and **W. F. Handly,** "Uniform Crime Reporting: Suggested Improvements," *Sociology and Social Research,* 46 (January 1962), pp. 135–143.

Anthony M. Platt, *The Child Savers:* University of Chicago Press, 1969.

Anthony Platt, "The Triumph of Benevolence: The Origins of the Juvenile Justice System in the United States," in Richard Quinney, ed., *Criminal Justice in America: A Critical Understanding,* Boston: Little, Brown, 1974, pp. 356–389.

Ned Polsky, *Hustlers, Beats, and Others,* Chicago: Aldine, 1967.

Austin L. Porterfield, *Youth in Trouble,* Fort Worth: The Leo Potishman Foundation, 1946.

C. Gordon Post, *An Introduction to the Law,* Englewood Cliffs, N.J.: Prentice-Hall, 1965.

Roscoe Pound, *Social Control Law,* New Haven: Yale University Press, 1943.

President's Commission on Law Enforcement and Administration of Justice, *The Challenge of Crime in a Free Society,* Washington, D.C.: U.S. Government Printing Office, 1967.

Richard Quinney, *Criminology: Analysis and Critique of Crime in America,* Boston: Little, Brown, 1975.

Richard Quinney, *Critique of Legal Order: Crime Control in Capitalist Society,* Boston: Little, Brown, 1974.

Richard Quinney, "From Repression to Liberation: Social Theory in a Radical Age," in Robert A. Scott and Jack D. Douglas, *Theoretical Perspectives on Deviance,* New York: Basic Books, 1972, pp. 317–341.

Richard Quinney, *The Social Reality of Crime,* Boston: Little, Brown, 1970.

Richard Quinney, "Structural Characteristics, Population Areas, and Crime Rates in the United States," *Journal of Criminal Law, Criminology and Police Science,* 57 (March 1966), pp. 45–52.

Richard Quinney, "There's A Lot of Folks Grateful to the Lone Ranger: With Some Notes on the Rise and Fall of American Criminology," *The Insurgent Sociologist,* 4 (Fall 1973), pp. 56–64.

Richard Quinney, "Who Is the Victim?," *Criminology,* 10 (November 1972), pp. 314–323.

C. Bernaldo de Quirós, *Modern Theories of Criminality,* trans. Alfonso de Salvio, Boston: Little, Brown, 1911.

Leon Radzinowicz, *Ideology and Crime,* New York: Columbia University Press, 1966.

Leon Radzinowicz, *In Search of Criminology,* Cambridge, Mass.: Harvard University Press, 1962.

Leon Radzinowicz and **Marvin Wolfgang,** eds., *Crime and Justice,* 3 vols., New York: Basic Books, 1971.

Walter C. Reckless, *The Crime Problem,* 4th ed., Englewood Cliffs, N.J.: Prentice-Hall, 1973.

Walter C. Reckless, Simon Dinitz, and **Barbara Kay,** "The Self Component in Potential Delinquency and Potential Non-Delinquency," *American Sociological Review,* 22 (October 1957), pp. 566–570.

Albert J. Reiss, Jr., *The Police and the Public,* New Haven, Conn.: Yale University Press, 1971.

Sophia M. Robison, "A Critical View of the Uniform Crime Reports," *Michigan Law Review,* 64 (April 1966), pp. 1031–1054.

Pamela A. Roby, "Politics and Criminal Law: Revision of the New York State Penal Law on Prostitution," *Social Problems,* 17 (Summer 1969), pp. 83–109.

Julian Roebuck and **Thomas Parker,** "A Typology of Police Corruption," *Social Problems,* 31:3 (1974), pp. 423–437.

Arnold M. Rose, "The Use of Law to Induce Social Change," *Transactions of the Third World Congress of Sociology,* 6 (1956), pp, 52–63.

David J. Rothman, *The Discovery of Asylum: Social Order and Disorder in the New Republic,* Boston: Little, Brown, 1971.

George Rusche and **Otto Kirchheimer,** *Punishment and Social Structure,* New York: Columbia University Press, 1939.

Jean-Paul Sartre, *Search for a Method,* trans. Hazel E. Barnes, New York: Knopf, 1963.

Leonard Savitz, *Dilemmas in Criminology,* New York: McGraw-Hill, 1967.

Max G. Schlapp and **Edward H. Smith,** *The New Criminology,* New York: Liveright, 1928.

Calvin F. Schmid, "Urban Crime Areas: Part II," *American Sociological Review,* 25 (October 1960), pp. 655–678.

Trent Schroyer, "A Reconceptualization of Critical Theory," in David Colfax and Jack Roach, eds., *Radical Sociology,* New York: Basic Books, 1971.

Karl F. Schuessler and **Donald R. Cressey,** "Personality Characteristics of Criminals," *American Journal of Sociology,* 55 (March 1950), pp. 476–484.

Harry Manuel Schulman, "The Measurement of Crime in the United States," *Journal of Criminal Law, Criminology and Police Science,* 57 (December 1966), pp. 483–492.

Edwin M. Schur, *Crimes Without Victims,* Englewood Cliffs, N.J.: Prentice-Hall, 1965.

Edwin M. Schur, *Law and Society,* New York: Random House, 1968.

Edwin M. Schur, *Our Criminal Society: The Social and Legal Sources of Crime in America,* Englewood Cliffs, N.J.: Prentice-Hall, 1969.

Edwin M. Schur, *Radical Non-Intervention: Rethinking the Delinquency Problem,* Englewood Cliffs, N.J.: Prentice-Hall, 1972.

Alfred Schutz, "Concept and Theory Formulation in the Social Sciences," in Maurice Natanson, ed., *Philosophy of the Social Sciences,* New York: Random House, 1963, pp. 231–249.

Herman and **Julia Schwendinger,** "Defenders of Order or Guardians of Human Rights?," *Issues in Criminology,* 5 (Summer 1970), pp. 123–157.

Thorsten Sellin, *Culture Conflict and Crime,* New York: Social Science Research Council, 1938.

Philip Selznick, "Legal Institutions and Social Controls," *Vanderbilt Law Review,* 17 (December 1963), pp. 79–90.

Philip Selznick, "Sociology and Natural Law," *Natural Law Forum,* 6 (1961), pp. 84–108.

Clifford R. Shaw, *Delinquency Areas,* with the collaboration of Frederick M. Zorbaugh, Henry D. McKay, and Leonard S. Cottrell: University of Chicago Press, 1929.

Clifford R. Shaw, *Natural History of a Delinquent Career:* University of Chicago Press, 1931.

William H. Sheldon, *Varieties of Delinquent Youth,* New York: Harper & Row, 1949.

James F. Short, Jr., and **F. Ivan Nye,** "Extent of Unrecorded Juvenile Delinquency: Tentative Conclusions," *Journal of Law, Criminology, and Police Science,* 49 (November–December 1958), pp. 296–302.

Allan Silver, "The Demand for Order in Civil Society: A Review of Some Themes in the History of Urban Crime, Police, and Riot," in David J. Bordua, ed., *The Police: Six Sociological Essays,* New York: Wiley, 1967, pp. 1–24.

Jerome H. Skolnick, *Justice Without Trial,* New York: Wiley, 1966.

Jerome H. Skolnick, *The Politics of Protest,* New York: Ballantine Books, 1969.

Alfred Stern, "Science and the Philosopher," in Paul C. Obler and Herman H. Estrin, eds., *The New Scientist: Essays on the Methods and Values of Modern Science,* Garden City, N.Y.: Doubleday, 1962, pp. 280–301.

David Sternberg, "The New Radical-Criminal Trials: A Step Toward a Class-For-Itself in the American Proletariat?" *Science and Society,* 36 (Fall 1972), pp. 274–301.

John R. Stratton and **Robert M. Terry,** eds., *Prevention of Delinquency: Problems and Programs,* New York: Macmillan, 1968.

David Sudnow, "Normal Crimes: Sociological Features of the Penal Code in a Public Defender Office," *Social Problems,* 12 (Winter 1965), pp. 255–276.

Edwin H. Sutherland, "Crime and the Conflict Process," *Journal of Juvenile Research,* 13 (January 1929), pp. 38–48.

Edwin H. Sutherland, *The Professional Thief:* University of Chicago Press, 1937.

Edwin H. Sutherland, *White Collar Crime,* New York: Holt, Rinehart and Winston, 1949.

Edwin H. Sutherland and **Donald R. Cressey,** *Criminology,* 9th ed., Philadelphia: Lippincott, 1974.

Gresham M. Sykes, *Crime and Society,* 2d ed., New York: Random House, 1967.

Gresham M. Sykes, *The Society of Captives: A Study of a Maximum Security Prison,* New York: Atheneum, 1965.

Paul Takagi, "A Garrison State in 'Democratic' Society," *Crime and Social Justice,* 1 (Spring–Summer, 1974), pp. 27–33.

Paul Takagi, "The Walnut Street Jail: A Penal Reform to Centralize the Powers of the State," *Federal Probation,* 39 (December 1975), pp. 18–26.

Frank Tannenbaum, *Crime and the Community,* Boston: Ginn, 1938.

Paul W. Tappan, *Crime, Justice, and Correction,* New York: McGraw-Hill, 1960.

Paul W. Tappan, "Who Is the Criminal?," *American Sociological Review,* 12 (February 1947), pp. 96–102.

Gabriel Tarde, *Penal Philosophy,* trans. Rapelje Howell, Boston: Little, Brown, 1912.

Ian Taylor, Paul Walton, and **Jock Young,** *The New Criminology,* Boston: Routledge & Kegan Paul, 1973.

Telford Taylor, *Nuremberg and Vietnam: An American Tragedy,* New York: Quadrangle Books, 1970.

Frederick M. Thrasher, *The Gang: A Study of 1,313 Gangs in Chicago:* University of Chicago Press, 1927.

Edward A. Tiryakian, "Existential Phenomenology and the Sociological Tradition," *American Sociological Review,* 39 (October 1965), pp. 674–688.

Simon H. Tulchin, *Intelligence and Crime:* University of Chicago Press, 1939.

Austin T. Turk, *Criminality and Legal Order,* Skokie, Ill.: Rand McNally, 1969.

Austin T. Turk, *Legal Sanctioning and Social Control,* National Institute of Mental Health, Washington, D.C.: U.S. Government Printing Office, 1972.

Clyde B. Vedder and **Barbara Kay,** eds., *Penology: A Realistic Approach,* Springfield, Ill.: Thomas, 1969.

Emilio Viano, "Rape and the Law in the United States," *International Journal of Criminology and Penology,* 2:4 (November 1974).

George B. Vold, *Theoretical Criminology,* New York: Oxford University Press, 1958.

Hans Von Hentig, *Crime: Causes and Conditions,* New York: McGraw-Hill, 1947.

Harwin L. Voss, "Socio-Economic Status and Reported Delinquent Behavior," *Social Problems,* 13 (Winter 1966), pp. 314–324.

Harwin L. Voss and **David M. Petersen,** eds., *Ecology of Crime and Delinquency,* Englewood Cliffs, N.J.: Prentice-Hall, 1971.

James S. Wallerstein and **Clement J. Wyle,** "Our Law-Abiding Law-Breakers," *Probation,* 25 (April 1947), pp. 107–112.

Max Weber, *Law in Economy and Society,* edited by Max Rheinstein, Cambridge: Harvard University Press, 1954.

Herbert Wechsler, "On Culpabiltiy and Crime: The Treatment of *Mens Rea* in the Model Penal Code," *Annals of the American Academy of Political and Social Science,* 339 (January 1962), pp. 24–41.

James Weinstein, *The Corporate Ideal in the Liberal State, 1900–1918,* Boston: Beacon Press, 1968.

Stanton Wheeler, "Criminal Statistics: A Reformulation of the Problem," *Journal of Criminal Law, Criminology and Police Science,* 58 (September 1967), pp. 317–324.

Stanton Wheeler, "The Social Sources of Criminology," *Sociological Inquiry,* 32 (Spring 1962), pp. 139–159.

Leslie T. Wilkins, *Evaluation of Penal Methods,* New York: Random House, 1969.

Leslie T. Wilkins, "New Thinking in Criminal Statistics," *Journal of Criminal Law, Criminology and Police Science,* 56 (September 1965), pp. 277–284.

Judith A. Wilks, "Ecological Correlates of Crime and Delinquency," in President's Commission on Law Enforcement and Administration of Justice, *Crime and Its Impact—An Assessment,* Washington, D.C.: U.S. Government Printing Office, 1967, pp. 138–156.

Alan Wolfe, *The Seamy Side of Democracy: Repression in America,* New York: McKay, 1973.

Marvin E. Wolfgang, "Criminology and the Criminologist," *Journal of Criminal Law, Criminology and Police Science,* 54 (June 1963), pp. 155–162.

Marvin E. Wolfgang, "Uniform Crime Reports: A Critical Appraisal," *University of Pennsylvania Law Review,* 111 (April 1963), pp. 708–738.

Erik Olin Wright, *The Politics of Punishment: A Critical Analysis of Prisons in America,* New York: Harper & Row, 1973.

Jock Young, "The Zoo-Keepers of Deviancy," *Catalyst,* 5 (Summer 1970), pp. 38–46.

Richard M. Zaner, *The Way of Phenomenology: Criticism as a Philosophical Discipline,* New York: Pegasus, 1970.

SUBJECT INDEX

NAME INDEX

77 78 79 7 6 5 4 3 2 1